TERi GONZALEZ

WINNING

~WITH~

Arabian Horses

WINNING

~ WITH ~

Arabian Horses

DON BURT

SIMON & SCHUSTER

NEW YORK LONDON TORONTO SYDNEY TOKYO SINGAPORE

SIMON & SCHUSTER
Simon & Schuster Building
Rockefeller Center
1230 Avenue of the Americas
New York, New York 10020

Manufactured in the United States of America

10   9   8   7   6   5   4   3   2

Library of Congress Cataloging-in-Publication Data

Burt, Don.
Winning with Arabian horses / by Don Burt.
Includes index.
1. Arabian horse—Showing.   2. Arabian horse—Exhibitions.
I. Title.
SF293.A8B87   1989
798.2′4—dc20   89-8773
CIP

ISBN: 0-671-76578-1

Illustrations by Craig Christiansen

Designed by Nina D'Amario

This book is dedicated to my coauthor,
writing partner, and best friend,
my wife, Ardys,
and
to all exhibitors past, present, and
future who truly love the Arabian horse.

Acknowledgments

Much of this book was compiled through the lectures and teachings of such notables as Dr. G. Marvin Beeman, Dr. Deb Bennett, Dr. Ronald Blackwell, and Dr. Milton Kingsbury, together with the educational procedures and materials of the American Horse Shows Association and International Arabian Horse Association.

A few special illustrations are in memory of noted artist, horseman, judge and friend Rich Rudish.

Last but not least, this book would not have been written had I not spent the last thirty-eight years standing in the arena making decisions.

Contents

Preface

The Arabian is the oldest light-horse breed and the oldest purebred horse. A growing industry for the past decade, the number of Arabian owners has increased 20 percent per year. It has emerged from being a pastime populated by artists, school teachers, and doctors to a multimillion-dollar business that attracts corporate executives and professionals. Arabians are also a very family oriented involvement. Many people are as interested in the versatility of the Arabian as a riding and show animal for the whole family as they are in any investment possibilities. The Arabian horse, once the property of ancient kings, has again come into its own.

UNDERSTANDING THE HORSE

One of the greatest pleasures of the horse business is having the opportunity to share with others the joy of the horse. In order to fully enjoy the horse, it is essential to know how its mind and body functions. The ability to train the horse is limited only by the lack of knowledge, time, and desire. There is no magic secret. You must have all three components—knowledge, time, and desire—in order to be effective. Knowing how to be most effective in handling and training horses greatly lessens frustration and time and increases the pleasure of working with them.

I don't treat horses any differently from how I treat people. I demand respect from the horse and give it in return. As should be done with anyone, I don't try to hold them in place. The horse must be allowed to use its natural abilities and talents. Just as with any athlete, know their capabilities; don't try to force them beyond their ability.

It is also important to be aware of your own limitations; and we all have them. We are all still learning. The hardest thing to do is to keep from holding the horse back, to keep from interfering with the horse to be its best. That is the most common mistake everyone makes. Often the horse is overcued and held back at the same time, thus creating confusion and frustration.

To work successfully with horses is to understand their basic instincts. No matter what romantic inclination you might have, horses in reality do not have emotions of love or hate as we know them. They do not have the ability to reason or understand, nor do they perceive dishonesty, revenge, or animosity. In that sense, the horse's relationship to us is neither friend nor enemy but, instead, simply one of trust or mistrust.

Three basic instincts—fear, mating, and hunger—determine a horse's reaction to man and the environment. Even though the instinct of fear (the opposite of trust) determines the approach for training the horse, you can't be successful if the horse is afraid of you. Trust must be established between horse and trainer in order for the horse to feel secure and unthreatened.

Historically, fear was the instinct that protected the horse from lions, tigers, wolves, and other predators. Horses are not naturally aggressive or combative, and will not try to escape or hide from threats or danger unless they are blocked or cornered. Only if they cannot escape will they strike back. On the other hand, horses are constantly seeking a comfort zone, or security. If you provide a comfort zone, and establish trust, they are no longer fearful. They will not come to man unless they believe there is nothing to fear. When the horse trusts you, he will come to you. Only then can you effectively work with him.

The other two instincts, mating and hunger (along with fear), determine the total behavior of the horse toward man and the environment. Although all three instincts are intended to provide the horse with a better chance of survival, the primary instinct of fear or perceived danger will override the other instincts of mating and hunger when it is present.

Often in training procedures, we actually teach the horse to mistrust by giving mixed signals (usually unintentionally), out of ignorance of how they function. This is done by asking a horse to both leave and stay, at the same time, by position and pressure. Or, man will call the horse to him and then try to punish him.

If a horse has a clean mind, it has not been cluttered and confused by man. If a horse has bad habits and a tainted mind, the problem has been caused by abuse or punishment to the horse. Most problems stem from trying to punish the horse. Horses do not understand punishment as we mean it; they only understand abuse. Horses are a reflection of how they have been handled. A horse of any age, even one off the range or only one day old, that has a clean mind will respond to the basics of position and pressure.

There are three things you need to understand before taking a horse in hand. First, don't resort to punishing the horse. None of us is quick enough to apply punishment to the horse the instant that the undesirable behavior takes place. They cannot relate to the punishment applied after the act. The horse responds to cues, rather than punishment. So, what is intended as punishment becomes a cue and only confuses the horse. If you become angry with the horse, walk away from it. If you are angry before you start working the horse, don't start.

Second, learn how the horse's eye functions. Unlike the human eye, the horse's does not move in the socket; he must move his head in order to focus. His eye is trifocal and focuses slowly; he must position himself to see long distances or close up. If he is facing into the light, the pupil closes down, allowing only limited vision. If he is jerking his head when you are working in front of him, he is only trying to focus on what is there. Develop a skill at reading a horse's eye, because it will tell how he will react. Understanding its limitations will save much time and frustration for both of you.

Third, you must realize the horse can only think in one place at a time. Bear in mind that the only instincts he knows are fear (trust), mating (companionship), and hunger (food), in that order. If a horse is eating and a mate approaches, he will forget eating and become interested in the mate. But, if something frightens him, he'll then forget the mate and flee or hide if possible. However, if the horse is forced to, he will fight. Understanding these responses will greatly increase the effectiveness and pleasure of the time spent handling horses.

Thus, judging and showing Arabian horses is simply a matter of knowing how the horse's mind and body works.

Introduction

The Arabian horse is one of today's most versatile breeds. Its popularity is at an all-time high and its uses are many and varied. The Arabian horse industry has expanded significantly and, in many areas, outgrown itself in the process. One important factor in this growth has been the Arabian horse show, which furnishes a proving ground, so to speak, to help establish product values.

Throughout this growth period, the changes in both quantity and quality, the elevation of costs for participation, and the escalation of that which is at financial stake have been staggering.

During this expansion, the people governing the horse shows have conscientiously attempted to address the issue of fairness of judging. Today, this problem has escalated due to prize money programs affording the exhibitor the opportunity to win substantial purses. Add this to increased numbers, better quality, and higher financial expenditures in all areas, and there is a situation in which judging takes on the weight of essential importance.

It is important to understand that the Arabian horse industry has reached the end of one historic cycle and the beginning of another. Following elevated market values and high peaking, the Arabian horse market experienced a nosedive.

Where we once had the luxury of being able to rely on chance and circumstances generally beyond our control, we must now establish certain safeguards and essential criteria that will protect the Arabian horse industry's position and provide for positive continuing development. As this cycle begins, it is obvious that we must rely on knowledgeable judging to protect the validity of the industry.

As frightening as it may sound, the truth of the matter is the future of the horse show business lies in the hands of the judges. Breeders will breed for and trainers will train for whatever the judge will place on top.

What happens today in judging manifests itself in years to come. When trends are established, both good and bad, we have to live with them for a long time. I've seen both positive and negative fads drift in and out of the industry over the years. So, the old saying, "blame it on the judge" isn't far wrong.

The concern is discerning the bad trends from the good, allowing the good to last and discarding the undesirable. This is a judge's duty, to know good traits from bad. Knowledge is the key to that end.

On a personal note: When I grew up in the horse business, to have a horse show we simply found an empty lot, put four posts in the ground, ran a rope around, and called it a horse show arena. Next, we took the person who had the worst string of horses and made him the judge (because he couldn't win anything anyway). Then, because of a lack of affordable transportation, we would ride one horse and lead two, tie them to a tree, show all day, and ride back to the barn. As you can see, the industry has expanded significantly.

There will always be a need for knowledgeable personal judgment as to which individual most closely meets the standards set forth. It is towards this end that this book was written together with the hope that the reader will be able to relate to the horse as the judge sees it.

Table of Symbols

*Asterisk	When used before a horse's name, denotes importation from any country to the United States (e.g., *Bask)
+	Legion of Honor
+/	Legion of Supreme Honor
++	Legion of Merit
+++	Legion of Supreme Merit
db	Means desert bred when used after a horse's name.

Egyptian, Spanish, Polish, Russian, Crabbet (English), and American or Domestic Arabian refer to the source (country) from which the individual horse or its parentage came.

The Lands of Origin

Learning Arabian bloodlines presents a special problem to the novice. The Arabian horse has existed for centuries in a number of countries, with each perpetuating its own strain of horses. The beginner must assimilate English, Spanish, Polish, Egyptian, and Russian pedigrees in order to understand the Arabian horse in America. In an effort to make these various lines of Arabian breeding more easily comprehendible, the following bloodlines have been isolated according to their country.

CRABBET

The Crabbet Stud in England, started by Lady Anne and Mister Wilfred Blunt, continued to flourish under the guidance of their daughter, Lady

Judith Wentworth, who took over the horses and the breeding program after Lady Anne's death.

The nucleus of the Crabbet herd had been imported from Egypt by the Blunts. The chestnut stallion Mesaoud, bought from Ali Pasha Sherif in 1889, was to become one of the most influential sires of the breed.

The next momentous purchase was that of Skowronek. Lady Judith Wentworth, with her keen eye for horseflesh, picked the gray stallion. Skowronek sired an incredible string of stallions whose prepotencies have been felt in many countries. His sons *Raffles and *Raseyn have legacies in the United States. Another son, Naseem, added style and beauty to Russian horses, and his grandson Negatiw (by Naseem) helped the Russians and the Poles perfect their Arabians.

Equal to her stallions were Lady Wentworth's mares. Razina, bred to Naseem, produced the stallion Raktha, who in turn sired the great breeding horses Indian Magic, *Serafix, and *Silver Drift. When later bred to Naufal, Razina produced Riffal, sire of Oran. Oran was a progenitor of horses known for their great motion. His descendant, Oran Van Crabbet, was a park horse legend in America during the 1960s.

The influence of these Crabbet horses was worldwide. Australia, Holland, Spain, Poland, Russia, and the United States all owe the strength of their foundation stock, in varying measures, to these English horses. In America, an exceptional impact was made by *Serafix, the sire, grandsire, and great-grandsire of national champions too numerous to list. Another import, *Raffles, was shipped with some mares imported by the Selby Stud in Ohio. *Raffles, who had failed to sire any foals in England, was thought to be impotent, which, combined with his small size (under 14 hands), made him useless in Crabbet. Through the excellent care and patient handling of Jimmy and Selma Dean, managers of the Selby Stud, *Raffles began to settle mares and himself originated a dynasty. His sons and daughters faithfully reproduced his classic type, but with increased size.

POLISH

Polish Arabians started with importations of desert stock going back to the early 1880s. A large number of conflicts and invasions made keeping the horses together difficult, but Poland persevered, maintaining very accurate records of the animals' lineage. An influential group of horses imported from Arabia in 1931 included the stallion Kuhailan Haifi, sire of Ofir and Kuhailan Afas, great-grandsire of Comet. Ofir sired many good horses during his lifetime, but three of his very special sons (known as "the three Ws"): Witraz, Wielki Szlem, and *Witez II were foaled in Poland before Ofir was exported to Russia. Comet was known for the line of exceptionally high-motioned horses he sired; many of these horses have been imported to the United States, doing very well in performance classes. During these golden years, Polish greats such as Trypolis, Aquinor, Amurath Sahib, and Balalajka were bred and put into service, producing increasing numbers of outstanding individuals.

Among the more famous Arabians bred in Poland and influential in Arabian breeding through the years, Ofir and Comet come to the forefront, as well as *Witez II (one of Ofir's best sons), *Bask (by the Ofir son Witraz), Pietuszok, and Wielki Szlem, to name a few. A little-known fact is that the great Crabbet stallion Skowronek was actually bred and foaled in Poland in 1909; he did not arrive in England until he was a four-year-old.

Poland has exported Arabs to the United States since the end of World War I, but the biggest influx came in the early to mid-1960s as breeders began bringing in greater numbers and developing herds of pure Polish horses in this country. *Bask was the most remarkable Polish Arabian to land on these shores. Imported by Lasma Arabians of Arizona, he was named the 1964 U.S. National Champion Stallion and sired horses possessing his own great beauty and ability. He produced a host of National Champions (and champions at all levels below that) in this country and Canada that is unequalled by any other stallion.

Among other well-known Polish stallions that have produced successful horses in this country are *Naborr (by Negatiw), who has many National Champions to his credit; Czort (by Wielki Szlem), sire of many successful racing Arabs and the 1976 U.S. National Champion Stallion *El Paso, and Aquinor, sire of *Elkin and *Elkana, the 1972 U.S. National Champion Stallion and Mare, respectively, and the 1981 U.S. Reserve National Champion Stallion *Czeremosz.

EGYPTIAN

In 1941, the Royal Arabian Society (RAS), predecessor of the Egyptian Agricultural Organization (EAO), took over the breeding programs begun by the royal families, guiding the Egyptian Arabians in their present direction and overseeing exportation of the animals. Importation of Egyptian breeding stock into the United States began in 1932 through the efforts of Henry Babson and W. R. Brown. Early importations included the stallions *Fadl, *Zarife, and *Nasr and the mares *Aziza, *Mahroussa, and *Roda. These classic individuals are found in the majority of Egyptian pedigrees today.

In this country, *Ansata Ibn Halima, *Morafic, *Talal, *Ramses Fayek, and *Bint Maisa el Saghire have had an astounding impact. They offered a direct and immediate infusion of the best Egyptian blood into existing American herds. Among these early imports, the Nazeer-sired horses had the strongest effect; sons such as *Ansata Ibn Halima and *Morafic went on to sire dynasties of their own.

Nazeer himself (Mansour x Bint Samiha) spend his early breeding years in relative obscurity. It was not until age twelve that he was discovered by the director of the El Zahraa Stud and his importance as a sire recognized. As prominent as Nazeer was to Egyptian breeding, so also was the exquisite mare Moniet El Nefous (Shahloul x Wanisa). Like Nazeer, she never left the homeland, but through her sons and daughters she has helped to shape Egyptian breeding programs in many countries. Bred to Sid Abouhom, she produced the two daughters Maya and *Bint Moniet El Nefous, the latter being imported to the United States by Richard Pritzlaff of New Mexico, another early breeder of straight Egyptian stock. Four sons of Moniet El Nefous were imported to this country: *Fakher El Din (by Nazeer), *Soufian (by Alaa El Din), *Tuhotmos (by El Sareei), and *Ibn Moniet El Nefous (by *Morafic).

The number of straight Egyptians in this country is small, compared to the total number of purebreds registered. For this reason, one does not see these horses in competition as frequently as those of other backgrounds. They are maintained as breeding animals to perpetuate their numbers, and although sales of Egyptians are not as visible on the show scene, individuals such as National Champion Stallion Ansata Ibn Sudan and National Champion Mare *Serenity Sonbolah come immediately to mind as vivid examples of the Egyptian Arabian.

SPANISH

The Spanish government and its military imported and bred horses, beginning in the 1880s, that became the basis of the Spanish Arabian. Private breeders were allowed to use some of the better stallions for breeding purposes, however.

Horses were imported from several countries, including the bay stallion *Ursus, who proved to be the most important of Spain's Polish importations. Following his use by the military, *Ursus was sold to a private breeder, Don Jose Maria Ybarra, and went on to sire one of two major Spanish sire lines. The *Ursus son Gandhy (x Gomara) sired Malvito and Maquillo, themselves influential breeding horses. Both have descendents in North America, with the 1979 U.S. and Canadian National Champion Mare *Abha Hamir and Supreme Spanish National Champion *G.G. Samir both tracing to Maquillo.

The most successful Egyptian stallion imported to Spain for use in their breeding program was *Seanderich. His best-known sons were Eco and Illustre; there are representatives of this line in the United States today. Illustre, in particular, produced athletic lines with great racing, jumping, and trotting abilities.

As the military was developing its intensely bred band of horses, several private breeders were also striving toward perfection in the breed. One was the Duke of Verague, whose most important contribution was the importation of five Skowronek daughters from England. At least one of the Crabbet mares (*Jilil, *Namira, *Nasleda, *Reyna, and *Shelifa) can be found in most Spanish pedigrees.

It was approximately 1930 when the first importation of Spanish horses was made to the United States by Mr. and Mrs. James Draper of California. The group was small: four mares and one stallion. In 1965, John Rogers of California imported two mares and one stallion, and a group of twenty-six horses (twenty-three mares and three stallions) known as the Steen Imports arrived at the Steen Ranches in Nevada. These latter horses and their descendants are recognizable by the suffix "De Washoe" (De Washoe is the county in which the Steen Ranches were located).

As of the end of 1980, approximately 175 Spanish horses had been imported to this country, making a total U.S. population of about 250. With the small numbers and the concentration toward carrying on the lines, many of these horses are being kept on farms for breeding purposes rather than being campaigned on show circuits. There have, however, been significant wins for Spanish Arabians: The former U.S. and Canadian National Champion mare, *Abha Hamir, was mentioned earlier. The Spanish bred mare S.B. La Ina (by *Barich de Washoe) earned the title of 1981 Canadian National Champion Mare. *A.N. Malik (a Spanish stallion imported by Jay Stream) sired the Junior Champion colt at Scottsdale in 1981. *El Moraduke, owned by Owens Arabians in Arizona, has been a Top-Ten Halter Stallion in the United States and Canada.

As numbers of Spanish individuals in the United States increase, they will become more visible. Those people who are breeding these horses comment on their type, presence, and good attitudes. They are found to be extremely easy to work with and, consequently, an ideal horse for the amateur owner who wants to train and show his or her own horse. As breeding animals, their prepotency has been impressive. As Bill Owens of Owens Arabians put it, "With the Spanish, you had better like what you see because that is what you are going to get. With their heavy concentration of blood, you get a genetic explosion. In one step you get what you want."

RUSSIAN

What American breeders have discovered in Russia, just within the past decade, are precisely bred, successful blends of Crabbet, Polish, Egyptian, German, and French bloodlines.

Although Arabians have existed in Russia as far back as the Seventeenth century, actual breeding programs at the government-owned Tersk

Stud began in 1944. The Stud was founded in 1921 and acquisition of purebreds for breeding purposes began in 1930. Horses were imported from France, England, Poland, and Germany, with specimens selected on the basis of athletic ability and physical beauty. In less than forty years, the Russian program has succeeded in producing exceptional individuals that are now in demand worldwide.

The six major sire lines found in Russian stock are an international mix, each horse adding a particular quality to the end product. From Poland came Ofir, Priboj, and Arax. Kann was French, Naseem English, and Aswan Egyptian.

Ofir sired Witraz, Wielki Szlem, and *Witez II, three sires of monumental importance, before he was exported from Poland to begin his breeding career at Tersk in 1940. He was used by the Russians for his smooth build, strong hindquarters, and well-structured hind legs. Priboj blended Polish substance through his sire, Piolun, and his Crabbet style and trotting ability from his dam, Rissalma. He thus offered the Russian program balanced action, a good head, and structural soundness. Arax, the youngest of the three Polish horses, did not arrive in Tersk until 1958, when he was six years old. His length of hip, huge dark eyes, and superb overall conformation added correctness to the Tersk herd.

The French stallion Kann, although at first glance appearing to offer little, was basically a correct horse with good legs and a particularly deep shoulder. His addition to the Russian horses was function rather than type.

For type and classic beauty, the English stallion Naseem (by Skowronek) fit right in. Imported at the age of thirteen from the Crabbet Stud in 1936, Naseem was used for seventeen years until his death at the impressive age of thirty-three. His greatest attributes were a long, well-arched neck, fine throatlatch, and beautiful head. His body was good, although not as correct as some of the Polish horses. The Russians, judiciously crossing the two types, were able to achieve excellent structure with the classic Crabbet front end.

The Nazeer son Aswan, a gift to the Russians from the Egyptian government in 1964, resides at Tersk and contributes type, style, and tail carriage to the Tersk horses. He has sired over 300 foals, with at least thirty daughters in the broodmare band.

It was not until Howard Kale of Arizona traveled to Tersk in 1975 and began his attempts to purchase several individuals that Russian horses gained recognition in America. Earlier imports had not been accepted for registration in this country by the Arabian Horse Registry or World Arabian Horse Organization (WAHO). Finally, in 1980, *Muscat, imported by Kale, achieved a grand slam of sorts by being named Champion Stallion at Scottsdale, the Canadian Nationals, and, ultimately, the U.S. Nationals.

Through perseverance and unrelenting efforts, the door has been opened for Russian Arabians. *Marsianin, by Aswan, was awarded the

1981 U.S. National Champion Stallion title; *Pesenka, by Salon, won 1980 Reserve U.S. National Champion Mare; and *Padron, an Aswan grandson, won 1981 Canadian National Champion Stallion.

These horses are noted for their strong, balanced movement as well as their classic conformation. Because of their recent arrival, for the most part, few have been presented as performance horses.

Russian imports have made a tremendous impact in this country. Russian breeders in the United States have carefully and knowledgeably promoted these horses, presenting them at open houses so that everyone—owners and enthusiasts alike—can see their qualities firsthand.

DOMESTIC

In concluding our discussion of the different countries that have produced Arabians, we come inevitably to the "Domestic" Arabian horse. Defining "domestic" is a touchy business since there are no Arabians truly indigenous to this country. "Domestic" has therefore come to refer to those horses born of animals that have been in this country for a generation or two, and whose lineage has not been maintained as straight or pure in any direction.

One of the most famous "domestic" stallions, Ferzon, traces heavily to the Skowronek son *Raseyn, with a remaining line to Nasik—all original Crabbet stock. Fadjur would hardly be considered Egyptian, yet his grandsire *Fadl is of old Egyptian lines, and his dam traces to Crabbet horses descended from Abbas Pasha/Ali Pasha Sherif stock. Multi-National Champion Khemosabi is a Fadjur grandson on his dam's side, with lines to Skowronek on top. The great-moving Abu Farwa can be traced to Naseem and Gulastra, again Crabbet. The Real McCoy is another firmly established domestic sire, yet his grandsire on top is *Raffles, he has three lines to Skowronek and some desert-bred (db) individuals appear on his pedigree too. Even *Bask, imported from Poland, has so many progeny, to grandget and great-grandget and beyond, that those individuals can be termed domestic Arabians due to the distance by which they are removed from the imported horse. All of these horses were born in the United States (with the exception of *Bask) of sires and dams born in the United States, and in most cases their grandsires and granddams were also foaled here. Although the label "domestic" might, unfortunately, appear less desirable than straight or pure animals with asterisks before their names, good breeding is good breeding. American breeders need stand second to none when it comes to producing top quality Arabians, using the foundations selected by their forebears.

CHAPTER
~1~

Judges

INNER THOUGHTS

Over the years, I've had several comments on and many questions about what judging is really like—"the inside scoop," so to speak.. To begin with, judging definitely has its moments, depending on your tastes for that particular place or time frame. You become a celebrity to some, a jackass to others, but more likened to the Wizard of Oz. You arrive at the location and are spirited off to an unknown destination for fear of influence, or to keep you pure from "the evil that lurks in the hearts of men." You're wined and dined with elegance (usually), and the country boy in you from last week becomes the debonair sophisticate who knows it all. You spend more time with your wardrobe because, after all, "clothes make the man."

You descend, not arrive; you don't go to, but actually appear at the horse show ready, eager, and apprehensive. Incongruous, yes, but true. You're introduced as "honorable," "best," "most sought after," "famous," and on and on until you wonder whom they're talking about.

As the first class enters the ring, you stand in quiet awe awaiting the winner. The gate closes and—lo and behold!—not a crowd-pleasing winner in sight. A quick look at the ringmaster tells you that's the entire class. Then all dreams and illusions disappear, and reality taps you on the shoulder. With the gate closed, there is no escape as the entrants line up, eagerly awaiting to be chosen "best" in the class. You tell yourself, "everyone only wants what they deserve," no favors or gifts: They all know their own horse and performance (but do they really?). You breathe a sigh of relief as your background and experience come to your salvation,

1

like a bugle in the distance when you need the cavalry to come to the rescue. That is, if you are a horseman to begin with.

The class sorts itself out. You're satisfied, and you await the next onslaught. As sure as night follows day, the expected surge comes as the gate opens and, again, you're eagerly searching for that elegant individual who will save you from ridicule. But, alas, the gate closes and once more you're in solitary, sorting out the impossible, trying to please everyone.

Then, you suddenly realize that you're not trying to please everyone, only yourself. As a horseman, you actually *do* rise above it and think, "to thine ownself be true" (or at least that's what you should do).

You finish the day's judging chores, whether at dinnertime or after midnight, and attempt to unwind. Some shows expect you to attend certain functions, while others shudder at the thought of you even nodding at an exhibitor. If you are not the only judge, then usually a nightcap or a sandwich (or both) with your colleagues is in order to climax the hard day. The next morning you're up at the crack of dawn or before. You fight off jet lag with a quick shower and a cup of coffee, and you're ready again.

As the show progresses, it doesn't take long to tell who belongs to what horse, or what parents belong to what child. After a few years in this business, you can pick out the pseudo-horseman or trainer and, most assuredly, the local complainer and/or know-it-all. He judges the horses from the backgate—everybody else's horse, that is, because his horse is always perfect. You can also tell which juniors have been partying instead of resting and riding; who is romancing whom on the side, as well as which husband and wife are fighting.

From your vantage point in the ring, you soon see all: The girls who smile and wink at you as they ride by, the trainer who wants to buy a horse from every judge, and the poor owner who has a turkey but has been pumped up to think it's a champion. At times some people become overly friendly and others overly cross. But, as a judge, you always know who the promoters are anyway, so it really doesn't make any difference.

Judging is a lot of fun, especially when you judge with others. After a while you end up joking and, if you know the other judges well enough, you carry practical jokes from one show to another. This tends to relieve the tension and helps to lift your spirits, especially if the weather is bad, your feet and back ache, or you're still trying to find a winner.

You, as a judge, become in reality the trendsetter. You actually have in your hands the future of what the horse business is to become (not you alone, but judges collectively). For instance, if all judges decided to ignore the walk, pretty soon no one would walk except to move from one gait to another. If you ignored the backup, the same thing would happen. This, in fact, has happened in many classes. For example, in park classes, horses that did not trot have won. Instead, they paced, racked, or whatever, but they did not trot. Consequently, we had a complete

Owner pumped up to think his turkey is a champion.

discrepancy in how a park horse should go. The same held true for the four-beat lope in the pleasure classes. All judges are guilty, through no fault of their own, because sometimes you must tie horses who do things you really don't care for but, in a given situation, they may be just the "least lousy." Hence, they win the class.

Life is full of compromises, and so is the horse business. After all, judging is only comparison. There are times when you must stick your neck out for what you actually believe in, even though you know all the backgate gossips will have a field day in telling on you. If a junior rider ends up beating all the pros, if he or she truly has the best go in the class, then you must tie it that way.

The horse business is a way of life, a love, and judging all over the country enables you to see all kinds of horses. Even when it's hot, 110 degrees in the shade (and there's no shade) with 90 percent humidity, or freezing in the rain, when the gate opens and that special class comes in with everyone performing to their best, you become just as anxious as the spectators to see who will win. Your eyes dart from horse to horse. "What a class!" you say to yourself. With your enthusiasm at a peak, you actually feel the excitement as you put the numbers in their places, because you've finally found the winner.

That one class makes it all worthwhile, the one great horse that makes up for all the bad footing, the bad lighting, and the poor quality of the past. You are part of the best taking place. Yes, in judging, there are all the good times and a few bad. But you will always have the one satisfaction in knowing that the old axiom is true: "You may not always be right, but you are never wrong."

I know that I am relating to you a slightly slanted viewpoint, one which brings to mind the time my youngest daughter was asked the prevailing question in school, "What does your dad do?" She readily answered, "My dad's a judge," not realizing at the time the importance of mentioning what kind. So, whenever I attended any school function, I was immediately addressed as "Your Honor" until they found out I was a judge of horses and not of the judicial system.

But even at the beginning of a horse show, you are referred to as "Your Honor," which makes you subject to praise by the winners and undertoned innuendos by the losers. Judging requires total concentration, so you can't allow the praises or petty thoughts to creep into your mind. Those who talk negatively are usually looking for a reason why they didn't win, forgetting that maybe someone else had a better horse or trip in that particular class. On a given day, in a given class and at any particular time, champions can fail and the meek can inherit the "blue."

But let's return to other outside pressures not touched on before, or to the shell game—Is the hand quicker than the eye? There are many pressures such as merchandising, local champions, popular trainers, and undefeated horses, which brings to mind an instructive personal judging experience.

As I walked up and down the halter line quietly inspecting each horse, I came to one in particular the crowd went wild cheering and clapping for. I had never seen the horse before, or the handler, and as I went by him I simply quipped, "Oh, brought the family, eh?" referring to the private cheering section. Naturally, I thought my comment was pretty funny at the time. But later I heard the word in the barn was this particular handler and I were long-time friends because I was overheard asking him about his family. I learned to keep my mouth shut after that.

As a judge, these kinds of things should roll off like water from a duck because you know that most exhibitors have better sense. Somehow, though, you involuntarily develop an outer crust to counteract the many little items over which you have no control. Judging is hard work, physically as well as mentally. I can't think of any other business that forces its leaders to make, on an average, 300 to 500 separate decisions in a single day, every day, with only about a minute for analysis, decisions that are open to public scrutiny and debate. Some judges wrongfully get uptight, never smile, and seemingly look unsure.

As a judge, you are a stylist and the actual future of the horse show industry. What you do in the arena, no matter what size show, will have a bearing on breeding programs, training methods and the whole spectrum. A judge should not think of himself as a follower, or he'll be way out in left field. To be a leader he must find an area where it all comes together; background, experience, and keeping up with the times. He must be currently on top of the trends and then form his own opinions.

Judging may be strenuous and tiring. But, it is especially rewarding when the show is over, and you know you have placed the horses as you honestly saw them (not caring what others may think or say).

Occasionally, you sneak a peek in the mirror just to make sure that you still look the same—no horns and no tail. You adjust your suit of armor, heave a sigh of relief, and then look forward with great anticipation to the next show, and the unexpected experiences you will have.

Accentuate the Positive

Since using the positive approach to evaluating a horse or group of horses, instead of the negative style of yesterday, an ongoing educational program (not only for judges but exhibitors and spectators as well) must be maintained.

For years judges customarily would find faults, give penalties, and utilize errors until the horse that emerged victorious was often not necessarily the best but merely the "least lousy." Judges are now instructed to accentuate the positive, to give credit for good qualities, and emphasize what a horse does right instead of placing all the weight only on the negative. Even in the halter division, credit for what a horse *has* should outweigh what he has not, that is, when the good qualities exceed the bad. This philosophy is a positive way of looking at a horse, requiring judges to become better prepared scientifically—to know more about how a horse is put together, and for what function. It has forced some changes in the procedures practiced in judging, weighing all the ingredients instead of simply looking at the "down" side. Faults are easy to spot and evaluate, but the gray areas of "how *good* is good" compared to how "*bad* is bad" and all else in-between becomes more difficult to actually define. We have, for years, placed unknown values or relationships on faults. For example, back at the knee is worse than over at the knee; toe-out worse than toe-in. But now, the degree has a direct bearing and needs to be related to shoulder, neck, back, hocks, etc. The whole is the sum of its parts. The arrangement of those parts equals conformation, and causes the degree of correctness or the degree of nonsymmetry to take on a much greater role.

The exhibitor and spectator must also keep up with the ever-changing tide, especially when being critical. Granted, a certain horse may have a little wrong here and there but could just possibly have more good qualities than the average one standing behind him. When the judge uses that positive approach, he in a way sticks his neck out because of actually putting values on the gray areas heretofore generally overlooked. Rule books don't tell you, nor do any other volumes I've read, that a certain bad quality is better than another bad one. They don't tell you that a hollow back is a much greater fault in young horses than toeing-out a little behind; or how straight shoulders correlate to postlegged; or a thick throatlatch to no withers. More than this, they don't say how a good shoulder, good neck, good hip, or good back correlate to a right front foot toeing-out a little or if he stands a little straight behind—all food for thought in the halter division.

YOU BE THE JUDGE

Some people keep a card file on judges and their likes, dislikes, idiosyncrasies—everything. I'm sure some even have such information on computer by now.

Analyzing the judge has always been a favorite pastime among exhibitors. More often than not, the way they arrive at their decision as to which judge likes them or doesn't like them is based on false impression, along with assumptions that only defeat their purpose.

Judges are tagged with all kinds of labels such as, "Oh, he only likes chestnut horses. Don't you remember that class when the first three placings were all chestnuts?"

That's how labels get stuck. Critics don't consider the fact that it was only one class and the three chestnuts were probably the best of that particular class. It would have been the same conclusion if the horses had all been gray.

There are, however, ways to analyze a particular judge, regardless of whether you agree with his placings. How he sets up the ring, the class, and even the mood of the show can give insight to a judge's habits and traits.

The first thing you have to analyze is where he stands for the classes he's going to judge. If, for instance, he has a definite plan (such as in halter), telling the exhibitor to walk here, trot here, line up here, he probably will be precise and exact where the horses are concerned. Also, he'll probably be a little more detail conscious as he inspects each horse and will place more emphasis on smaller details such as correctness.

On the other hand, the judge who is a little lax in his instructions, who doesn't really care how you enter, and relies on the ringmaster to put the horses wherever he happens to want them—uphill, downhill, facing into the sun, whatever—probably will be lax in the horses' detail department, maybe overlooking some defects that might not be too important to him.

Consider the enthusiasm the judge displays as he looks at the horses and the methods he uses on each horse. Is it the same for each? Or is it the same for some and different for others? All these are clues as to how to show to a given judge. How he watches horses travel gives you an idea as to how much emphasis he places on that phase. The judge who studies the horses' footfalls and closely scrutinizes how they move, both at the walk and trot, obviously cares more than the one who glances at the walk and views the trot only a few paces.

When the judge pulls horses out for the final lineup, does he do it firmly and confidently with little switching around? Or is he willy-nilly, switching many back and forth before the final tally? And, I might add, what about the influence of applause, especially when the judge is switching back and forth?

These all become part of truly analyzing the judge.

The rail classes are the next dimension. Again, where a judge stands gives you a good idea of what he's looking for and at. It's obvious that the judge who stands in the corner (looking into the arena) sees more than the one who stands looking at one side only or who stands in the corner and looks only at the rail.

Most judges try to stand in the corner of an arena for equitation classes on the flat. The reasons for standing there are twofold. First, it gives the opportunity to see most of the ring with only a small portion being behind your back. And, even while a rider is not in your line of vision for that instant, if your hearing is exceptional (as mine is), it isn't hard to discern what's happening from the trainer coaching on the rail to the rider fussing at the horse.

Ideal judging position—standing in corner looking into arena.

Ingate

The second reason for this vantage point is that you can see a rider coming straight toward you or going straight away from you. This gives a good picture whether or not the rider sits square in the saddle and uses all of the aids, or cheats on one side.

Which corner the judge stands in needs to be studied. First impressions are important, so if he stands by the gate, he sees exhibitors enter, one at a time. If he's in the corner at the end of the ring opposite the in-gate, he sees two or three riders coming in at a time. Facing the side rail, the judge sees the first impression, but then is only interested in a pass, so what you as a rider do the rest of the way around the ring is of little importance to him (unless he turns around unexpectedly and catches you doing something you shouldn't).

The next item after the judge positions himself is how long he has you maintain the walk. This gives you an idea of how important the walk is, and the same is true of the trot and lope or canter.

You can be tipped off where a certain judge places importance if you know what to look for. Does the judge stand still or change positions? What about the lineup? The judge who instructs the ringmaster as to exactly where he wants the horses lined up has analyzed the ring and has planned his next procedure. He will probably put more emphasis on the back-up (in those classes required to back) than the judge who leaves it all up to the ringmaster. The latter, walking down the line to back, really pays little attention to what the horse does; he's simply fulfilling a requirement.

The way judges give instructions in the individual work classes separates them. Precise, detailed instructions tell you that a judge will be

Ingate

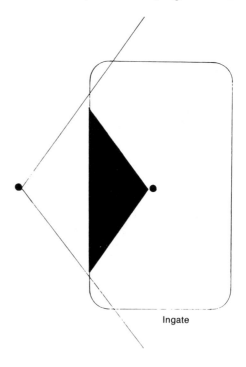

Ingate

This position affords the judge an opportunity to see two or three riders coming into the arena at one time and about three quarters of the ring.

Judging position facing the rail on the long side of arena. This figure also shows the relative field vision of the spectator to that of the judge.

quite critical if they are not followed. Mumbling ''do-what-you-want'' instructions give the opposite impression.

A judge sitting in a chair across the ring where he can barely see the walk-overs in a trail class tells you he really doesn't care whether you touch the logs or not. It's the same with the back-up between poles or any other maneuver that requires exact placement of the feet.

Where he stands (or sits), in the Western riding class again, tells all. He should be on the side where he can see all the lead changes, or missed ones, but should not be on the end of the arena. The judge can only judge what he sees. It then becomes obvious whether he wants to see a lot or just a little.

In over-fence classes, if you don't see the profile, you miss half the class. Faults like hanging legs, dropping shoulders, and hollow backs can be seen only from the side.

Then, last but certainly not least would be the judge's basic attitude. Is he confident, polite, neat, precise? Or is he lackadaisical, uncaring, cocky, curt, devil-may-carish? Is he late, slow, fast, unsure, ignorant of the rules? Does he visit with the ringmaster or exhibitors? Is he sloppy, mixing up numbers? I could go on and on about individual traits, both good and bad.

Analyzing the judge, even one whom you've never seen or heard of before, is much more than seeing the outcome of his placings; it involves objective thought. Today, we have many people analyzing, or, more bluntly, judging the judge. The criteria they use should be in proper perspective, and not based simply on who won.

Ingate

Judging position standing in corner facing the rail. This position is the least desirable—the epitome of tunnel vision.

You can't judge on that basis unless you actually see what the judge sees at every turn, and that can't be done from the grandstand or back gate. It's not what the judge chooses but how he goes about it that counts, for both you the exhibitor and you the judge.

VIEWS FROM "THE TOP"

I was invited to judge a show and also to be the guest speaker at a special exhibitor dinner after the show was over. I've been a speaker on many occasions, once the night before a show, but never right after.

As we were having dinner, I looked around the room at the sea of faces. There were happy ones and, yes, sad ones too, all trying to search my face out in the crowd. I was introduced, though by now everyone must have known who I was, and my opening remark was: "Please save all your questions until the end and we'll have an open discussion period."

I went through the by-now-familiar routine that judging is only an opinion, not a matter of right and wrong. I touched on what I personally like to see in a pleasure horse class, because I knew we would have questions about that division. I went on to the halter phase, giving my viewpoint on the relationship of form to function and yes, I even touched on the controversial park horse classes. I tried to relate the whole talk to all types, discussing the pros and cons of each. I talked for about an hour or so and, satisfied with myself, I said, "And now, are there any questions?"

Hands went up as if I were giving out free blue ribbons. To my surprise, the questions did not center around "Why did you tie that horse in that class?" or "Why didn't my horse get a ribbon?" Instead, they were a genuine quest for my inner thoughts and knowledge of exactly what goes on in a judge's mind as he proceeds with his chores. I tried to be very open, with a "tell it like it is" format.

One stimulating question was "Does advertising a horse have any influence on judging?" I can speak for only myself, but, no, it really doesn't to me because I neither read the ads nor do I look at the show results. But I am an exception, I think. I know what I like, based on my own experience, and I look for the individual who comes closest to that standard. Some exhibitors do an excellent job of merchandising their show horses and I think that's fine, but when it comes to judging, "best" should still be best on that particular day in that particular class. A good horse can let down at any time and a not-so-good one can be brilliant, and whoever performs, at that time, should be the winner. If a judge has a preconceived notion of who is supposed to win, he should not accept the job of judging.

We have several polished super-showmen who attempt to intimidate a judge—not necessarily in a derogatory way, but their particular style of showing a horse is very intense and sometimes overbearing. If you listen, you can hear them say, especially in halter classes, "Stand up, you undefeated champion" or "Let's make it ten wins in a row, that's just right, boy, stand up." But, to answer the question, I guess advertising and merchandising do work on some judges, but I really hope not too often.

Many hands shot up in the audience, but I had noticed a trainer who never once raised his hand, so to change the pace I called on him and asked, "Don't you have any questions?" He smiled and replied, "Oh no, I had a good show." Everyone had a good chuckle with that, as I turned back to the hand-wagglers for another question: "What do you think is the weakest point of an amateur showing in the halter classes?"

"Most amateurs don't show their horses to their best advantage," I answered. "Most are nervous to begin with, even though they have had experience, and when they walk toward the judge some knees even rattle (handlers', that is, not horses'). But the most common error is only showing half the horse, the front half. Oh, the handlers get the front legs in line and the ears up, but then usually a foot is cocked up so the horse looks like he's got a hip down. The handlers rarely look at or think about the hindquarter, but to a horseperson and most assuredly the judge, the hindquarter is as important as the front end; to a performance horseman, it's extremely important because he knows that the hind end is the horse's driving force, and without a good hip and hind leg you don't have much horse."

The questions were open and varied, and as the hour was getting late we had to wind it up. But I hope perhaps other clubs or organizations putting on shows will adopt a similar format and allow exhibitors and judges to get to know each other on a different basis. It all goes along with my basic concept of open communication, and maybe someday we'll be in a position for the judge to comment about a class as the ribbons are given out, such as is done with cattle and other livestock. It sure would stimulate audience participation!

Politics in Show Biz?

Traveling around the United States on judging assignments, I've had the opportunity to ask many questions relating to the exhibitor's thoughts on how he feels about showing in general, the good parts and the bad.

One of the most controversial subjects, and a topic about which few are silent is, "Do you think politics play a part in the horse show world?" There was an overwhelming mass feeling that there is a great deal of politics going on at all levels, but mostly where the major shows are concerned and then relating mainly to halter, park, pleasure horses, and equitation.

This seemed to me to be the natural relationship because those are completely opinion classes, not judged on an individual work basis such as reining or trail. The feeling puzzled me somewhat and, as I dug deeper into the reasons, I tried to understand the comments on the somewhat clouded issues, even though I did or did not agree.

The most outspoken group was the relatively new owner who bought a horse or two and all that goes with it, scanned the rule book and a few horse publications, and went off to a show. Needless to say, no prize would have been the probable result. After this happened a few times, and they conversed with a few other nonwinners plus the backgate tongue-waggers, the attitude started to take effect: "Well, the judge is a friend of the people who do all the winning" or "He's a trainer and this judge always places trainers because they'll be judging him next week so he has to let them win" or "He sold them some horses a while back so he lets them win now so he can sell them more."

Most people listen and what they hear makes sense, at least at the time, because they don't think it through or follow a logical course. Sure, there are politics in showing just as there are politics in everything we do (in fact, our nation and all our associations are run with politics). Just because it is that way doesn't mean that all politics are bad, dirty, or to be looked down on. First, we must clarify what we're calling "politics," and not make overall assumptions.

We may very well have some unscrupulous judges, but I've only met a few. Most judges and, most assuredly, the ones who do the majority of shows, are of very high integrity. It is true they know people in every area because, over years of traveling, showing, and judging, lasting friendships are made. But because of these friendships, for a judge to place a horse only on that basis, it would do only harm to the respect friends have for each other to award a ribbon that each party would be ashamed of.

Just as with my after-dinner question-and-answer forum, I think we should encourage judges and exhibitors to "get to know each other" whenever we can. All shows would be much smoother if officials and participants understood each other and their own individual likes and dislikes. The judge's opinions should not be the "best kept secret in town" until the awards are given out. Communication, or the lack of it (in most cases), has a great deal to do with establishing rapport.

AN EYE FOR A BOLD PROPOSAL

"What position or vantage point is best from which to judge?" is an often-asked question.

I've always been an advocate of "what you see is what you get," depending on where you're looking and on what your mind is concentrating. Not only is what you see what you get, but it's also how much others see or don't see.

Some judges actually handicap themselves by their judging position, to say nothing of handicapping the exhibitor by reason of where they look. All too often the spectator-exhibitor sees more than the judge, which also leads to all types of problems and criticism.

Going back to the basics, we, as judges, are trying to pick a winner—that is, in our opinion, the best horse in the class. Everyone agrees to that. But how we view a particular horse in a class definitely will influence our opinion.

Starting with halter classes, judges historically view the horses coming toward them from the in-gate, whether they have all come in and lined up as a group or are coming toward us one at a time. However, the spectators or exhibitors see either the hind view or the side view first while others get their first impression from a near-front view. Which comes first is really of no consequence. It is, however, important for a judge to view the horse in the best environment, and not just by rote. If you're looking directly into the sun in an outside arena, you're not going to see the same things that you'll see with the light coming from over your shoulder. If the arena slopes downhill to where you are standing, you're further disadvantaged by allowing horses to stand up on slanted terrain. The arena must be used to your advantage as far as sun, terrain, silhouette on the wall, or any other situation that will cause distortion in your viewing is concerned.

Performance classes constitute an entirely different story. After trying every conceivable position except standing on my head, I have made some startling discoveries. Inside the ring, you see a completely different horse show from what is seen from outside. Another revelation is that at arena floor level you also see from a different perspective than when your viewing position is a little elevated. The worst possible place to judge a pleasure or rail class of any kind is inside the ring by the in-gate or out-gate facing into the corner. An arena encompasses some form of a 360-degree oval, rectangle, or open field. My contention has always been that the judge has an obligation to see as much as possible of the entire class, not only a corner.

The major problem areas for rail horses are by the gate and in the corners. If a judge simply looks at that one spot, he or she is obviously trying to catch mistakes, or more than likely force them. A judge so doing sees only one or two horses at a time and then for only a couple of strides. It's the epitome of tunnel vision. Instead of seeing 360 degrees, it's more like 10 degrees, with the rider being able to stop and have lunch in the remaining 350 degrees before making a pass.

The next worse way to view a rail class is by looking at a spot on the rail and seeing a profile for only a few strides. Viewing a segment of 15 or 20 degrees is still not seeing all the class, and it is definitely not

Ingate

Unfortunately, sometimes a view can be blocked by a centerpiece or gazebo in the middle of the arena no matter where the judge stands.

seeing what others are capable of seeing. This is not new, because every judging seminar has been encouraging judges to stand in a corner just off the rail and face the major portion of the ring so they can view horses coming toward them, going away, and in profile. This view encompasses a much better view of the class, using 350 degrees and losing a horse during only 10 degrees. This same premise holds true for nearly every other individually worked class.

After much thought and a lot of trial and error, my conclusion is that nearly all but halter, trail, and cutting classes are better judged from outside the ring, and from a viewpoint that is almost at a corner and elevated to the height of the normal horse's eye. Hunter and jumper classes should be judged from a slightly higher position in the middle of one side of the arena, to allow a broadside, or profile, view of the horse going over fences. This, coupled with the position on the opposite side of the arena from the in-and-out or a combination, allows the best possible judging view.

Judging reining classes from much the same position provides a better view of how a horse uses the arena, the size and symmetry of the circles, the smoothness and length of the run-down, a much better view of the turn-around, and an easier place for counting the number of spins. Also, for what it's worth, the judge's view is exactly the same as that of the spectator-exhibitor.

The advantage in the rail classes, whether judging horses or riders, is that no one needs to wander around to see the whole ring. There is no 10 degree segment that's out of sight; all horses are looked at in the same way (unless a judge wants just to focus on one as he goes around). Another advantage for viewing the class just outside and elevated is the ability to see across the arena when there is a gazebo or judge's stand in the center. The distraction caused by people moving about and the activity going on in the center while the horses are performing is lessened.

There are some disadvantages, though (until the physical needs are determined), in the fact that the only place that's outside and elevated at most shows is in the stands, where people are milling about, talking, and peeking over your shoulder. These problems are easily handled, if thought of early enough, by having a ringmaster with the judge and an area of seats that has been set aside.

At shows where seats in the stand are nonexistent, I've found the bed of a pickup truck with a couple of chairs (as at most cutting horse competitions), parked just outside the ring a workable solution. In fact, at some shows in Europe, the judge sits in a judge's car on a truck bed with glass enclosure, table, and chairs, and a driver to position the official wherever the best view is deemed to be. In most rail classes today, judging inside the arena at floor level is the most preferred by judges and exhibitors. But always remember, what you see is definitely what you get, wherever you are!

"When does the judging really start?" Ask most judges and they'll tell you, "When the gate closes." That's what the rule book says, but I think maybe a more realistic approach is that judging never stops. We are all judging something most of the time—dogs, cats, art, houses, cars and, of course, each other.

Judges are subconsciously forming opinions the first time they see a horse or rider. The exhibitors also go on first impressions of the judge— his physical appearance, professionalism or lack of it—as he judges the first class. So, what a horse does or how he appears at that initial meeting is very important.

Even when the judge is walking from his car to the office or from the office to the arena his mind is working. If he passes horses being unruly, it registers; if people are arguing or displaying bad manners, that clicks too, or at least subconsciously.

Some people go to great lengths just to let the judge know which horse is theirs. I've sometimes thought if they'd only put that much creative energy into finding a better horse—but, I guess that's human nature.

Judges do not begin to sort out the class until the gate is closed but, as the horses come in, they certainly do categorize them in their minds. Good or bad mover; too fat; too skinny; nervous; nice, that's one to watch; or, Oh, my God, that's not the class, there's not a good one in the bunch.

In rail classes, the first clue comes when the horse enters the arena. Does he respond easy to the leg and go right into the gait called for or does he back off, resist, charge, throw his head up in the air, or prance around. All of these traits are witnessed at first glance and, as the horse proceeds the first way around the arena, are usually an indication of how

the "go" will be. Good movers, willing and happy, have a higher percentage of good gos than resentful, crabby, bad movers. Therefore, the
entrance becomes extremely important; it is the first impression.

The reining horse that comes jogging into the ring with his mouth
open offers a negative image to the judge; and similarly so, the sulky one
that sulks coming through the gate.

What amazes me is that some people deliberately put their horse in
a bind before they ever get to present him. Time after time I see riders,
especially in pleasure or equitation classes, who come up to the gate, but
instead of entering they stand there posing or just waiting. They may be
waiting for a better position, but to a judge who has stood on his feet for
eight or ten hours, holding up at the gate for any reason is an obstacle
you put in your own way. The judge wants you to be punctual, so he can
be too.

In this quest for recognition, many trainers walk their students to the
gate and stand there giving so-called "last-minute instructions," obviously
overdoing it. But most judges realize it's an attention-getting device to
let them know who rides with whom.

The Granddaddy of all ruses, though, is the fanatic who follows his
horse around the ring leaning over from every box seat. So intent is he
on letting the judge know which horse is his, he is oblivious of the tripped-
over toes and sat-in laps piling up in his wake as he pushes his way up
and down the aisles.

Which brings to mind an incident that happened some years ago
when trail courses were not posted, which kept the exhibitors in the dark
until the instructions were given. One exhibitor went to any extreme to
find out what the judge or course designer had dreamed up the night
before. He would hang around the horse show office hoping to overhear
someone giving a list of material to the ring crew to load on the truck, or
he'd stand just around the corner of the judge's box trying to dislodge
any tidbit of information that would give him the edge over the other
participants in the class. This particular event was held in conjunction with
a county fair so there was a variety of animals and things to choose from
to build a course suitable for the stake's $1,000 prize money. As the
judge for this prestigious class, I was well aware of this person's famous
shenanigans. Not too far from the arena there were elephant rides and
camel races among other midway games. It was the evening prior to the
big class, and the head of the ring crew came to me as I was about to
leave for the day. I hadn't really given much thought to the course, as I
planned to work on it that night. The ring crew head and I were talking
generally when, out of the corner of my eye, I saw the exhibitor slip into
a stall not five feet from us. I could visualize him, crouching near the wall
with his head cocked and his ear fine-tuned in our direction. I decided to
have some fun, insuring an equal obstacle course for all. So, in a little
louder voice for our eavesdropper's benefit, I said, "Oh yes, tell him I

need the camel about 8:30." I winked at the crew chief and drove off.

Hearing my last remark and waiting until the coast was clear, the overachiever set out to make a deal with the camel owner. He rented a camel for the night and, after everyone was gone, or so he thought, he proceeded to accustom his horse to the camel. All night he worked until the horse and camel behaved like long lost friends.

The next morning as the riders all lined up for their instructions, I stood before them and laid out the course—gate, bridge, back, and so on. When finished, I asked if there were any questions. Our rider's hand went up and he blurted, "What about the camel?" I, of course, replied, "Who in their right mind would put a camel in a trail-horse class?" The lineup tittered, for by now the word had gotten around about what he had done. Quieting down sheepishly, the rider accepted his well-learned lesson. We still reminisce today.

First impressions are, more often than not, lasting ones. Sometimes you misjudge, but not too often. Judges have to work hard at not letting one bad class affect a horse's placing in later classes. First impressions are different for every class; even though it's the same horse, he's competing with a brand new group. Where horses are concerned, you have an immediate gut reaction whether or not you like the horse. The same applies to riders; instant classification as the rider comes in the gate—stiff, phoney, off balance, can't ride, or fantastic. Judges find it easy to forgive minor errors by good horses and riders. They also have a tendency not to, however, at the other extreme.

You can gain points in a judge's mind if you make it easy for him to give you a ribbon. Don't make him walk all over the ring or chase you down to find out your number. Or, when he does find you, he can't read it because you've whittled it down so in size or contoured the numbers (the logic of which escapes me) so that all the white has vanished, leaving him groping for the black numerals.

Riders should plan their entrance just as an actor or actress does, and I most certainly don't mean you have to be first or last in the ring to be noticed. Promptness is a major quality all judges appreciate.

Forward to Reverse

Often the simplest of requests, such as the announcer asking a class to reverse, can cause a myriad of problems not only for the judge but for each individual in the class. Some rules dictate the method to be used, such as "only at the walk" or "away from the rail." But most do not, thus leaving it purely to the whim of the judge or competitor.

Different parts of the country create unique fads that cause confusion for judges when they are hired into that territory. I remember my first experience with creative reversing; it happened to be a Western pleasure class. I had walked, jogged, loped, and (after bringing them back to a walk) asked them to reverse. They all reversed but as soon as the horses were facing the other way, they stopped and stood. No command had been given. I queried my ringmaster, "Why are they all stopped?" "That's the way we do it here, pard," was his reply. Seems someone who had judged there before disqualified everyone who moved after the reverse. So, the trainers all schooled their charges to turn around and stop—a habit created by an overzealous judge and perpetuated by too-quick-to-follow teachers.

After restarting the group, I asked my local "custom's agent," "What would they have done if I had called for the reverse at the jog?" "They'd a stopped, 'count a they're s'posed to, ain't they?" "No," I said, and asked for the reverse again with the additive, "continue to walk, do not stop." I've repeated my preference to this day so there can be no confusion as to how I want the reverse performed. I pondered the reality of what would have taken place had a couple of riders from those parts of the country drifted to other parts where they didn't automatically stop. Judges must be aware that they can and do cause confusion and create future calamities by not being explicit in what they want the riders to do.

When asked to reverse (if not specified explicitly), the gait prior to the reverse command is the same gait you maintain during and following the reverse. If you are walking, it should be maintained throughout the reverse and continued in the opposite direction until the next gait is called. If jogging, you will jog right on through the transition keeping your rhythm.

Because most rules are silent about the reverse, many ignore it, some abuse it, but most use it as a true component in judging the class. Those who ignore it probably don't even watch after the announcer passes the

"Hold it guys, he only said reverse, not 'and walk,' so don't get in a hurry!"

word. They converse with their ring partner, make notes on their pad, or walk from one place to another. Those who abuse it most likely have some secret plan, sneaky in scope, hoping to trap the unsuspecting. They're the ones who still call for the reverse at the lope, which became taboo years ago when we quit judging solely on errors. Judges who continually use the "aha, caught you that time" method of judging are obviously insecure in their abilities.

The reverse has a positive use in all classes. For the Western pleasure, it is a great time for the rider to demonstrate control, level of training, correct use of the mouth, and the horse's ability to handle. The pleasure horse is not required to do a reining half turn or offset at the walk, but simply a smooth, forward motion gait, maintaining form and impulsion. The reverse at the jog is a beneficial tool, both for the horseman and judge. The ideal is a smooth, unrestrained maneuver with the horse handling the turn, without duress or resistance in form and balance. The exhibitor can also use the reverse to gain a better rail position or working advantage regardless of the gait called for. To many, though, it's an opportunity to interfere with someone, take an undo advantage, panic, hide, or be creative to the detriment of others and a problem for the judge.

In the English sections of pleasure, many cross the ring to get set for the pass. Some mistakenly stop, though, and wait for the call to canter, especially if they are near a corner, making the proper lead easier to obtain. Judges who watch for this fix in their minds that the transition is probably ragged to say the least, and see achieving the proper lead as due to luck rather than talent.

The reverse is extremely important in the driving classes, not so much as a judging tool on performance, but more of a safety valve. Horses not totally under control or drivers not entirely proficient in show ring procedures can cause major disasters if left to their own devices when reversing. Therefore, the password is reverse with caution and judges and ringmasters must be observant during these procedures. If the class is small and the arena large, one can easily reverse (still with caution) the driving horse at will. If the opposite is true, the reverse should be done on the diagonal under the direction of the ringmaster.

The reverse often becomes the time for some to take advantage, as exhibitors have been known to do. If the reverse is behind the judge's back, it's not beneath their dignity to grab two handfuls of rein and sneak in a jerk or two, not subtly but with a bang, bang on the mouth. Some judges quickly turn around and in doing so catch the culprit in the act and eliminate the possibility of a prize.

In the olden days, there were classes called command classes (some still exist today) where judges would deliberately try to outfox the exhibitor by the commands. They were graded on promptness of execution and the horse's ability to do no more or no less than commanded. The reverse was a favorite area of a judge's entrapment procedure. Those classes were referred to as the fun classes, for everyone knew strange commands were the order of the day. In regular classes, however, outrageous requests by the judge are frowned upon and those who rely on that type of judging are soon singled out.

Reversing is not limited to the rail classes. Trail horse course designers include many changes of direction using the reverse while negotiating obstacles. This can be a "positive" for an exhibitor to show how agile the horse is and a good judging aid when plus points are needed. The reining classes also change direction after spins and rollbacks. Their reverses must be in form, balanced, waiting and happy—not throwing the head up, lurching, gaping the mouth, charging off out of control, hesitating, sulling, or refusing to go.

How the judge asks for the reverse is also food for thought. If the judge waits for all the horses he or she has in contention to be totally visible, then judging that portion has a definite meaning. If, on the other hand, the judge continually allows his winner to be hidden, either by obstruction of a centerpiece or behind his back, protectionism is his M.O. The "go the other way" portion of any class should be meaningful to the judge and a place for a sharp exhibitor to chalk up some brownie points. Judges should be cautioned to use the reverse for the horse's benefit and not just as a test to see who survives.

Balance/Counterbalance

It becomes obvious to the judge as he watches the horses enter the arena (regardless of the class) which horses are in contention and which aren't. True, the judging doesn't start until the gate is closed. But those that are out of balance, out of frame, compensating for a misplaced center of gravity, tip-off imminent trouble. As the saying goes, "the cream rises to the top," so the horses that are in balance are able to maintain cadence for the duration of the class.

The immediate criteria and the most observed clue is the placement (good or bad) of the saddle. Many (most occurring in the Western pleasure, stock seat equitation, and hunter-type rail classes) are defeating their horse's performance from the start by having the saddle too far forward. This restricts the horse's shoulder movement and forces him to carry more than his normal 65 percent of the weight on the forehand. When the saddle is too far forward and the rider perches in the restriction zone, it is physically impossible for the horse to be balanced. Not only does it force the motion downhill but choppy strides ensue. As the horse is asked to move forward (when the center of gravity should be moving back), he must take even shorter strides just to keep up and a mixed-gait is the result.

As I've said before, all horses do not have the same balance point because of conformational differences that make the placement of the saddle and rider the key to balance. Because the horse's center of gravity moves farther back as his forward motion increases, it is necessary for the saddle and rider not to restrict the horse's front end freedom. The shoulders, neck, and head are all affected as well as the rear driving force. When the saddle restricts, it forces a jabbing movement that is felt from the horse's feet, through the pasterns and into the knee. As the jabbing-the-ground is happening, it forces the horse to trail its hocks out behind to maintain some semblance of rhythm. This causes the short front-end stride and a strung-out-behind look that we see in many horses. It is always better, for the horse's motion, to have the saddle too far back rather than too far forward, but better yet, to place it where it is an aid, not a hindrance, to good balance.

Because balance is that innate ingredient all athletes must have to perform gracefully, it is best achieved by allowing the horse to function properly. Without getting into a discussion of physics or becoming too technical, the balance of a horse can be observed in many ways. The most obvious is what he does with his head. The horse's head is one way he controls his body. When the head goes down it makes the hindquarters easier to come up, like the bucking horse. The lower his head the freer the rear. By the same token, when the head comes up it tightens the rear quarters, not just raising the nose, but raising at the poll drives the hindquarters down. The back also reacts to the head position. If the head goes too low, the back becomes too round and if the head comes up too far, the back hollows out.

If your horse has to adjust his way of going to compensate for saddle, rider, or both, it puts a strain on other muscles not normally used when the horse is free. As soon as these muscles become tired the horse becomes more resistant. The rider, who expects more, and the horse, who is able to do less, enter into a battle which could have been avoided if only they were balanced together.

In the race horse industry, for example, because of the study of how horses function, changes of riding style have occurred. If you look at old pictures of race horses, you find the jockeys sitting up straight, but the last several years they drop over in the crouch. This is for one reason only: It has been proved the horse will run faster with the rider in this position. It gives the horse more freedom and balances horse and jockey as one unit. One famous race horse trainer was asked why his horses all seemed to run well year after year. His answer was to buy good stock, watch them, and find out what they do naturally. He then trained them accordingly, capitalizing on their natural movements.

Just because we have show horses and not race horses doesn't mean we should not progress our thinking or our study to capitalize on what the horse does naturally. If you're in front of the motion, your horse is off balance, just as much as when you're behind it. Don't fall into the trap that all balance points are the same or stay the same when the horse is working. Different jobs require different balances, as witnessed by the judge.

Obligations and Duties of the Judge

The primary obligation of a judge is to give his honest opinion of what he sees in front of him at the time a class is in progress. Contrary to many opinions, the judge is not there to decide right from wrong, but only to give you (the exhibitor who pays an entry fee for this judgment) his opinion of who or what is the best horse or rider in relation to the others in the class. He should not consider past performances or where the horse or rider stand in the "High-Point Race." He should only consider what is taking place in front of him at that particular time, and relate it in the form of who gets first, second, third, and so on down the line. In that regard, the judge has the obligation to give the exhibitor his undivided attention, and not visit with the ringmaster or other people around him.

A judge has an obligation to spectators, too. Although some of you might think this is insignificant, a judge who shows consideration for those who are sitting on hard seats or standing around the arena will tie a class with promptness—making certain, though, that everyone has had a chance to be seen and to show his horse to its best advantage. Many judges go so fast that no one really has a chance, and many go so slowly that everyone wonders if he knows what he's doing. The judge, while being prompt, has the obligation to make a class as interesting as possible to the spectator (who in all probability is also an exhibitor). Even classes that are only held on the rail can be made interesting through various maneuvers by giving a little thought to individual tests when required. Nothing is more boring than a judge who works his class on the rail so fast that no one ever gets a complete round, but then, after the horses are lined up, takes forever to figure out who wins what prize.

The next obligation that a judge has is to the management, club, association, or persons who have hired him to do the show. He should always be on time and be prepared to do his best by familiarizing himself with the arena, the announcing system, and local procedures. He should have all the necessary equipment to begin a class promptly. His obligation to the management also dovetails into his obligation to the exhibitors, to be completely familiar with all the rules of the various associations licensing the particular show and to conduct the classes according to these rules.

PRINCIPLES OR ETHICS

The two areas of principle where judges find themselves in the most trouble are:

1. The judge accepts a show or class that he is not qualified to do.
2. The judge accepts a show or class believing he is qualified and finds, after it begins, he is in over his head.

Therefore, the entire matter of principles or ethics is personal, a subject that lies in the mind of each of us.

Some "don'ts" or areas gathered out of experience to be avoided when officiating that will make the job a little easier on you, the judge, and the show committee:

1. Don't accept a job you're not qualified for.
2. Don't be a houseguest of an exhibitor just prior to a show.
3. Don't spend time in the barn area during a show.
4. Don't spend time during the show with your friends if they are exhibitors, even though you're completely honest.
5. Don't talk to exhibitors in the ring.
6. Don't judge people (except in equitation classes)—judge horses.
7. Don't attend social functions during the show unless invited and accompanied by a steward or other official.
8. Don't judge according to applause.
9. Don't acknowledge friends in the grandstand. (They just might own the horse who's winning.)
10. Don't take judgment advice from the ringmaster.
11. Don't drink alcoholic beverages in public, and preferably not at all during the show.
12. Don't be disrespectful to an exhibitor due to lack of knowledge on his part. Remember, you are the pro.
13. Don't become involved in lengthy explanations or discussions with exhibitors following a class.

There will always be that one exhibitor who talks about everything and everybody, but if you follow a few simple guidelines, you will find you can keep yourself above reproach. Again, when in doubt, use logic—think of how a situation may look to someone else who doesn't know the inside information.

MECHANICS

What constitutes the ideal judge?

1. Integrity and strength
   a. Ability to stand on own convictions and judgment
   b. Ability to be beyond influence or touch by anyone
   c. Ability to judge horse and not the exhibitor
   d. Ability to judge horses as he sees them at that time and not as others have judged them or how they performed at previous times

2. Conduct and background outside the show ring
   a. Dignity and presence
   b. Stature in the horse world
   c. Character and reputation
   d. Relationship with exhibitors and officials
   e. Avoiding embarrassing situations
   f. Physical stamina
   g. Motivation

3. Conduct and presence in the show ring
   a. Dress neatly, be dignified, and businesslike
   b. Promptness; work with dispatch
   c. Have a system and follow it
   d. Consider and observe every horse in the class
   e. Allow, even make, exhibitors show to their best advantage
   f. Don't make or disclose embarrassing defects
   g. Exude confidence in your ability and firmness in your decision
   h. Make your reasons for decisions obvious to all
   i. Serve your own conscience, the exhibitor, and the spectator

4. Thorough knowledge of rule book

A good judge must also understand the mechanics of running a show and of running each class in order to make accurate judgments. If your approach is correct, it makes it easier to select the best horse in each class, but judging becomes difficult if you set out in an uneasy, haphazard way. Develop a step-by-step method to work from and mark each class accordingly, including a simple, quick method of recording your observations. You must have total confidence in your own ability and show no sign of uncertainty or panic if you're suddenly confronted with hundreds of horses or have several hundreds of thousands of dollars riding on your judgment. Again, you should always try to make your decision obvious to the audience.

Use the ringmaster, steward, and announcer to the best advantage. Be completely familiar with each show's premium list and time schedule, and stay abreast of any management decision as the show progresses. Arrive at a show allowing enough time to make restroom stops, meet with the announcer, steward, ringmaster, paddock steward, and other officials. Know the ring, and take time to analyze the setup, in-gate, out-gate, lay of the ring, and any possible areas of distraction.

RESPONSIBILITIES

Webster defines "integrity" as honesty, sincerity, and completeness. The quality of integrity is a judge's primary attribute. Of course, a judge who is licensed to judge a breed or division must have a thorough knowledge of that breed or division. However, if he or she is the most knowledgeable person in the world—but lacks integrity—the breed, the show, and the exhibitor suffer.

It bears repeating that horses must be judged on what a judge sees in a specific class on a specific day. The judge must disregard past performance and reputation of a horse; he must judge the horse *only* on its performance in the class he is judging at that time. The judge must have the integrity and courage to tie a champion horse down if that horse fails to merit a first-place ribbon.

Except in equitation classes, the rider should be inconsequential to the judging. Nationally known trainers and exhibitors should not be given more favorable consideration than those who are relatively unknown. Professional trainers who are judges must be especially aware of this requirement. A judge might know that he and a trainer or exhibitor whose entry he is judging today will be changing places at a show in several weeks, hence: the exhibitor will be the judge and the judge becomes the exhibitor. Therefore, the judge is admittedly under pressure to favor that trainer or exhibitor's entry. Although the accusation of "swapping out" is heard many times throughout the show season, it is unjustified in most cases, but occasionally it becomes obvious to everyone that a judge has favored a particular stable or exhibitor. Exhibitors are reluctant to return to shows where they have experienced bad judging, even though the judge is not the same one as in the previous year.

Many stories are told of attempts to influence a judge. Most of them are figments of the imagination, but unfortunately there have been times when judges have been enticed to place a particular entry. If such a situation occurs, it is the judge's responsibility to report it at once. Obviously, doing so is distasteful, but if the sport is to remain as such, he has no other choice.

Ring procedure and the judge's method of judging are an important part of the impression a judge makes on management, exhibitors, and spectators. In breeding and collection classes, you as the judge may enter the ring immediately or wait until all horses in the class have entered and the gate is closed. The preferred method is to enter immediately, so horses can be observed as they enter the ring. Most exhibitors prefer to have the judge in the ring when they make their first "pass."

The experienced judge usually will observe the entries going the first way of the ring, making short notes on his card and making mental notes on the entries he feels are ribbon contenders. He can begin to put numbers down on his scratch pad or the reverse side of his card. When the call to "line up" is made, you as the judge should no longer observe horses until you walk the line. This procedure will discourage the few exhibitors who make a practice of making several more passes before lining up. (Some exhibitors do this, hoping that you may be further influenced toward their entry.)

After the class has lined up, you should walk the line observing conformation and backing horses, if such specifications are called for. In pleasure classes, backing is important as it is part of the desirable requirements of a pleasure horse and should count in the final placing.

It is most important that the "order of precedence" be observed in judging each class. For example, pleasure, amateur, and ladies' classes list *manners* as the first consideration, followed by performance, quality, conformation, and presence. In junior-horse classes, the first order of precedence is *quality*, with manners the least important. In open classes, *performance* generally is first in the order of precedence. The class specifications should be printed on your card for your reference in each class.

After you have your final observation, walk to the rear of the lineup and mark your final placings on your card. Once the placings are made, it is well to check them before handing the card to the ringmaster. Doing so may avoid having the wrong number on the card or the inadvertent transposing of numbers.

Sign the card and hand it to the ringmaster. Then leave the ring—or retire to the judge's stand but remain in the immediate area in case a problem arises with the placing. Never leave the immediate area of the ring until all ribbons have been awarded. A sufficient number of incidents have occurred over the years—such as the announcer's calling the wrong order of placing—to warrant being present to correct such a situation immediately.

The ringmaster is an important aid. Thus, before the show begins, discuss exactly what is expected of him, especially in halter classes. Once the class is called, however, you should have no further conversation with the ringmaster, other than to request change of gaits and ask for a lineup. Judges have been criticized for conversing with the ringmaster during the process of a class; your full attention should be on the entries. Incidents have occurred when ringmasters have attempted to influence a judge's decision, but by having it understood in advance that you will not converse with the ringmaster during the class, you can avoid this situation.

Sometimes a Learner Judge or a Recorded Judge is approved by the show committee to be present in the ring. The Learner or Recorded Judge must be in a position to observe the class in the same perspective as the officiating judge. No conversation should ensue between the two judges until the officiating judge has marked and turned in his card. Nevertheless, this is a learning experience for the other judge, and the officiating judge should be as helpful as possible. Never resent the presence of a Learner or a Recorded Judge in the ring with you.

In breeding or halter classes, the ring procedure is also important. This procedure may vary according to your personal preference, but it should be the very same for all breeding classes. Here too, the ringmaster should be briefed before the class as to the ring procedure you will follow. One method is to observe the entries as they enter the ring; then line them up on the long axis of the ring away from the rail, head to tail. The ringmaster should have each entry leave the line, walk to you, set up, and then after inspection trot away. The entry then will return to the end of the line. In this method, the line continues to move up until all entries are back in their original positions.

You then should walk the line, selecting horses for the ribbon awards and having them form into a new line. It is not necessary at this time to have the entries in the order of final placing. Horses not being considered for an award should be excused at this time. The remaining entries then can be observed once again, and the final placings can be made on a new line. This method may have to be adjusted, depending on the number of entries and the size of the ring; however, the method finds favor with both exhibitors and spectators.

Whatever method used in judging both halter and performance classes, you should adopt a consistent pattern. You should move about the ring with a confident air. Work the entries at each gait only long enough to observe all entries at that gait—a class should not develop into an endurance contest. Most qualifying classes can be judged without a workout. If, however, there are a large number of entries in the class (more than twenty-five, for example), you may want to take another look at your top contenders before placing the class. If such is the case, make this first workout comparatively short. After lining up the horses, you should walk down the rear of the line asking entries in contention to step forward a few paces. You may then ask that the back line be excused. After they have left the ring, work the remaining horses for final placing. In such cases, however, remember that the first workout (before the other horses are excused) must not be considered as you arrive at your final placing. The horses remaining in the ring must perform all required movements (as called for by the rule book) and be judged on their performance after the other horses have left the ring. You must work the remaining entries at least once around the ring at each gait called for; then do the same the reverse way of the ring. The Arabian breed calls for working entries at all gaits both ways of the ring in a workout.

CHAPTER
~2~

Halter Classes

THE IMPORTANCE OF CONFORMATION

What is conformation? As defined by Webster's, "it is the formation of anything by symmetrical arrangement of its parts." What conformation does can be summed up by the relationship of form to function.

When trying to analyze the horse-show business, always use this rule of thumb: Horses on the open market are classified according to their jobs. Some structural features place definite limits on a horse's capabilities, while other structural features distinctly enhance his abilities in a specific field. Horses, then, must go as they are designed to go. This includes balance, which is the horse's ability to coordinate his action and go in form.

Therefore, *conformation* equals *form to function*.

Years ago, judging conformation was left up to nature, as in "the survival of the fittest." Today's judging system is based on opinion rather than nature's hard cold facts. But as man has taken over the task, many judges have no fixed target of why one horse is better than another, or for what purpose.

Conformation is, however, factual, and in that sense, not opinion. If it relates directly to "form to function" by selection of the best performers, form relates directly to what purpose the horse will be used for. The most significant application is that conformation is a major factor in the soundness of the limbs, that degree of soundness often determining the useful life of a horse. Most unsoundnesses are the direct effect of stress, strain, and concussion on the musculoskeletal system. Therefore, the underlying cause of these injurious factors is faulty conformation.

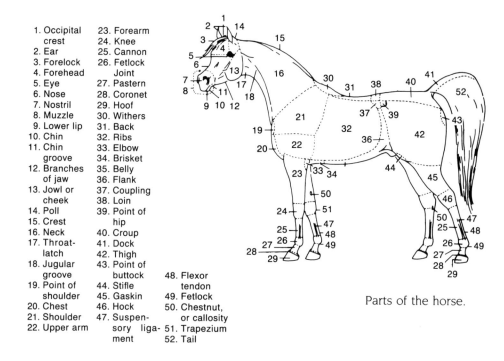

1. Occipital crest
2. Ear
3. Forelock
4. Forehead
5. Eye
6. Nose
7. Nostril
8. Muzzle
9. Lower lip
10. Chin
11. Chin groove
12. Branches of jaw
13. Jowl or cheek
14. Poll
15. Crest
16. Neck
17. Throat-latch
18. Jugular groove
19. Point of shoulder
20. Chest
21. Shoulder
22. Upper arm
23. Forearm
24. Knee
25. Cannon
26. Fetlock Joint
27. Pastern
28. Coronet
29. Hoof
30. Withers
31. Back
32. Ribs
33. Elbow
34. Brisket
35. Belly
36. Flank
37. Coupling
38. Loin
39. Point of hip
40. Croup
41. Dock
42. Thigh
43. Point of buttock
44. Stifle
45. Gaskin
46. Hock
47. Suspensory ligament
48. Flexor tendon
49. Fetlock
50. Chestnut, or callosity
51. Trapezium
52. Tail

Parts of the horse.

Before we get into actual conformation judging (and we "take a horse apart"), let us review a list of conformation and structural defects and how they apply to judging.

1. "Soundness" can be defined as that state in which there are no deviations from the normal that have resulted in, or that will predispose the horse to, pathological changes that interfere with intended use.

2. Soundness is often classified as working soundness or breeding soundness, since a horse that is sound for breeding purposes is not necessarily sound for working, or vice versa.

3. In judging horses, the degree of soundness and the effect of blemishes must be carefully evaluated, and their values properly weighted in the type of class being judged.

4. Good judgment must be used to determine the importance of unsoundness and blemishes.

    a. For example, a splint or bog spavin is a minor condition when not accompanied by poor conformation or unsoundness.

    b. A blemish is of minor significance if caused by some foreign agent (wire cut, etc.), but is quite significant if caused by faulty conformation, such as wounds over the inside sesamoids caused by the horse winging in, to the extent that he hits the side with the opposite foot.

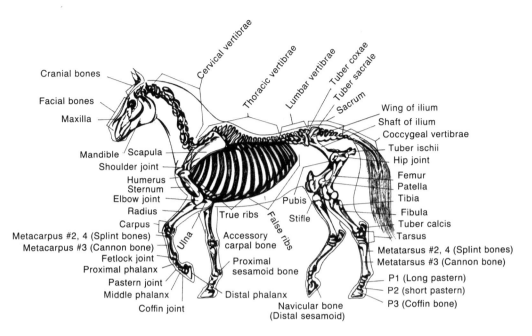

Skeletal parts of the horse.

5. The following unsoundnesses and blemishes are undesirable, but do not necessarily constitute disqualification. (However, when these defects are associated with faulty conformation, they should be carefully evaluated.) Some will be found in both lists:

a. Unsoundnesses
   - Side bones
   - Ring bones
   - Contracted feet
   - Navicular disease
   - Cocked ankle
   - Laminitis
   - Splints (when accompanied by pain)
   - Wind puffs
   - Bog spavin
   - Curb
   - Thoroughpin
   - Stringhalt
   - Bowed tendon

b. Blemishes
   - Dished or deformed feet
   - Toe cracks and quarter cracks
   - Splints
   - Wind puffs
   - Bog spavin
   - Capped hocks
   - Thoroughpin
   - Stocked or swollen legs
   - Bowed tendon
   - Scars from leg interference
   - Capped elbow
   - Sweeny
   - Hygroma of knee
   - Blindness or defective vision

FUNCTION

The observation that "winners can come in all shapes" may be true, but generally it would be more correct to say that it is the exception. Good conformation in a horse does not guarantee good performance, but it is safe to say that far more winners come from the ranks of horses with good conformation than from the ranks of "nondescripts." Horses with good conformation are more likely to be good athletes, and they are apt to remain sound and capable of withstanding the stresses of such a demanding sport.

Conformation, again, simply means how the horse is put together—how his bones, tendons, muscles, and ligaments are shaped, and how they fit together. Conformation usually determines whether the horse will be a good or poor athlete, agile or clumsy, fast or slow.

A well-conformed horse has a pleasing overall appearance, with no obvious faults that detract from his total makeup. A horse with good conformation usually has a certain amount of "presence"—that undefinable bit of something which at first glance makes an impression that it will be able to perform admirably. It is this presence, coupled with fluidity and gracefulness of movement, that helps convince a judge that he has picked a winner.

Let us look a little closer and dissect the Arabian horse's various parts individually in order to obtain an in-depth idea of conformation, and how conformation may possibly enhance or hinder the ability to perform well and remain sound.*

A horse has a proportionate head, which helps him maintain balance. He raises or lowers it to counterbalance whatever is happening at the other end of the body, as well as to adjust his speed or direction. The good head allows room for wide nostrils and windpipe, giving the access to a large flow of air during exertion. A horse cannot breathe through his mouth very readily (as a human does when out of breath), so he needs to be able to take great gulps of air through his nostrils when running hard.

The head should be of a size proportionate to the horse's size, with well-defined features. In judging an Arabian horse's head, the horseman looks for a small-to-medium-size, finely formed ears, eyes set wide apart with good width of forehead, a finely formed face, and relatively small muzzle. A face that is too narrow will interfere with the horse's flow of

---

*In looking at the horse's anatomy, it is interesting to note that almost every part of the horse (except the tail) corresponds to a similar part of the human body. The stifle is the same as the human knee and has the same kneecap (patella). The horse's "knee" on his foreleg is comparable to the human wrist and even has the same seven bones. The hock joint in the hind leg is similar to the human ankle. The cannon bone in a horse is like the human middle finger, and the fetlock joint compares with the middle knuckle on that middle finger.

air when breathing hard, due to narrowing of the nasal bones. Ears should be carried alertly. Eyes should be prominent, clear, and large.

There should be no unevenness or mismatch of upper and lower jaw. A horse with an overbite ("parrot mouth") or undershot jaw will have trouble eating and will usually be a poor keeper and thus hard to keep

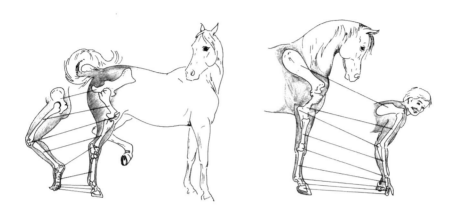

Parts of the horse corresponding to similar parts of the human body.

(A) Good Arabian head. (B) Poor head—big lop ears, deep-set pig eyes, small nostril, short mouth, and pendulous underlip.

Comparing the head of (A) a typical "cold-blooded" horse with (B) a typical Arabian.

fit. A jaw deformity may not be obvious unless the horse's mouth is opened and examined to see how the front teeth line up.

The lower jaw should be well defined. The space between the two sides of the lower jaw should be wide so there is adequate room for the larynx and its large muscle attachments. Horsemen of early times used to say that a man should be able to lay his closed fist between the two halves of the jaw beneath the larynx; a wide open space between these upper ends of the lower jaw bones is regarded as a good characteristic for a horse that needs to have adequate wind. Width and roominess between the two sides of the lower jaw at this spot will depend partly on the way that the horse's head is set onto his neck. If the angle at which the head meets the neck is too abrupt, the lower line of the neck is often too fleshy, thus making the neck meet the throat too low. This constricts the windpipe and interferes with the horse's breathing when he is running hard. This unsightly head and neck hookup is often found in horses with a short, thick neck and upright shoulder (old timers called this acute angle of head and neck "cock-throttled").

The angle at which the neck and head meet is one of the most important aspects of a horse's general conformation. The head should be set into the neck at such an angle that the horse can flex at his poll. The neck is the vital link between head and shoulders for regulating balance; a horse must be able to swing his head up and down like a pendulum to regulate and shift his weight and balance at each stride. A long neck is often considered more desirable than a short one because the longer-necked horse is generally able to balance himself better; a short, thick neck can be a hindrance to balance and good action. A neck can be too long, however, putting the horse's center of balance too far forward. The neck should be of a length proportionate to the horse's overall build and conformation, just as his head should be the right size and weight to match the rest of his body.

Neck and head should complement one another. A horse with a long neck and heavy head will have poorer balance than a horse with a long neck and lighter head. A coarse or heavy head will require a heavier, shorter neck to carry it. A short, thick, or heavy-crested neck is not very flexible.

The way the neck bones are positioned, along with their muscle attachments, determines to a large degree how a horse will carry his head and neck; it also determines much of the extent of forward movement in the front legs. Thus, the carriage and gait of the whole body is influenced directly by the conformation of the head-neck-shoulder relationship.

For good maneuverability, there must be a reasonable length of neck and a well carried head. A short-necked horse must move his front legs faster and more often to keep up with a long-necked, longer-angled, longer-striding animal. Over short distances, the short-striding animal may be able to keep up, but he will tend to tire over an extended period by having to take twice as many steps as his competitor. Usually the short strider does not compete well over longer periods unless he is an exceptionally strong horse with great heart and endurance.

Even though a major interest in a horse's conformation must be his feet and legs, close attention must be paid to his body and its principal structures, for these play an important part in the form and function of his legs. A horse's body must be well proportioned, a major factor in how the limbs are handled and whether or not there will be leg interference when the horse travels. Therefore, body and leg conformation must be compatible. A long-bodied horse should be long legged, and a short-bodied, short-backed horse should be shorter legged. If a short-backed horse has legs that are too long for his body, he will be more likely to

(A) Abrupt angle of head meeting neck—not desirable, constricts breathing. (B) Proper head and neck connection. (C) Arrow depicts space between sides of lower jaw. Its width will partly depend on how the head is set onto the neck.

(A) Clean throatlatch/good neck. (B) Abrupt throatlatch/neck bulges below jowl—will be less supple, less responsive, and will interfere with breathing. (C) Undefined throatlatch/short, straight neck—will have trouble rounding his back and engaging his hindquarters.

Neck and throatlatch. (top) Good; (bottom) poor.

overreach when he moves, striking his front feet with his hind. A horse that is too long-backed may have a swing to his gait that changes the forward movement of his legs enough so they are not traveling perfectly straight, making him prone to limb interference.

When judging the body of a horse, look for a deep heart and girth and well-sprung ribs. A horse needs plenty of room for his lungs to expand. Horses that are wide through the ribs and deep through the flank are usually better doers than horses that are narrow and "bacon-sided" with very little spring of rib.

The shape of the ribs varies in individual horses as to length and

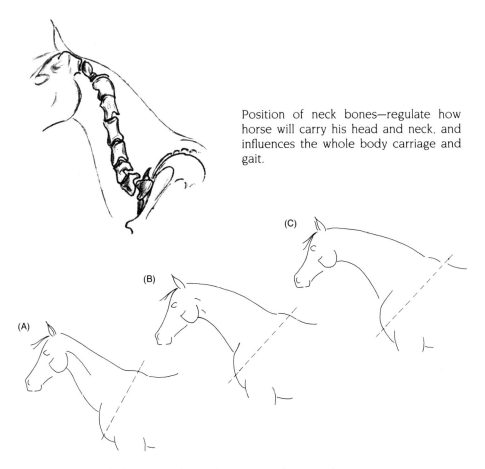

Position of neck bones—regulate how horse will carry his head and neck, and influences the whole body carriage and gait.

(C)

(B)

(A)

Head, neck, and shoulder relationship. (A) Neck set on low; (B) average; (C) set on high.

curvature. The greater the rib curvature, the greater the "spring of rib" and total space within the chest cavity for lung expansion.

Staying power and endurance depend partly on sound and fit muscles, but even more so on a horse's having plenty of space within his chest for lung capacity. There are two types of efficient chest structure. The wide, deep chest provides considerable lung room, and so does the "barrel" chest. The closer the rib cage is to cylindrical shape, the more volume it will have. Viewed from front or back, the rib cage should appear wide, not narrow; it should be wide enough to be seen from a front or rear view of the horse. Ribs of moderate length that lack curvature may give an impression of depth of chest, but the sides will be flat and the chest capacity limited. A wide thorax (chest cavity) provides the greatest lung room. Consequently, a flat-sided chest has the least capacity.

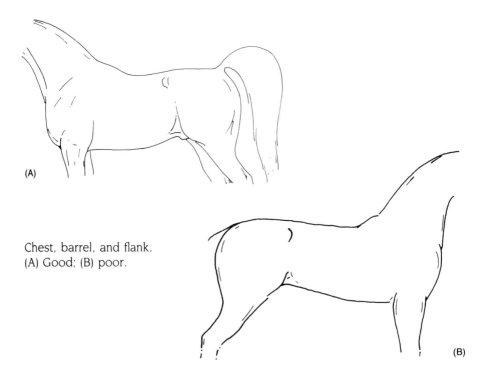

Chest, barrel, and flank.
(A) Good; (B) poor.

Many old-time horsemen liked to measure the girth of a horse. The rule of thumb they used was that a horse of 16 hands should have a girth measurement of at least 6 feet in circumference to give adequate room for lung expansion.

At least eleven pairs of ribs are not attached to the breastbone, but are held together by bands of cartilage; this permits these ribs to expand more fully than the ribs in front. These pairs produce the greatest increase in lung capacity when they rotate into their position of full expansion at each deep breath. It is therefore important that the ribs extend well back along the abdomen, giving maximum chest capacity and lung room. This is why a horse that is deep through its flank, with ribs well back, often has more endurance and staying power than the "wasp-waisted" horse that is narrow through the flank. Many individual Arabians, and some thoroughbreds, have an additional pair of ribs, with a subsequent increase in lung room and that "well-ribbed-up look" that makes them deep through the flank.

A horse that is narrow in the chest may also be narrow in his front end. If he is, the front legs may be too close together where they come out of the body (an old expression was "both legs out of the same hole"). There should be sufficient width between the front legs, yet the front of the horse should not be too wide and heavy. Width of chest cavity and width of breast are two different things; a horse can have good width of rib cage without being wide in the breast. A wide breast is a disadvantage in a riding horse because it reduces speed and agility. Nor should the horse be too heavy in front. He should be wider at the hindquarters than at the front, for he needs strength of loin and quarters. It is best if his center of gravity is not so far forward; he will have freer use of his front legs if his weight is balanced farther back. Remember, every horse has a different balance point or center of gravity depending on their conformational qualities, angulation, length of back, and length of neck.

A horse's body should ideally be wedge-shaped, narrower in front and wider behind. The sternum (breastbone) lies between the forelegs and carries the lower ends of the first eight pairs of ribs. If the breastbone is too wide and the pectoral (breasts) muscles are too bulky, the horse will be too wide and heavy in front. A wide front will be an advantage for a draft horse that leans into a collar and depends on slow strength and power to get his work done, but it is a definite disadvantage in, for example, a reining horse that needs speed and agility. A breast that is too wide will give the horse a rolling gait and he may paddle outward with his front feet. He also will have more trouble moving his legs freely at great speed. Anything that hinders free, true straightforward action of legs will cut down a horse's speed.

Extreme heaviness of muscle on thighs, arms, or forearms is not necessarily good for performance; it actually hinders free action. Heavily muscled horses may have early bursts of energy, but they will tire sooner than trimmer horses. Maneuverability and endurance come from long, lean muscles, not bulky ones. Long slender muscles denote speed and staying ability, while round heavy muscles are more associated with weight-carrying ability and power.

The withers, which are composed of the spines of the third- to ninth-dorsal vertebrae, are very important, for they not only hold a saddle in place but also play a major role in how the rest of a horse's front end is put together. The withers begin shortly after the neck ends; the first two dorsal (back) vertebrae have short processes and are not part of the withers. The spines of the third to fifth dorsal vertebrae gradually increase in height, and then decrease again to the tenth dorsal vertebrae, after which the upright parts of the vertebrae (dorsal and lumbar) remain short and nearly the same height down the length of the back.

Good withers should be well defined and of moderate height. Withers that are too high and sharp are associated with deficient spring of rib cage (corresponding to a narrow chest cavity), while withers that are too low and thick will usually interfere with freedom of shoulder movement and be associated with poor foreleg action.

The withers provide an anchor for the muscles that attach the shoulder blade to the horse's body. Without well-defined and well-formed withers, it is almost impossible to have a well-laid-back shoulder. The set of the shoulder blade depends on whether the withers are set forward or extend well back, and this set of withers in turn depends on the actual height of the spinal bones.

Withers should always be well shaped and covered with muscle at the sides instead of being too thin and sharp. A horse with withers of good height usually has a long sloping shoulder that is well laid back. Withers of good height also provide better suspension of the thorax between the forelegs. The thorax (rib cage) is suspended between the front legs entirely by muscular attachments rather than by bones and joints, providing a "shock-absorbing" effect because the muscular attachments have more give for absorbing concussion than bones do.

The shoulder blade provides some buffering action in counteraction concussion. The horse's body, suspended as it is between the forelegs by means of muscles holding the shoulder blade to the withers and ribs, depends on this "give" whenever the horse puts weight on a front foot. The shoulder blade is only loosely attached to the ribs, and can glide upward and backward over the outer surface of the ribs whenever weight is placed on that foreleg. This gliding action helps spread and lessen the effects of concussion. The more upright the shoulder blade, the shorter it must be, with less backward gliding movement over the ribs. And an upright shoulder has little room for much shoulder flexion when the short shoulder blade is directly over the joint instead of behind it.

Good withers and sloping shoulders usually go together. Angles in a horse's body tend to be similar throughout the entire body, and a horse with good withers usually has a good shoulder and pasterns as well. A shoulder that is too straight and upright limits the horse's freedom of action and gives a shorter, choppier stride. A horse with short straight upright shoulders often has a short neck and short upright pasterns as well, although there will occasionally be exceptions.

A good horse usually has a long mid-line and a short back. In other words, he is "close coupled." If he has a well-laid-back shoulder and good withers, his back will tend to be short. Low withers and a more forward upright shoulder (withers and shoulder placed more forward) leave more room for a long back. A long back can be a weak back unless the horse is quite strong across the loin.

Loins should always be muscular and slightly raised, never hollow. A mare may have a slightly longer back than a stallion or gelding. A moderately long back is found in individual Arabians and can be an asset rather than a detriment to speed. Some length is necessary to provide a long rib cage, with very little space between the last rib and the angle of the hindquarter.

A horse must have some length of back for fast work, permitting a longer stride of the hind leg, but the loin area must be short. The loin is the least supported area of the back. Horses with long loins are the ones that usually give the impression of slackness and weakness in the back, and too much length behind the saddle.

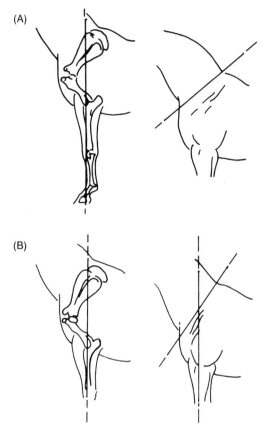

Shoulder and withers. (A) Good—a desirable slope of shoulder. The shoulder blade or scapula should slope back to such an extent the leg can swing forward easily and freely, like a pendulum from the shoulder joint. (B) Poor—straight or perpendicular shoulder.

The classical Arabian horse's back should show a definite shape and contour, never arched and only very slightly concave just behind the withers, then slightly convex over the loins, all well covered with muscle. Too much concavity in the back puts strain on the muscles. If a back is too long, the propulsion from the hind legs may be somewhat diminished in efficiency. A short back, by contrast, indicates strength and solidness. It rarely becomes hollow, and there is no wasting of propulsion and power from the hind legs. But a back that is too short diminishes the rib cage and lung room, as well as reducing flexibility, handicapping free action in the hind legs, and encouraging the horse to forge, especially if he has much length of leg.

The backbone is made up of seven neck vertebrae, eighteen dorsal vertebrae (each carrying a pair of ribs), six lumbar vertebrae, and the sacrum (a bone made up of several fused vertebrae). There is both lateral and up-and-down movement of the spine in a young horse, but mature horses have very little spine flexibility. Almost all flexion in any horse's back comes in the area between the last dorsal (rib-carrying vertebrae) and the first lumbar (loin area) joints, plus a little movement between the first, second, and third lumbar vertebrae. Some movement is also possi-

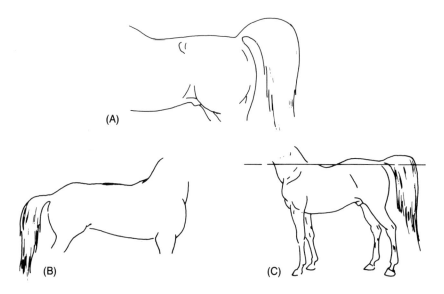

Back, loins, and croup. (A) Good—Back short, level, and well muscled on each side of spine. Mares may have longer backs than stallions, and somewhat deeper, particularly after carrying several foals. Loins are short and strong; croup is long, level, and same height as withers. (B) Poor—Back roached or humped; loins dropped; croup too short, and sloped. (C) Poor—Back too long and low; weak loins; croup too high, higher than withers.

ble between the last lumbar bone and the sacrum. The front half of the spine is, practically speaking, rigid.

Because of the rigidity of the back and lack of spinal flexion, a horse's hind feet can come forward only as far as the middle of his abdomen. The hind leg moves in a pendulum fashion from the rigid pelvis at the hip joint, but most of its swing comes from the stifle joint. Due to the mass of muscle surrounding the thigh, the upper leg bone (femur) has limited movement. The stifle works in unison with the hock; when one flexes, the other flexes. The horse's hocks support and distribute his weight, and it is through hock action that most of the horse's athletic activities are made possible.

The croup is the highest point of the rear end of the horse, the point where the pelvis meets the sacrum. The croup should not be unreasonably high, but relatively flat and surrounded by the muscle. Running down from the croup toward the tail (at the rear) and the hips on either side are muscles called the ''quarters.''*

---

*The croup and quarters are often confused and spoken of as one (in an all-inclusive term like ''rump''); technically, however, the ''croup'' is merely the highest point, the upper extremity of the pelvic bone.

Most good performance horses have quarters that tend to be long and level. But whether the quarter is level or sloping, in order for the horse to have maneuverability, the line from the point of the hip to the point of the buttock should be long. The angle made by this line and the line from the point of buttock to stifle joint should be sharp. As with the shoulder, the sharper the angle of the quarter, the more freedom of movement and the better the action in the legs. The angle in shoulder, quarters, and pasterns governs whether the horse will be smooth and free-flowing in his gaits and whether or not he will stay sound and active with strenuous use.

Angles in shoulders, quarters and pasterns also help determine how much concussion the bones of the feet and the leg can take (concussion is a major factor in the breakdown of vital structures in the feet and legs, causing lameness and sometimes ongoing unsoundness). These angles greatly determine the horse's action and freedom of movement. A shoulder that is steep puts the front legs too far under the horse, cramping his stride and making him unable to reach out in front as he should. When traveling at speed, a good horse's front feet should be able to reach out well past his nose.

Ideally, a horse should be the same height at the withers as he is at the highest point of the hip (croup). Nearly all young horses are at first a little higher in the croup, but by the time they are three- or four-year-olds, the dorsal spines of their withers will have grown higher and the

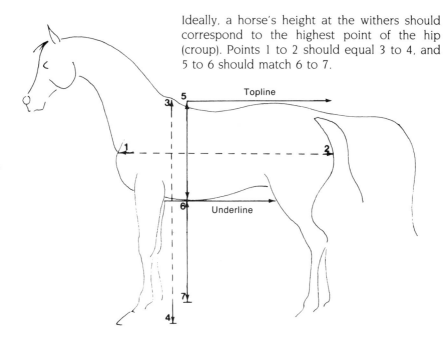

Ideally, a horse's height at the withers should correspond to the highest point of the hip (croup). Points 1 to 2 should equal 3 to 4, and 5 to 6 should match 6 to 7.

bones of the forelegs completed their growth, so that by this age the withers may be level with or even a tiny bit higher than the croup.

In some horses, however, a high croup is a hereditary trait. The horse finishes growth and remains an inch or more taller at the croup than at the withers. Some horsemen feel that a high croup is a sign of speed in a horse if the muscles of the loin and quarter are well developed. Yet the fact that a horse has a high croup does not always mean he will have a longer stride. The range of hind leg movement actually depends more on the length of the tibia (the leg bone between stifle and hock) and the upper end of the tibia within the stifle joint.

Whether the croup is high or low, the angle that the upper part of the pelvis makes with the sacrum (a bone at the end of the spinal column) can still vary quite a bit. Whether or not a horse with a croup slightly higher than his withers will be exceedingly smooth is a matter that can vary with each individual horse.

A well-balanced horse has about the same distance from fetlock joint to underline as from his underline to the top of the withers. In other words, the depth of his body is about the same as the length of his legs down to the fetlock joint. Some say the ideal horse is a "square" horse, one that is roughly the same height at the withers as the distance from the point of the shoulder to the point of buttocks. The length of his body is thus the same as his height from the ground to the withers.

Ideal height and size in a performance horse has been debated for centuries. A larger, taller horse may have greater stride, but often a smaller horse has better balance. Weight is also a factor to be considered.

Some say the ideal horse is a "square horse," roughly the same height at the withers as in the distance from the point of the shoulder to the point of the buttocks.

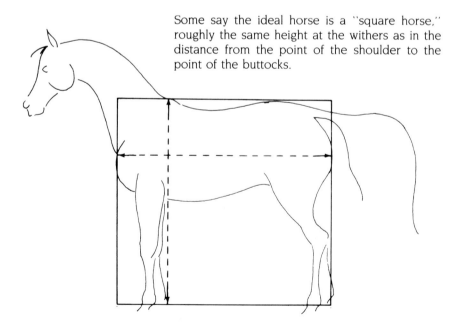

Halter Classes

There is an old question of whether the extra power and forc[e]
from a larger body and larger muscles is enough to compensat[e]
additional weight the horse has to carry. Perhaps no general [s]
can be made, for the answer—aside from the abilities inherent in a well-
made body—must also depend to some degree on the heart and determination of an individual animal.

The conformation of a horse's feet and legs is probably the most
important aspect of his overall makeup when judging his potential as an
athlete. A horse may have all the heart and endurance in the world, but
if a foot or leg breaks down because of weakness or inferior structure,
his potential will be unfulfilled.

A horse always should be evaluated while he is moving as well as
while he is standing still. He should have a good way of traveling, moving
"straight and clean." A horse with good conformation has straight feet
and legs that move forward in straight lines. Some points of bad conformation will show up more sharply when he is standing still. Faults that
give clues to imperfect structure include the horse's feet paddling outward or his hock rolling outward as he travels, and a closer look can be
taken to discover why there are deviations in gait.

A horse is only as good as his feet and legs. If they are weak, crooked,
or poorly formed, the horse probably will be unlikely to stand the stress
of strenuous activity and will go temporarily lame or permanently unsound. Poor conformation of feet or legs can contribute to some types
of lameness, and, in some cases, may actually be the cause of lameness
or unsoundness.

Feet should be well shaped and of a desirable size, proportionate to
the size of the horse. A horse is a large animal that needs enough hoof
to support his weight. Feet that are too small will not hold up under hard
training; the increased shock of concussion in the small area may cause
lameness from several problems, including navicular disease. A large or
heavy horse needs feet of adequate size for his weight, while a smaller
horse needs a smaller hoof. Feet that are too large will be clumsy.

The two front feet and the two hind feet must match in size and
shape, although front feet should be slightly larger and rounder than hind
feet because they support about two-thirds of the horse's weight. The
shape of each individual foot is directly related to the conformation, position, and action of the leg above it. An odd-shaped foot should arouse
suspicion as to soundness, as should any foot that is a bit different in
size than its mate. A horse that has been lame for some length of time
may develop mismatched feet because he places less weight on the lame
foot; as a result, the foot is not subjected to as much spreading action
and tends to contract.

Hoofs should be wide at the heels, never narrow or contracted. Wide
heels give and spring apart when the foot hits the ground, absorbing
some of the concussion. Otherwise all the shock and jar will be transmit-

ted directly to the bones of the foot and leg. The heel should not only be wide, but deep. A thin, narrow heel will not be as strong. The sole should be almost round, with a deep and well-formed frog, good strong bars, and definite grooves on either side of the frog. The bars, which help take additional weight upon the heels, act as wedges to keep the heels from caving in and contracting. Each time the foot takes weight, the frog forces the bars apart, lifts the plantar cushion, and exerts a pumping action on the blood vessels within the foot.

The sole should be slightly concave in the front feet, and even more concave in the hind. Flat feet are undesirable, for they are easily bruised. The navicular bone, over which the flexor tendon glides, lies within the foot above the center of the frog; a horse with flat feet is more likely to develop navicular disease than a horse with good concave soles. Navicular disease can occur in feet that have short, upright pasterns that cannot absorb enough concussion, especially if feet are too small. The problem can also occur if heels are low and weak, putting additional strain on the flexor tendons and increased pressure on the deep flexor that glides over the navicular bone.

The frog should be large and healthy, and exactly centered in the sole, with the point of the frog pointing to the toe of the foot. If the frog does not divide the sole into two equal halves, the horse is probably base wide or base narrow, with his feet growing unevenly because the legs are not quite straight.

A horse with good leg conformation has feet that wear evenly; the foot will break over squarely at the center of the toe and one side of the foot will not wear lower than the other or one side of the toe more than the other. To a great extent, the conformation of a horse's leg determines the shape of the foot and how it wears, and its flight—how it is picked up, swings through the air (straight or crooked), and how it is put down. The flight of the foot should be an even arc, reaching the highest point of its arc as it passes the opposite leg.

The angle of the pastern should be the same as that of the hoof. Ideally, the angle of foot and pastern should be about 45 to 50 degrees, but this can vary among individual horses and still be considered normal.

Foot and pastern angles should not be too sloping or too upright. A pastern that slopes excessively will be weak. If it does not slope enough, the foot will not have enough "give" and the horse will have a choppy, jarring gait that will likely damage the feet and legs from the increased concussion.

A horse with a well-sloped foot and pastern and a fairly long pastern will usually have a relatively low heel. He will tend to put more effort into breaking over because his toe is relatively long. The added effort in break-over will create a longer stride. The foot will be picked up briskly, reaching the highest point of its arc before it passes the opposite leg. Then the foot flight tapers into a long graceful stride, touching down rather gently.

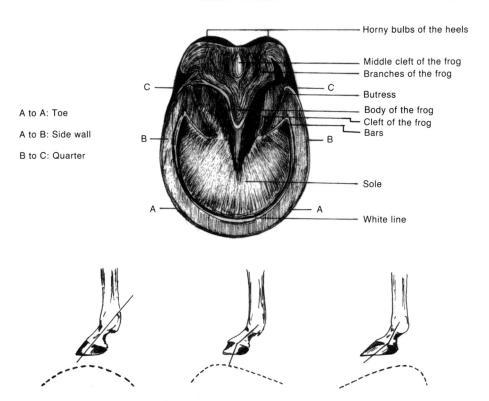

A to A: Toe

A to B: Side wall

B to C: Quarter

Horny bulbs of the heels

Middle cleft of the frog
Branches of the frog

Butress

Body of the frog
Cleft of the frog
Bars

Sole

White line

Structure of the foot—angles of pasterns and the arc a foot will follow as the horse moves.

This type of foot and pastern angle is usually found in horses with a correspondingly sloped shoulder.

By contrast, a horse with a straight, short pastern will often have a higher heel and shorter toe, and a more effortless breakover but a short stride and more jarring gait. The decreased effort needed to raise the already high heel will be reflected in the foot flight. The arc will be lower and more forward, not reaching its full height until it is past the opposite leg, after which it comes abruptly back to the ground with a jar. The shoulder is usually the same as the pastern—short and upright. This type of conformation makes a choppy gait and short strides, the horse needing many more steps to keep up with the longer-striding animal.

Length of toe makes a great deal of difference in the performance horse. Toes should never be too long, or the horse will be clumsy and apt to stumble; in a horse with sloping pasterns and relatively long toe, the extra length of pastern and toe and the resultant longer strides can make the difference. Dubbing off, or shortening a horse's toe, can make him fall short of the distance he would have naturally reached.

If front pasterns slope properly, there is less likelihood of strain and

Compared to other breeds, the Arabian has a rather large foot for his size. Unusually small "pony feet" are hereditary and very objectionable because such feet seldom stay sound under sustained, hard use. Very low flat heels and contracted feet or contracted heels are also objectionable for the same reason.

Examining the feet.

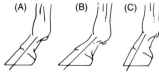

Side view of foot and pastern axis.

(A) Normal front hoof and pastern axis, approximately 47 degrees (hind nearer 50 degrees). (B) Hoof and pastern axis less than normal (less than 45 degrees in front or less than 50 degrees behind). (C) Hoof and pastern axis greater than normal (greater than 50 degrees in front or greater than 55 degrees behind).

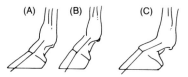

Examples of broken hoof and pastern axis.

(A). Broken hoof axis with toe too long and heel too low. (B). Broken hoof axis with toe too short and heel too high. (C) "Coon" foot. Weak pastern. The foot axis is steeper than the pastern axis. This is most objectionable because of the frequency of injury to the fetlock joint. The injury may be caused by stress, but is usually caused by the fetlock joint striking the ground because it is let down too low. A weakness may be the result of an injury, but is generally considered to be hereditary in origin.

breakdown, sore shins, damaged knees, splints, navicular disease, and other stress-caused lameness.

A long, flexible pastern is essential in the front foot, but hind pasterns should be a little more upright and solid, because the hind leg hock is the main structure that flexes and absorbs the shock, taking the weight when the hindquarter supports the horse. If the hind pastern is too long and flexible, the weight on a hind leg would cause the pastern to yield and break down.

The front leg has no joint that corresponds with the hock, with its ability to counter concussion and shock. The knee, which flexes in the opposite direction, is usually fully extended when weight is put on a front foot. In the extended front leg, the elbow joint is locked, so only the pastern (and moveable shoulder blade) acts as a shock absorber. This is the reason why front pasterns must be well sloped and flexible.

Front legs should be well balanced and straight, with proper length of bone and proper angles so that there is not undue stress on any one part of the leg. Both forelegs should bear weight equally. They should be perfectly straight when viewed from the front. A line dropped from the point of the shoulder should go down the center of the leg, bisecting forearm, knee, cannon, fetlock joint, pastern and hoof. Toes should point directly to the front. The feet should be exactly the same distance apart as the distance between the forearms where they come out of the chest. Front legs that move forward in straight lines have no loss of energy due to inward or outward deviation of foot flight, and there is no extra strain on any of the joints.

The elbow must rest squarely on top of the forearm and not turn in or out. It should appear clear of the body, and be well defined. A turned-in elbow makes the horse throw his front feet outward when the knee is flexed. Elbows turned outward are usually associated with the feet being turned in. A horse's not traveling straight is sometimes due to the set-on of the elbow being not straight. In these cases there is extra strain at the fetlock joint that can lead to further problems, including lameness or interference.

The forearm should be long, wide, thick, and well developed. The forearm is probably just as important for propulsion as are the muscles of the second thigh in the hind leg, for although the hind legs provide much of the power, the front legs help by pulling the horse along at all gaits. The arm muscles help drive the body forward, especially during the trot and gallop.

The cannon bones in front legs are mainly just for support. The horse has muscles in the upper parts of his legs; the muscles in front of the forearm are extendors that pull the lower part of the leg forward; the muscles at the back of the forearm bend the knee. All these muscles continue downward below the knee and hock, so a long forearm allows longer muscles and shorter tendons.

Correct conformation.

Over at the knee (buck knee).

Back at the knee (calf knee).

Front limbs viewed from the side.

Pastern too straight.

Standing over.

Standing under.

Cut out under knee, bone and tendons too small under knees.

Tied in at knees. Tendons too close to cannon bone just below knee.

A long, powerful forearm and a short cannon put less concussion and strain on the short tendons that would come from longer ones if the knee were at a higher level. A horse will have more agility if he has long forearms and short cannons, for it is the lengthy muscles (operating through tendons in the lower leg on the level system) that produce speed. Very few leggy horses with long front cannons have much athletic ability or stamina. A horse with long forearms and short cannons is usually a better athlete than the horse with short, stubby forearms and long, clumsy cannons.

The cannon bone in the hind leg, however, is longer than the front cannon, coming to the height of the chestnut (the horny growth on the inside above the knee) on the front leg. A longer cannon in the hind limb is beneficial for speed. The cannon carries the hind foot forward and back faster and farther when the length of the cannon slightly exceeds the length of the second thigh. The tendons are long, with more stress on them and the hock joint, usually no problem because the flexibility of the hock joint (working in the opposite direction as the knee joint) makes

Correct conformation. A perpendicular line drawn from the point of the shoulder to the ground divides the leg and foot into two equal halves.

Front limbs viewed from the front.

Toes out (splay-foot, or toe wide). Narrow chest.

Toes in (pigeon toe).

Knock-kneed (knee narrow).

Bow legs (bow-kneed).

Base narrow (feet too close together).

Base wide (feet too far apart).

Bench knees (off-set knees). Cannon bone is not directly under forearm.

strained tendons far more unlikely to occur in the hind leg. Tendon strain is always much more common in the front leg; thus, the "rule" of short cannons in front and longer cannons behind.

The front leg from elbow down is a very rigid structure when it bears weight. It needs a short, strong cannon, short strong tendons, and a good solid knee. The knee should be large, flat, and well proportioned, as large as possible without looking out of proportion to the rest of the leg.

A small pinched-in knee crowds the bone, tendon, and cartilage and hinders smooth, free action. The front of the knee should be very flat with no hint of roundness; the outer edges should look rather square. The back of the knee should be well molded and wide enough for the flexor tendons that pass on down the back of the cannon.

The cannon bone must be placed centrally under the knee. Too far to the outside ("bench knees," or offset cannons), and the extra strain on the inner splint bone will be likely to develop splints. If the cannon bone is too far back, the horse will be "calf-kneed" (back at the knees), which is very weak conformation; the head of the cannon, in this condition, lies behind the line of the radius and the front line of the foreleg looks concave at the knee. A calf-kneed horse usually cannot handle any overextension of the knee joint during any extended performance, and the structure may break down or fracture. Calf knees put great strain on the knee bones and ligaments, and the horse rarely stays sound with steady use.

Another deviation from straight front legs is "over at the knee" or "bucked knees." This condition may be inherited, or it can occur in a horse that has been run too much or otherwise overworked. This condition is not as weak as calf knees, but perfectly straight forelegs should always be preferred. Bucked knees, the result of stress, have the tendons behind the leg somewhat contracted; here too, the leg will not be as strong and sure as if it were perfectly straight.

Cannon bones should be wide when viewed from the side (the horseman's term is "flat bone," actually a combination of bone and tendon, giving the lower leg the appearance of being wide from front to back). The tendon should be set well back of the cannon bone for best action and strength of tendon. A common fault is being "tied in" close to the knee or hock, in which the tendon is too close to the bone, causing friction between bone and tendon and a condition that can cause wearing and other problems between the moving parts.

Undesirable "round bone" occurs when the cannon bone and tendon are too close together all the way down the cannon. This type of leg will not hold up as well as one with a cannon with tendon set well back from the bone. A horse that is "fine boned" has insufficient support—cannons that are too small in diameter. "Coarse bone" usually means a heavy, clumsy cannon. Good bone in a cannon is short, strong, flat, and proportionate to the horse's size.

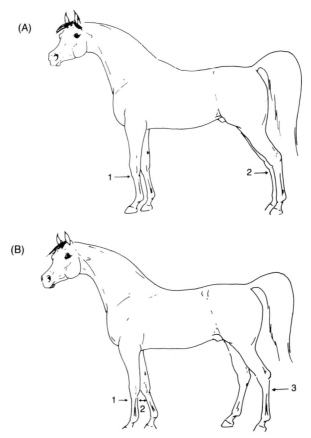

(A) 1. Buck knees (over-at-the-knee); 2. post legged. (B) 1. Back-at-the-knee (calf knees); 2. tied-in tendon; 3. sickle hocks.

Fetlock joints should be broad from all angles, rounded a little at the front, but firm and flattened on all sides. The sesamoid bones should stand out prominently with the flexor tendons gliding over them. If the fetlock joint is narrow from front to back, the tendons will be too close to the cannon bone and become subject to more stress and strain than in a well-formed joint.

Viewed from front or side, front legs should be perfectly straight. A horse that is "in at the knees" (knock-kneed) has added strain on the legs and rarely stands up under hard use. Bowlegs ("out at the knees") puts strain on the limb in the opposite direction and is often accompanied by base-narrow, pigeon-toed conformation.

Base narrow, an undesirable type of front leg conformation that puts the feet too close together, is found most often in horses with large pectoral muscles and wide breasts. Base-narrow conformation is very often accompanied by pigeon toes (pointing inward instead of straight to the front). Base-narrow, pigeon-toed conformation puts strain on pastern and fetlock joints on the outside portion of the foot. The hoof will be worn excessively low on the outside edge because it tends to land on the outside wall instead of flat on the ground. Base-narrow and pigeon-toed horses usually paddle outward with their front feet, while the pigeon-toed horse will usually paddle whether he is base-narrow or base-wide. Again, any deviation from straight action reduces a horse's agility.

Worse conformation than base narrow and pigeon toed is base narrow and splay footed (toes pointing outward). This puts even greater strain on the leg below the fetlock joint. The feet of a splay-footed horse wing inward as he travels, often causing limb interference (striking the opposite foreleg), especially in a base-narrow horse where the feet are so closely placed to begin with.

Base wide is poor conformation in which the legs are farther apart at the feet than at the forearms. It is usually found in horses with narrow chests. Most base-wide horses are also splay footed, a condition that causes a winging inward as the legs move forward. The inside of the limb is under great stress in a horse that is base wide because the ligaments of the fetlock joints and pastern are always under tension. Splay-footed horses generally wing to the inside whether they are base wide or base narrow. Their feet are excessively worn on the inside wall. A few horses are both base wide and pigeon toed, which is weak conformation due to the additional stress to the limbs.

Hind legs are less subject to lameness than front legs because they carry less weight and suffer less concussion and trauma. However, hind leg conformation is very important because it plays a role in how the horse travels (whether or not he interferes) and whether he will develop curbs or spavins. Hind legs, with their groups of muscle that are larger and more powerful than those in the front legs, provide much of the propelling power. Hind legs must hold the entire body weight at times, and are also important when the horse puts on the brakes for stopping.

The hind leg thigh should be long, well muscled, and deep. From behind, it should appear thick, with ample muscle development. The stifle should be well forward. The stifle and hock, which work together in unison, are the two most important hind leg joints for proper propulsion. Angle of stifle and hock will be the same; a horse with a straight stifle will also have a straight hock.

The second thigh (muscles above the hock), the part of the leg that furnishes much of the power for impulsion, contains the muscles that flex and extend the hock. The ideal length of the second thigh has often been debated by horsemen. Some like a long second thigh and a low-set hock while others prefer a shorter second thigh and higher hock (slightly longer cannon). From a purely mechanical standpoint, the shorter second thigh and longer cannon is more efficient. The position of the point of hock (high or low) actually varies only slightly, however, in horses that have been measured. A good general guide is that the point of hock should be level with the height of the chestnut on the front leg.

The hock joint, the hardest worked joint in the horse's body, must therefore be large and sturdy. The larger the joint, the greater the surface area for absorbing concussion, and the wider the joint surface, the less friction. The hock should be firm and well defined (but not fleshy), flat on the inner side and only slightly rounded on the outer side.

Proper hind leg angle is very important. Viewed from the rear when the horse is standing squarely, the hind leg should be well balanced and perfectly straight. A line dropped from the point of buttock should exactly bisect the leg. A straight leg gives equal distribution of weight on various parts of the leg—equal strain and pressure.

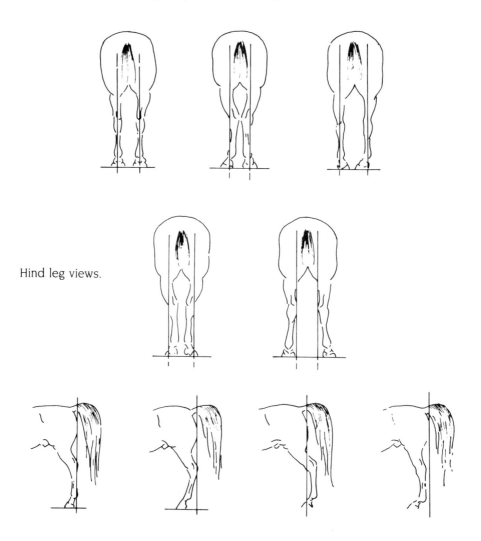

Hind leg views.

When viewed from the side, the back of the hock and cannon bone should be perfectly straight up and down, perpendicular to the ground if the horse is standing squarely. If a line is dropped from the point of the buttock, it should touch the point of the hock and follow the back of the cannon on down, the ideal degree of angle in the hock joint.

If the hock joint is too straight (set too far underneath the buttock) or too angled (not perpendicular, with the cannon bone angled and feet too far underneath the belly), there can be the following serious consequences:

• Viewed from the side, if the hind leg is too straight, a line dropped from the buttock falls in back of the cannon; the hock is set forward almost under the stifle joint, and the hind leg as a whole is practically as straight as a fence post. This type of conformation can lead to bog spavin because of extra strain on the front of the hock joint capsule. This type of leg can be easily injured by hard use.

• Stifle and hock joints are synchronized and have the same degree of angulation; thus a horse with too straight a hind leg (hocks and stifles too straight) may be likely to suffer dislocation and locking of the stifle joint. This is called upward fixation of the patella. The patella (''kneecap'' over the stifle joint) slips upward, locking the joint so it cannot flex. When this happens, the leg is extended back behind the horse and the stifle and hock cannot bend.

• The joints may be locked, or may just catch temporarily, the horse may hop along for a few strides with his leg extended out behind him, and then it comes free and he is able to travel normally again. Young horses with straight stifles may suffer from this problem at certain phases of their growth, the patella jumping on and off its proper position. In some of these horses the problem disappears as the bones grow and the horse matures.

• The opposite problem—too much angle in the hock joints—is a type of conformation called ''sickle hocks.'' This leg structure predisposes a horse to curb, bone spavin, and bog spavin due to the extra strain on the hock joint. Sickle hocks is often called ''curby'' conformation because it puts strain on the ligaments and hind parts of the hock, causing curb (the resultant permanent enlargement due to injury to the plantar ligament) if the horse is worked hard.

• If a horse is sickle hocked, a line extended up the cannon bone is at such an angle that it completely misses the buttock. The horse's feet are too far underneath his body, not directly under the hocks and buttocks as they should be, and the cannons are angled backward instead of perpendicular to the ground. Sickle hocks is a detriment to performance; straighter hocks and stifles can move faster. Too much angle in the stifle and hock joints means considerable loss of time and energy in straightening the joint at each stride. A straighter leg can swing farther and faster, moving in pendulum fashion much more rapidly and with greater length of stride.

   • Some horses have hind legs that are "out of the country." The cannon is vertical as it should be (rather than angled as in sickle hocks), but it is too far back behind the horse. This condition is not as weak as sickle hocks but is still undesirable in an athlete.

The horse's leg and foot structure, if it is well conformed, distributes concussion properly and works to lessen the stress and strain on any one part. Poor conformation always puts added stress on certain parts, which may eventually cause breakdown and resultant lameness and unsoundness when these stressed areas are injured from excessive wear and tear.

OBSERVING THE HORSE

When judging a horse for conformation, the following distinct routine is recommended: Start with a side view observed from a distance of eight to ten feet. The second view is a front view observed from five to six feet. The opposite side view is a scanning view as you pass along the far side from the front to the rear. The third full view is a rear view. Two additional views are the obliques. When this approach has been made, you will have started on the near side of the horse, gone to the front, scanned the off side, examined the horse from the rear, and returned to the right and left front of the horse.

From the left side view, the first step is to look at only the body. Divide it first into thirds; the first third is from the point of the shoulder to the girth line, a line drawn between the back of the withers down under the chest, behind the foreleg. The middle third is from the girth line to a line drawn from the top of the croup down the flank. The rear third is from the last line described to the point of the buttocks.

Step two, while observing the body, is to draw an imaginary line (like the children's game of connecting the dots with a pencil). Starting at the point of the shoulder, make a straight line to the point of the buttocks, to the top of the croup, from the top of the croup to the withers, and from the withers to the point of the shoulder, all taken in at one glance. This figure is a *trapezoid*.

The front sloping line from the point of the shoulders to the withers is an indication of the horse's speed and endurance. The line from the point of the buttocks to the top of the croup is an indication of the horse's power. The line from the top of the croup to the withers is the top of the bridge and an indication of topline strength. It should be slightly longer than the saddle to be placed on his back. Therefore, the key to this trapezoid and its usefulness to the horse is the bottom line, the longer the better. A horse that divides evenly into one-thirds will have a short topline and a long bottom line.

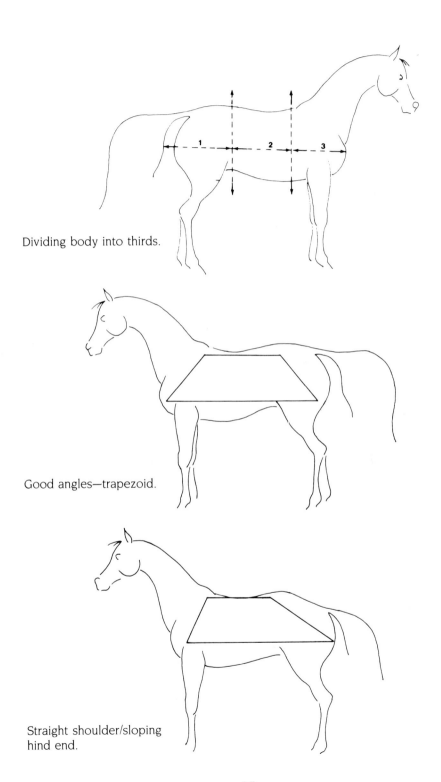

Dividing body into thirds.

Good angles—trapezoid.

Straight shoulder/sloping hind end.

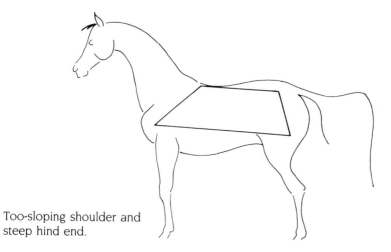

Too-sloping shoulder and
steep hind end.

At this stage we have finished observing the body of the horse on the left side. Now direct your gaze to the ground plane of the forefoot. Work from the bottom of the foot taking in each part of the horse that you can name from the ground to the top of the shoulder.

Next, observe the neck to see how it attaches to the body; whether it is smooth, whether the neck comes from the bottom of the chest or comes out of the horse with a positive stop. Work your way out the neck observing the side view of the head, throatlatch, poll, etc., clear to the lips all in a systematic order.

Moving to the ground plane of the hind leg, work your way to the top of the croup, and lastly observe the attachment of the tail or tail set.

Next, move to the front of the horse and again start at the ground plane taking one leg and then the other at each level to their attachments on the body. Observe the chest, shoulders, and withers by crouching slightly to see whether there is a good inverted heart. Come up the ventral surface of the neck, taking in the area of the trachea, both jugular veins. Then switch your gaze to the poll and work down the face ending on the lips. This completes the examination of the horse from the front.

Move slowly past the off side of the horse taking in the neck as you go by, then casually observe from the ground plane of the right forefoot to the point of the shoulder, from the ground plane of the hind foot to the top of the croup. There's little point in examining the tail from the right side, as it will probably look the same as it did from the left side, so move on to the rear.

The first step in examining a horse from the rear is to observe the heels of all four feet (this is the only time that the heels of all four feet can be examined). Work from the ground plane up each hind leg to the top of the croup. The last view of each hind leg is to peer over the croup if possible, and observe the angle of the withers, the only time that the angle of the withers can be properly evaluated.

Moving back up the off side of the horse to the head, while standing on the right side of the horse's head looking backward, observe the inside of the left foreleg for splints and the inside of the right hock for jack spavins, bog spavins, and the outside of the hock for thoroughpins.

Move around the head of the horse to its left side and face the rear. Observe the inside of the right foreleg for splints, inside of the left hock for jack spavins and bog spavins, and the outside of the left hock for thoroughpins.

Several factors that will influence your impression of the horse being observed should be taken into consideration or avoided when possible. First the horse should be standing on level ground. Obviously, a horse that is standing on uneven ground will give the impression of being taller on the portion that's facing uphill. In addition, you should be standing on ground at the same level as the horse, which will give you the proper perspective of the horse's size.

Second, the horse should be standing on firm ground so that its feet are not hidden in grass, straw or soft sand, or mud. If you are to observe the feet, coronet bands, and the heels of the standing horse, they must be on solid ground to be visible.

A third consideration should be to look for any unusual shoes or trim jobs. (Emphasis on all four limbs of the horse begins at the ground plane.)

After a cursory look by sectioning the horse into thirds and drawing the imaginary trapezoid comes a deeper probe. For instance, check for angulation. A horse with a long sloping shoulder has a good shock absorber system, especially if he has a good pastern angle. The shock absorber system obviously is related to his prolonged soundness. It also is related to a comfortable ride. More importantly, it is directly related to his maneuverability.

The horse with the long sloping line from the point of the buttocks to the top of the croup must, in order for this line to be long and sloping, have a long full rear third.

Imagine, if you will, that a horse has placed his hind feet on the ground while galloping and is preparing to propel his body forward; visualize a long rubber band stretched from the top of his croup around his rump over the point of his buttocks down the hind leg over the point of the hock, down behind the fetlock underneath the heel and imbedded into the coffin bone. The fuller the rear end, the tighter the rubber band will be stretched.

This rubber band obviously becomes more taut, with thus more "snap" power if the croup is located farther forward, if the rear third of the horse is longer, and if he has ample muscle structure behind. When this rubber band is released his body is propelled forward and as the hind legs are extended to the rear, the rubber band becomes slack. Therefore, the length of the rear third, the long angulation of the rear line of the trapezoid, is the horse's power.

Again, on the ground plane of the left foreleg, observe the type of shoe, if any, or type of trim job, and the soundness of the hoof. Check the angle of the hoof in front and the presence or absence of chips, cracks, or ridges. Cracks very easily can lead to unsoundness. Chips may indicate if the horse has been shod in the past, or they may show that the horse has a brittle foot and has difficulty in holding a shoe. Of course, the problem may just be a matter of a lack of attention. However, it bears further investigation. Ridges in the foot coupled with a hollowed dish to the front line of the hoof makes the horse suspect for founder.

Feet and pastern soundness.

Side bones: Ossification of the lateral cartilages resulting from injuries that cause calcium to accumulate and harden.

Toe crack: A split in the front part of the hoof wall. May be partial, complete, high, or low.

Quarter crack: A split in the quarter area of the hoof wall which runs towards the heel.

Seedy toe: A separation of the wall of the hoof near the toe.

The cause of a crack to start on the bearing surface is usually due to improper care. The crack originating at the coronary band is usually caused by an injury.

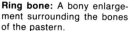

Ring bone: A bony enlargement surrounding the bones of the pastern.

Examine the coronet band for evidence of breaks and scars. A scar through the coronet band could lead to irregular growth of the hoof, which could make a very unsound foot. The area just above the coronet band is examined for enlargements which might indicate sidebones or ringbone; the pastern for enlargements, scars, and wire cuts; the fetlock for smoothness and evidence of strength (coupled with strength and angle of the pastern). A long weak pastern will give a smooth ride, but also is a sign of weakness and early breakdown. A short straight pastern will give a choppy ride with a lot of concussion and, for obvious reasons, will not be a sound horse for long.

Remember, when a horse is in motion, especially at the gallop, that the weight on the front legs is increased. The weight is transferred down the forearm through the knee, down the cannon bone to the fetlock. At this point the weight is transferred across a joint and at the same time angled forward and placed on the ground inches ahead of the straight line of the foreleg. Therefore the ankle must be strong, and the pastern angle must be correct.

Move upward, observe the width from the front of the cannon bone to the back of the tendons in the area just above the fetlock. Make the same visual measurement just below the knee. Directly behind the cannon bone lies the suspensory ligament, which should be observed along with the superficial and deep flexor tendons that lie directly behind the suspensory ligament. These four parts should be the same thickness just above the fetlock as they are just below the knee. Many conformation defects and many injuries can be found when these measurements are not the same. A horse that is tied below the knee will be narrower below the knee than he is just above the fetlock. A horse that has bowed a tendon also will be larger just above the fetlock than he is just below the knee. A horse that has had a high bow or injury to a check ligament may appear larger just below the knee than he does just above the fetlock.

You can start at the ground plane and work upward, or drop an imaginary plumb-line from a given point on the horse then follow it down the leg and come out to a hypothetical point on the ground. This works very well if the horse is a model that stands with all four feet placed exactly and stays that way during the entire examination. Most horses being observed are not quite such willing subjects, so it is best to work from the ground upward.

There should be a smooth transition from the cannon bone into the knee. The line through the knee should extend on up the forearm while maintaining a straight line. The knee should appear to be neither forward or back, which would indicate either over at the knees or back at the knees, respectively. If you have to choose one over the other, the pref-

Canons—common blemishes and unsoundnesses.

(Left) Splint: A bony enlargement in the groove formed by the splint and cannon bone. It may be high or low, forward, or back (occasionally on the outside).

(Right) Bowed tendon: An extension behind the flexor tendons, caused by tearing or stretching.

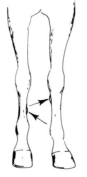
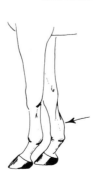

erence would be for a horse that is over at the knees as there will be little interference on the forward edges of the carpal bones. A horse that is back at the knee will put additional pressure on the forward edges of the carpal bones, leading to chips, slab fractures and calcium deposits.

The forearm should be well muscled and should blend well into a large muscle mass of the upper arm at about or just above the body level. The upper arm should be well muscled and blend smoothly into the point of the shoulder. The shoulder itself should be smooth and should show no evidence of indentation along the line of the spine of the scapula. Such an indentation found on one side and absent on the other should make one suspicious of some degree of sweeney (a sprain of the shoulder muscle on the outside of the joint).

Next observe how the neck comes out of the body, starting with a positive stop between the base of the neck and the beginning of the chest. Flexibility is the key when you examine a neck; the thicker the neck, the less the flexibility. It is also important to check the amount of crest in relation to the age and sex of the horse, as geldings and mares with heavy crests may present many problems. The horse with a thick cresty neck is usually obese, also having patchy fat around the tail end. Such a horse is a likely candidate for founder, as well as not generally being likely to have a great deal of endurance. He is a horse that, though an easy keeper, would rather spend the entire day eating and little or no time working. The mare with a thick cresty neck, showing an evidence of masculinity, is often a difficult breeder.

Moving on out to the front of the horse, notice the presence or absence of swelling in the poll and the cleanness of the throatlatch. A deep thick throatlatch could indicate that a horse has an exceptional amount of fat around his air passage that would hinder his breathing capacity for performance. Likewise, a horse with an exceptionally sharp throatlatch, especially one who carries his head tucked, would have an insufficient amount of air traveling to the lungs.

Next, observe the alertness, cleanness, and the presence or absence of growths in the ears, the top line of the face, the set to the eyes, and the cleanness of the cheekbone. The top line of the nose should be straight, nostrils full but relaxed in the standing horse. The lips should meet. It is also surprising how many times you can pick up the presence of a parrot-mouth or an undershot jaw just by looking at a horse from the side.

Moving to the rear of the horse, start with the ground plane. Again, note the type of shoeing or trimming, observe the hoof wall and coronet band for defects. Look for enlargements, growths, scars of the pastern, and observe the pastern angle. It is quite common now for horses to be a little weaker in the pastern behind than they are in the front.

Regarding the hock, it should be noted that there is no more than one angle involved in the normal hock angle. A horse that appears to have three lines and two angles (with one entire line being the face of the hock) is usually a sickle-hocked horse. There should be one line from the hock to the fetlock, and one line from the hock to the stifle. Sickle-hocked horses usually have one angle from the fetlock to the hock, another angle and another line from that point through the hock to just below the gaskin, and a third line from the gaskin to the stifle. Conversely, horses that are extremely straight make nearly a straight line from the fetlock to the stifle.

The point of the hocks should be observed for capping; in some cases the thoroughpin can be seen from a side view. The face of the hocks should be smooth; the well-developed gaskin can be a reflection of the horse's age, breed, sex, and degree of training. The stifle should be observed to see when the leg is in full extension whether there is a noticeable dimple in front of the stifle in the region of the flank. It is important that a horse be able to lock his entire hind leg in full extension with no pain and then to maintain this stance. When this is accomplished, a small indentation (dimple) in the stifle will be evident.

Curb: An enlargement below the point of the hock. This fullness is due to an enlargement of the ligament, tendon sheath, or skin. Can be caused by structural defects such as cow-hocks or sickle-hocks.

Hocks—common blemishes and unsoundnesses.

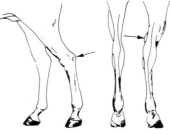

Capped hock: An enlargement on the point of the hock, usually caused by bruising.

Bog spavin: any inflamation or swelling of the soft tissues of the hock.

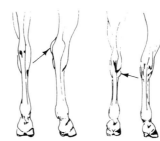

Thoroughpin: A puffy condition in the hollows of the hock. It can be identified by movement of the puff, when pressed, to the opposite side of the leg, Caused by strain on the flexor tendon.

Bone spavin (jack spavin): A bony enlargement that appears on the inside and front of the hock at the point where the base of the hock tapers into the cannon bone.

Then examine the musculature of the hip, the smoothness over the whole bone area, the curvature from the top of the croup to the tail, and the tail set.

Next, move to the front of the horse and begin at the ground plane. This time, take in all four feet observing for cracks and ridges. However, note the shoeing job, the presence or absence of toe cracks, chips, other defects of the foot and coronet band.

Observe the fetlock in its relation to the cannon bone above and pastern below. It should be smooth and blend well, remembering the transfer of weight. Keep in mind, all horses "go" as they are designed to "go." Every movement the horse makes is directly related to his conformation. Attitude and heart are the only variables or unseen relationships. Breaking a horse into parts is simply undoing the formation of the arrangement of those parts and studying each area as it relates to a given function.

TYPE VERSUS INDIVIDUAL

The age-old controversy and the still unanswered question concerns which kind of horse is best. On this subject everyone fancies himself a judge and is dedicated to his favorite type of horse; Arabians are better than Morgans, or Quarter horses are better than thoroughbreds, ad infinitum. This is not confined to what particular breed or color is best, for even within the breeds there is controversy.

Within the Arabian breed, there can be several types of horses; big, stout-muscled ones and fine-boned, leggy ones or various combinations of each. Should a judge in a halter class, for instance, use only one type of horse, regardless of the individual? If he pulls a big long English-type horse out and puts him at the head of the line, does that mean that all the horses to which he awards ribbons in that class have to be of the same basic type, simply because he is so opinionated that he only sees or cares to look at the one type?

This happens more often than not. Why should a judge not look at each horse individually, even though he favors a particular type? It is possible that the second place horse is of a different type within the same breed, but one with the same basic structures as the horse on top.

Some breeders have a tendency to overlook how a horse moves or travels and only see the structure from a breeder's standpoint, with little regard for an eventual ride. By the same token, some performance-oriented judges place a great deal of emphasis on how a horse travels, how his feet move, whether he is balanced, or whether his back is formed to carry a saddle, yet overlook the points sought in a breeding program.

There is also the combination person who lets it be known he not only "feeds 'em and leads 'em" but he "rides 'em and slides 'em" and

Ideal Arabian (top); and grossly fat Arabian (bottom).

maybe this, after all, is the correct balance one should seek, when asking an opinion about a horse.

Performance horses today must be much more than a mechanical robot type. They must possess the ability to be schooled in a particular direction and must look good doing whatever is required. Therefore, the breeder should keep in mind what the horse is really for, which certainly would include being ridden.

In the largest of all the types of classes at horse shows, the pleasure horse class, we always find many different types of horses.

This produces a variety of horses, most all of them doing everything they're supposed to do, but with each one of these horses, there are people who look only at one type of horse, regardless of all the rest of the class, and pay little attention to how good another type may be performing. There also are individuals who look only at the classes that have action and are bored stiff by halter classes or the like.

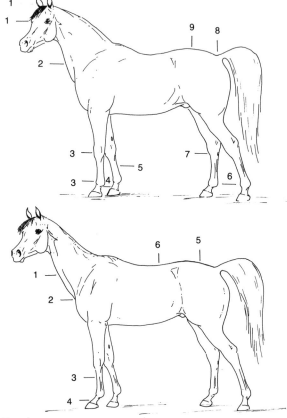

1. Coarse head; heavy; thin ears;
   pig eye
2. Thick, coarse neck set on low
3. Puffy knees
4. Short, straight pasterns
5. Tendons not defined
6. "Second-hand" fetlocks
7. Filled hocks
8. Tail set on low
9. Apple rump

1. Ewe neck
2. Straight shoulder; long back
3. Long cannons
4. Too-long pasterns
5. Short, steep croup
6. Long back

Conformation faults (top and bottom).

As I stated before, there are many different types of horses within any given breed. Each horse, regardless of type, should be judged as an individual, whether in a class limited only to halter showing or a class where performance is the prime target. Because a big free-moving, smooth-muscled horse wins the trophy for that class, it doesn't necessarily mean that a horse should be placed second only because he remotely resembles the winner in conformation with no consideration to how he performed.

Therefore, one must be careful to look at the individual and decide how good he is on his own merit and not lump all of one type into one common basket.

The Arabian division goes into detail about type and conformation and describes at length what the typical Arabian should look like. While in actual conversation with an Arabian breeder, he usually refers to type as meaning Egyptian, Polish, or Anglo, which is really relating it more to a stereotype. What I'm really trying to say is that everyone has his own idea of what "type" means, and this so-called type definitely finds its way into judging. Therefore, the background of a judge is important information for the exhibitor who pays money (entry fees) for the judge's opinion. You frequently hear discussions about judges in which people associate a judge's background with a certain kind of horse; in effect, he is being classified to a type (e.g., Western, English, dressage, hunter/jumper, etc.).

There should be emphasis placed on type, but I relate it more to breed characteristics, rather than just saying "type" (which is really only a matter of semantics). Type, then, is directly related to the breed characteristics, of which there are many, and the judge's background, which in most instances is *not* so widely varied.

"Type" is a word that is always changing meaning. I have seen many changes in desired type over the years in every breed. What was "in" three or four years ago is "out" today (for example, pretty headed, small horses that traveled close to the ground). All horses are getting better, for the most part, and I just can't help wondering what type of horse we'll be wanting ten years from now.

Type, in reality, is as the dictionary defines it: "A general form or character common to a number of individuals that distinguishes them as an identifiable class; a particular kind, class, or group." Expanding further, "A kind, class, or group, as distinguished by a particular character: a representative or typical specimen; a thing embodying the characteristic qualities of a kind, class, or group: as, 'The Arabian type': the standard or the model for comparison." Impression, image, figure, form, model, standard, archetype, quintessence, embodiment, specimen, representative, symbol, personification, essence, example, kind, character, nature.

Type is the inherent characteristic that separates the Arabian from other breeds of horse. It is considered to be foremost in the selection criteria for Arabian breeding stock, for if we lose type, we lose the Arabian. Emphatic consideration to this position is essential if the genetic integrity of the Arabian breed is to be perpetuated.

The overall picture and attitude, spirit, or pridefulness is the first impression one should get on type. *Stand away* from the horse to get that first impression. You cannot see the true composition of a horse by standing on top of it, any more than you can judge a fine oil painting by being too close to it.

The overall "essence" of the horse is the first impression of type: balance, harmony of composition, grace, and spirit. Thereafter, having assessed the overall harmony and "essence" of the individual, begin by judging the head, which is the *hallmark* of the breed. Proceed from there, paying particular attention to the arch and length of the neck, the length of back, the relative horizontal nature of croup, and the natural position of tail carriage.

Type can be summed up with this analogy: If you showed a horse to a group of novice equine aficionados and they said, "Nice horse, is it an Arabian?" You know the horse lacked type. If they said, "Lovely horse, it's an Arabian isn't it?" The horse probably had some Arabian breed characteristics. But, if they said, "Oh, look at that beautiful Arabian!" There would be no doubt as to whether the horse had "type."

Would definitely say this horse lacks type!

INNER THOUGHTS

An Eye for Halter Classes

Halter classes, popular as they are, are still the most controversial and openly discussed classes among owners, breeders, and handlers. The halter division is one area in which it is opinion alone that the judge exercises in placing his class. His background whatever it may be—breeder of a certain type, trainer of another type, owner or salesman of several types—comes to the fore, and his opinion is based largely on what he has been introduced to in the past.

Today, with the better breeding programs withstanding the test of time, and much thought given to the fitness of a halter horse (where largely before it was a matter of fat and gloss), it is a real challenge to the man who accepts the judging assignment.

There have been many changes in judging procedures over the years, and the halter division has not escaped these changes. In the past, the theory was to find the horse with the least amount of noticeable faults and stand him at the head of the line. Not so now. Most judges with whom I have talked take a different approach—they try to see how good an animal is, give him credits instead of debits, then sort out the best individual in a class instead of the least lousy. There is truly a difference.

The most difficult halter classes to judge are those in which you find no outstanding horse that relates to his breed type but, instead, a mediocre bunch that could be placed in many different ways, none of which would really be satisfactory. It is these classes that the grumblers delight in watching because, as is often heard over the mike, "As the judge sees it, the first award goes to so and so." Someone will say, "Yeah, but can that judge see? How could he place a horse with crooked legs over mine?" Not mentioning, or not even noticing that his own horse was lame.

Who is to say which is the worst fault? Short pasterns or a sloping croup, pigeon toes or cow hocks, narrow chest or small feet, short neck or long head? It all depends on who's doing the looking.

It is always much nicer and easier to judge a class with many top horses entered, as it then gives one the opportunity to base his opinion on what he really thinks, without any compromise or compensation as in the case of a poor class of average horses. It is almost impossible to judge a single horse against an unknown or a set of standards that are not clear; in other words, to put him against the theoretical perfect horse.

It's much easier to compare what you see with others that you see at the same time, and that is how a class is really judged—on the basis of comparisons. Comparisons, then, become a matter of opinion, good and bad.

Comparative judging—
one is always a winner!

As a handler, a lot can be learned from comparison judging. If your horse is quite typy, but a little small, and he is standing next to a large horse of average conformation, the comparison could very well work to the advantage of the bigger horse if the judge happens to think size is a basis of deciding the class. It could be more to your advantage to line up, until asked to change, next to a horse or horses that would be about the same size as yours, but perhaps not as pretty.

Color should have little to do with halter placings. Horses with nice heads definitely have an advantage over those of lesser quality, regardless of other attributes they may possess.

To a breeder, a mare should have characteristics that would make it easy for her to carry a foal; a trainer may look for other things this mare might possess that would enhance her ability as a working horse. Who is to say which is right or wrong? It really is of no consequence, because classes are not judged on right or wrong but solely on opinion and preference.

Heads of lesser quality!

A broodmare, on the other hand, should definitely have the qualities that make her, as the class she is in denotes, a "mother" but not forsaking her appeal as a performance horse that could and hopefully would be transferred to her offspring.

In gelding classes, we do not look for the same attributes that were just sought after in a broodmare. Well, maybe some of them, for all horses, regardless of the class, should possess eye appeal, balance, and grace, and this is where the gelding should shine. They would have to be important, because it shows up in performance—and that's all he has left. The looks and ability to make a top horse in whatever field of endeavor is laid out for him; pleasure, trail, reining, park, driving, or just riding over the hills—what he is for—should be the prime consideration when he is standing in front of you or moving on the line.

Stallion classes, where the sires of the next generation stand up to be counted, should be looked at with that in mind. (If more owners would look at their stallions with the thought of what they're going to perpetuate, we most certainly would have more geldings!) Stallions should have traits that can be passed on. Good traits, not simply traits; disposition, intelligence, presence, balance, and character as well as overall conformation, before he is allowed to reproduce.

Halter classes are classes of comparison from the youngest to the oldest, and comparison makes competition because we all don't see things just alike. So until a horse stands beside a lot of others, no one really knows what kind of a horse it is or how great an improvement is needed in his condition, his manners, his way of going, or his performance in order to make him tops in the judge's opinion.

By the same token, until you—as a judge or not—compete and compare, you really don't know your own shortcomings when forming opinions. Competition is the most powerful of all incentives for horses and people alike, and it is through competition and comparison that horses achieve progress. That is what halter classes are all about—look, compare—but most of all, see and form your own opinion.

Viewpoint

A judge is there basically to separate horses—which one is best, second best, and so on. He must decide when good qualities exceed the bad. To do so, the judge must be allowed to view the actual horse. Many showmen, professional and amateur, make this difficult to do either by plan or by accident.

Position is the key—position of the judge in relation to the horses entering the arena, position of the horse in relation to the judge and the other horses in the class, position of the handler to allow the judge to view the horse at its best. I personally don't care whether or not horses trot into the arena or walk and then trot. I analyze a class as it enters, but I don't start my actual judging until all horses are in.

I prefer the horses head to tail around the rail in order to clearly see the profile of each horse as it relates to all others in the class. However, every arena is different depending on the ground slope, sun position, or other obstacles, so some variation might be in order. I like them to be three-quarters of the way around the arena, and I use my ringmaster as the pivotal point to bring the class to order. I motion for the handler to walk the horse toward me, paying particular attention to how the horse tracks—i.e., wing, paddle, drag the toe, etc. When the handler reaches me, I simply say, "Set up there, anywhere," giving the handler the opportunity to position his horse to its best advantage. I like them to be prompt and not spend the day setting up. I follow my standard routine of looking at the eye so I won't get maimed, then the feet, etc.

I personally am extremely conscious of a horse's balance, that single

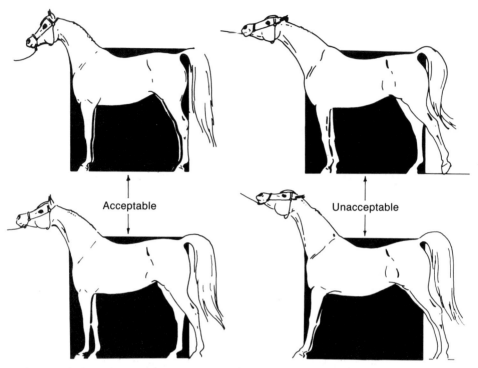

Showing halter stances.

ingredient that allows the horse to function. Many showmen, especially amateurs, are unaware of how their particular horse balances when standing. Most show the front end, the neck and head, and allow the hindquarter to sag, creep, shift, or do any number of things that demonstrate a lack of balance. They're conscious of the "flat-croup syndrome" and where they're told to place the feet to show a flat croup. Actually, the one-foot-behind-the-other position to flatten the croup line was created by photographers trying to get a good picture. While it is advantageous to some horses, it is not to others. All horses do not balance alike and therefore should not all conform to the same stance.

From the hipline, I look to see how a horse "wears himself" in front, again to show balance. One that stands with equal weight distribution on his front feet is impressive; if he doesn't, all the corrective showing in the world will not cover it from this angle.

After viewing the horse, I ask the handler to trot him off; I'm particularly interested in his first move. "Natural" is what you see during that period. The horse may have been stood up to camouflage some trait, yet when he moves off all the parts must come together. It is a most important view. As he trots, balance, or the lack of it, again becomes obvious.

I watch him trot straight away and on the profile. How he uses himself creates for good, fair, or poor movements.

One of the best ideas to surface in the last decade was to allow the judge to view the horses walking on a loose line with the handlers' whips down, not used as an aid. The real horse is seen: croups thought flat then drop off; necks thought long appear short. I study each horse as it walks "natural" and often change my opinion of what I thought I saw. Handlers still try to cover up areas by jerking and jigging or walking by the shoulder or hip, obviously attempting to conceal a weakness. When this happens, I pay more attention to the area in question. Then again comes the final stand-up or position, to look at overall elegance and balance of each particular horse relating to every other horse in the class.

Amateurs often create their own problems by not maintaining position. They crowd the horse in front when first coming in. They crowd the judge while he's inspecting, and they crowd the horse in front while walking. The converse is also true. They hang back all the time, not keeping the gap closed. Exhibitors should know that showing your halter horse to its best advantage at all times will gain you more ribbons. The judge wants it to be easy to put you on top. Have your horse stand, with you out of the way, not being jerked on or constantly moving about. Keep him on the ground, as it were. Even in most classic cases, natural animation is a plus, artificial a minus, and following instructions with poise and confidence a must.

The Idea of "Ideal"

Certain words have a way of bringing things into perspective or merely act as a simplification. I was listening to a talk (at a judge's seminar) and the lecturer used the words *ideal* and *optimum* to interpret the type and conformation portion of judging. All through the rules we find references and some percentage factors given to these areas. The most weight, naturally, is given in the halter or in-hand classes. The ideal or "standard of excellence" for most associations consists of a drawing: Arabian by Gladys Brown Edwards; Quarter Horse and Appaloosa by Oren Mixer; Morgan by Jeanne Mellin Herrick, to name a few. The ideal may be the mental image perceived in those classes that resemble the beauty pageants, but other criteria should be adopted in the riding sections. The lecturer referred to that as optimum, and it made a lot of sense. The horse having those traits or characteristics most conducive to the task involved—trail, cowhorse, hunter, etc.—would probably not equal the ideal at halter, but he'd be optimum using the traits necessary for that job. The optimum English pleasure horse in the Arabian division would likely have the same basic optimum as the costume horse, but not the same optimum as the Western pleasure horse or hunter. He could, however, come close to the ideal at halter using those certain important traits and characteristics. Then, looking at ideal versus optimum, the language allows us to use the true percentage factor for type and conformation to a more realistic degree. The trail horse, for instance, could have optimum qualities for that particular class, fitting the trail horse picture, but be somewhat less than the ideal in-hand.

This all leads to one of my favorite topics: Angulation, the end result of each horse's individual capabilities. All horses of various ages have the same basic bone length relationship regardless of breed, but the angle of the bones is what actually makes the horse work. Shoulder angles, when changed, affect the neck and back appearance as to length and workability. Angles in the hindquarters (hip, leg, etc.) have the same effect. They change not only the appearance, but the same workability as the shoulder angle. What would be optimum for a race horse would not be the same standard for a park horse. The angles would be quite different but could correlate to the ideal where breed standards are concerned. All of this is quite evident within the various breeds. Breeders and judges are picking certain traits (optimums) that relate to jobs, while trying to maintain breed characteristics (ideals). In the Arabian division, many evolutions are taking place. The park horse optimum, Western horse optimum, hunter style optimum are emerging as three separate distinctions of Arabians. You can have optimum traits for a given job without losing the ideal qualities of Arabian type. All breeds of horses are experiencing similar directional changes. Instead of just breeding horse to horse hoping for as close to the ideal standard as possible, the breeders of the future are directing their programs toward optimum efficiency for the given job. When this takes place you can actually tell early the direction the foal will probably take. Bones grow and muscles develop, but angle correlations don't change. Shoulder, croup, and hip angles stay the same. Length of reach and height of leg or knee (high, low, or reaching action) comes from the shoulder, neck, withers (back) relationship. Power or impulsion up and down and length of stride (hindquarter) are all related to the hip, croup, and hind leg angles. Naturally these angles are also related to the front or shoulder angles for a complete picture. "Optimum relates to ideal for the job desired" is a quote worth filing in your memory bank for recall every time you view a horse in relationship to another. From the judge's standpoint, using that type of philosophy means that halter horses can look like halter horses and hunters can look like hunters while maintaining breed characteristics. This could rid us of much confusion.

About Jerks and Jerking . . .

Are we handicapping good halter horses and preventing them from becoming good performance horses? We definitely are and I'll tell you how.

I have a friend who takes "outside" horses for training. One crop—brought in—was two- and three-year-old halter horses, who had had some success in that division, but their owner, desiring more from his horses, wanted to find a performance division to show them in.

These particular candidates were unbroke to the saddle and had only been shown in-hand by "one of the top trainers" in that field. Well, when the head-set portion of the training came about, push came to shove, with battles won and lost. All types of basics were applied, all types of bits and bitting apparatuses were used, and many wet saddle blankets piled up, but the problem was the same with each horse.

I stopped by one day and the trainer asked me to sit in and witness the schooling session. One of the horses was saddled, warmed up, and everything went well—walk, jog, lope, smooth changes, lope down to a jog, and then back to a walk. The transitions were smooth and the horse carried a nice head position. Into the lope again from the standstill with a fishing for leads for a stride or two then, all of a sudden, the horse propped, threw his head up, and bounced it up and down. The trainer, who had been through this before, simply waited for the confusion to pass, allowing the head to drop where it belonged and the schooling session continued.

The trainer, who believes in teaching the horse to be in the bridle (and not by hitting him over the head with a bat) was truly trying to figure out the cause and come up with a solution. As I watched the other horses go through similar antics, the same type of situation developed with each horse. It became obvious we had to go back to the basics or as I say, "When in doubt, use logic."

We verbally traced the history of each horse. All were owned and, for the most part, raised by one person. They were all put in training and shown in halter by one trainer and they all had primarily the same problems.

We looked for conformation defects or problems that might hinder them from maintaining a head-set for very long. We unsaddled the first horse and put a halter on him so we could look at his conformation. And, that's when it happened—like the sunshine after a storm. The trainer was going to lead the horse toward me, à la show ring style for in-hand classes, set him up, and trot him away. The horse only threw his head up and bounced it up and down just as he had done when being ridden.

We did it over and over—walk a couple of steps, set up, head bounce up and down, creep forward, move back, and then trot off, a routine he had learned since he was first haltered. We had found the reason.

Today many halter handlers jerk the horses continually to elevate the head and stretch the neck. They never let the horse alone—stretch, creep back, jerk again. I see it done every week with every age of horse. These horses were actually taught a defense mechanism from the very beginning. Every time something was just a little askew, a foot out of place or a tiredness in the back, it happened. The horse would brace for the jerk by putting the head up quickly to soften the coming jerk, bounce it up there as long as possible, and then relax completely after the ordeal was over. When ridden, the horse was doing exactly what he had been taught to do on the line.

I recall a championship show with very few of the horses, if any, left alone for a period of time. They were picked at constantly—jerk, cluck, come up here, kick the leg, jerk again. They were manhandled into a position for the judge to observe. Then, they were jerked again, trotted off and the same procedure started all over with the next horse.

We decided to experiment, so we drove over to another trainer's barn, one who specialized in halter horses. We went to look at some of the new show prospects. There it was, babies and yearlings being conditioned for the show ring. One by one they were brought in, jerked around, snatched again and again until they reached that point with their head up at an unnatural angle and then the trainer was satisfied. The only place the horse found relief was with his head in the air. "That's it," the handler would say, when this position was achieved.

Jerk and snatch once more and this time the trainer was looking and talking to us, not even seeing the horse. Sometimes I ask what may seem to be a lot of silly questions as I was always told that's how one learns. So I asked the trainer why he had just snatched the horse who was standing relaxed. Without even looking at the horse to see what he was doing, he answered, "Keeps 'em on their toes. Always keep them sharp, alive, and ready."

Keeps 'em on their toes—sharp, alive, and ready!

"Attentive?" I asked. "Good definition," was his answer. I said no more, as it was not my place, but it was obvious we were instilling problems in our halter horses that would show up the moment we tried to ride them.

Our minds and mouths were going a mile a minute as we went back to the "drawing board" to find the solution. After much searching and many more wet saddle blankets, trying every avenue, the only one that worked and had a lasting power was to untrain the halter training. Teach the horse to move naturally, staying in balance and form with his head in a natural position. Take away the resistance and anticipation of being jerked, snatched, whipped, or kicked around. This worked but it took awhile and, you know, those same horses are now winning in performance and still do well in halter without all that overdoing or overshowing.

No wonder some of our best halter horses never make it in performance.

Flagellant Waving

Everyone has the same description of what a whip is and what it's used for. Simply stated, it's an extension of the arm. I find, though, that arms do not all have the same connotation of use. Captain Hook used his iron claw to intimidate and mutilate those who disagreed with him, Billy the Kid used his in direct correlation with notches on his gun, and Mike Tyson uses his to punch out his opponents. Heads of state often extend theirs in gestures of friendship and diplomacy.

The same wide ranges of arm extension use are witnessed every day in the show ring. The whip has become to the handler what the telephone is to the busy executive—a tool, a crutch, and even in some cases, a trademark. We have some so adept that they appear to go through an entire ballet routine while simply standing up a halter horse. Others, attempting to look graceful, hit the judge or themselves with it, get tangled up in it when trying to open the mouth, or step on it when trotting away.

Some are even thought of as good luck charms and kept just for special classes.

However, there are those who think of a whip as being almost a swordsman's foil, with but a fine line separating their use of it from out-and-out abuse. I've seen many horses shown with fresh welts on various parts of the body. Often there's only a raised area, but on several occasions it's looked like a scene from *Rocky* III. Although I'm not a purist in that respect, discipline is one thing, but abuse is another.

The whip is a tool and is necessary in the proper hands. But when horses in the ring were whipped to their knees in front of the spectators or fell over backward trying to get away, the whip was being misused. The judge now can ask the handlers to put their whips down by their sides and let the horses walk around them naturally. Most comply and put their whips down, but some handlers whose arm extension evidently doesn't work too well keep putting them up and down, intimidating the horse, and to a degree, even the judges.

Horse show watchers have just about had enough of whip overuse in the ring. Everyone wanted the judges to do something about it. But in reality, when you're looking at one particular horse as it comes to you and sets up, your concentration is on the inspection. What goes on behind the judge's back is often missed, but not by everyone else. The judge may catch some goings-on out of the corner of his eye, but most of those who take advantage are masters and know when and where they can get away with it.

Unfortunately, people copy those who are considered the best showmen, meaning those who win frequently. The more they see their idols jerk, jump around, whip, and so on, the more they will do it too, usually without the knowledge or experience to know exactly what they're doing to the horse or the show.

Size: The Big Little Horse?

How important is size in today's judging process?

This same question has been asked at every seminar or group discussion and my standard answer is, "When all else is equal, size is an asset."

That is a direct answer to the direct question, but I always go deeper into the meaning, and specifically the words "when all else is equal," which then makes it become a rarity. Size, therefore, is not the sole criterion by which horses are judged. It all goes back to the theory of relativity. In fact, I see many horses that measure nearly 16 hands but, in reality, should be 14.3 hands.

Angulation is the key. For instance, if a tall horse has a long, straight shoulder (this being undesirable) coupled with a long, but very straight pastern and a long, spindly cannon bone, he may appear—to the untrained eye—big, and maybe even win at times solely because of his size. But if we dissect the true horse and put him together as he belongs, with the correct angulation, starting by sloping the shoulder properly, he would lose a couple of inches; when we give him the correct length of cannon bone and angle the pastern to correlate to the shoulder, he would lose a couple of more inches and he then would be (if in proper proportion) only 14.3 to 15 hands and a better-proportioned horse.

So, because of improper angulation, size would be a detriment and actually affect his ability to perform. Angulation then becomes more important than size when all else is equal.

Many people fall into the trap when judging that they must continue throughout all the places in the diminishing size ratio to stay consistent, starting with the biggest and continuing until the smallest or vice-versa. This is not consistency. It should be consistent to pick the most correct horse for first, the next most correct horse for second, and so on, caring little for only the tallness of the horse.

Size also affects different people—and, I'm sure, different judges—in several ways depending on background and, in some cases, location. If a person grew up with ponies and related every horse to that norm, 16 hands would seem gigantic no matter how well proportioned a horse may be. On the other end of the spectrum, to a person with a racetrack background, 15 hands would seem on the small side.

Judges' backgrounds, then, become a major portion of judging or how each individual relates his "druthers" to size, shape, mares, geldings, stallions, etc. A judge who spent his early career roping steers, for instance, would feel uncomfortable, at the start, in judging saddle seat equitation and vice versa. Many times a breeder may look upon a gelding as a cast-off, but a stock horse man would think him perfect for the job. Again, judging is relative to the horse's many uses.

People tend to relate the judge's decision to only one area—size, color, type, head, tail carriage, legs, or what have you. But in reality, the judge must take all of those things into consideration and then add balance when making his final decision.*

"Bigger" horses should relate basically to the length of muscle. Today, I think we are all looking for a little longer muscle in a horse because it gives him better movement and more grace if in the proper angle. Now, when we halter and ride the same horse, the way the horse moves is most important and the longer muscle aids in this movement. So, just by natural progression, if we increase the length of the muscle, we must also increase the area it fits into, and, hence, follow a trend toward a somewhat larger horse without sacrificing correct angulation for size.

But, as it always seems to happen, the pendulum swings from one side completely past the center to the other extreme before it settles where it should, somewhere in the middle. The repetitious and worn-out adage that "if a little does a little good, a lot should do a lot of good" has not escaped the size issue. I've even seen young horses allowed to grow so much heel that it changed their natural way of going. They not only developed contracted heels but were, in fact, crippled just to gain that extra inch or two. I often wondered if it was better to have a "big" cripple than a smaller, sound horse. The chase for the blue ribbon sometimes clouds our thinking, I'm afraid.

---

*Where size becomes confusing is when it is related only to height or massiveness. The appearance of being huge becomes apparent especially in young horses; some want to make yearlings mature, to look like three-year-olds and two-year-olds look like massive aged horses. This is wrong. The forced feeding and introduction of the promiscuous use of hormones is not in the best interests of the horse business.

The size question most assuredly manifests itself in the young horse and in what we, as controllers of nature, do about it. Size must be related to everything the horse is and should only be looked on as one portion of his entire makeup. Judges must accept the responsibility to put size in the proper perspective when placing classes. Horses are used for many purposes and different sized horses fit into various categories.

I've never seen a situation that related what a horse was good for based solely on how big or small he was. First he must be able to do the desired job better than another horse, as an individual. Horses are like people in that respect; each is an individual and must be judged accordingly. All seven-foot people do not make star basketball players nor do all five-foot people make winning jockeys. True, size does enter into special divisions, but we must look at each horse as he is in total proportion and correct angulation.

Yes, under most circumstances, "big" is an asset when all else is equal, but, make sure all else is equal before letting that become the sole determining factor.

CHAPTER
~ 3 ~

English Performance

ENGLISH PLEASURE

The Arabian English pleasure horse has evolved into being a significant part of the breed. Not only in the open classes but in amateur and junior exhibitor as well. In addition to performance, type and quality are important ingredients in these classes. It is not at all unusual to witness classes in which several horses could qualify for the blue ribbon (due to performance and quality), requiring the judges to consider very slight differences in order to place the class. It is no longer enough simply to perform the required gaits without error, they must be performed with ease, grace, and a pleasurable attitude.

The judge is looking for a horse that is ready to show as soon as he enters the arena. As first impressions, more often than not, are lasting ones, the overall appearance then becomes quite essential. The head should be carried in a collected, proud position, near the vertical—not in front and definitely not behind (overflexed)—just flexed at the poll. The horse should give the impression of total acceptance of the bit, be happy in attitude, well balanced, with style and animation. Excessive motion is not necessary but, more important, the stride should be collected and comfortable to the rider.

Each horse should travel according to his size and length of stride. The objective is twofold: (1) To create a pretty picture of balance and cadence with the hocks well under; and (2) to obtain enough speed and proper elevation without losing form, and enough speed and animation to give the appearance of being a pleasure to ride.

The horses are to enter the arena at a normal trot until all horses are in the ring. I bring them down to a walk, and then I ask them to again

81

Incorrect flexion at fifth vertebra; not flexing at the poll.

perform the normal trot, the strong trot, and then back to a walk before the canter and hand gallop. The walk is a four-beat gait, brisk, flat-footed and with good reach. Besides being brisk, it should be a true cadence, easy to ride, under control and at a speed that best suits both horse and rider. The walk should be maintained without constant breaking, urging, taking back, wandering, or showing signs of duress or resentment. The horses should be allowed to walk and not merely use it as a transition gait. The horse's expression should be happy, not fearful, and show a definite degree of relaxation. Horses that appear nervous or are retarded to a half-step-type of movement should be penalized heavily.

Balance is that condition which allows the horse to perform at his best. Collection plus impulsion equals balance. To be balanced, the horse must be collected to the degree that allows him the greatest freedom of movement while still maintaining form. Since the horse normally carries most of his weight on his front end and he is allowed to move forward without control, the weight load is increased. This results in a heavy-in-front movement or "traveling downhill" and, therefore, out of balance. You don't just pull back on the reins to have collection, and it does not mean overflexed or going slow. Collection is load-leveling or moving the center of gravity back to distribute the weight. To what extent varies, depending on how each horse is built. It relates to the length and slope of the neck, the length of the back, and the shoulder angle. Collection is accordian-like and comes from both ends—hence, the second part of balance is impulsion.

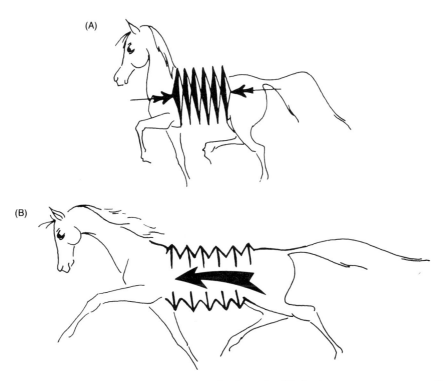

Collection is accordian-like. (A) From both ends; (B) depicts an over-exaggeration of extension.

True collection without impulsion is impossible. Therefore, without impulsion, balance is not possible either. Impulsion has nothing to do with speed. It is the degree of forward inclination required to obtain collection at any gait or speed. The proper impulsion is needed to drive the hocks up under the horse to keep him going square. All of this manifests itself in the top line and how level it stays as the horse performs. When all of the ingredients are combined in the right amounts—the correct degree of collection and rate of impulsion—the top line becomes level, and the horse is balanced.

Horses, depending on size and stride, will by necessity need to pass or trail behind other horses. The rider should pick the best spot to show the horse at the walk. A shorter-strided horse would probably show better just off the rail to not give the appearance of a plodder. A long-strided horse by comparison would be better on the rail, using as much arena as possible. Of course, it always depends on the traffic encountered in a given class. Circling may be necessary at times but should only be done to gain a better position. The judge knows if the rider is using a circle maneuver for other reasons.

Sometimes, when coming back to a walk, many riders will simply stop and wait, especially if the walk is only used as a transition to the canter. How the walk is achieved becomes nearly as important as the walk itself. Horses that have problems at the walk are the ones the judge automatically focuses attention on at other gaits (it's just a matter of habit). When viewed in that light, the walk takes on more importance.

The normal trot is a two-beat gait, performed at medium speed with moderate collection. It must be mannerly, cadenced, balanced, and free moving (posting is required). Since there is no mention of elevation, either for or against, the degree of desired elevation stems directly from the horse's athletic ability. Some horses easily achieve elevation, other horses can't because of conformation limitations or improper schooling and showing.

The horse should show its own "style" of motion, move efficiently with rhythm and pace, and give the appearance of being graceful and natural. The horse should trot off both ends, front and rear, maintain a level top line from ears to tail and have fluid motion. He should appear pleasant and gratifying, not confronting. The horse should "wear the bridle; wear his ears." This means not showing duress, either lugging or jawing off, not in front of or behind the bit but in steady headset position to allow the horse to go in form and balance.

English Pleasure horse using both front and hind ends—fair position.

The form we're talking about at the normal trot is the poll-elevated head to the vertical with impulsion, demonstrating the ability to move on but not noticeably pushed or hurried. The leg action resulting from the free-moving shoulder should be near the horizontal at the top of the knee movement but never above the horizontal (some will move slightly lower depending on shoulder and forearm conformation).

The normal trot should be a pleasant, easygoing trot, ridden with light contact and without evidence of undue restraint. Horses will be penalized for falling out of form, as will those who lack consistency, forge, or not handle the bridle with comfort.

The transition from the normal trot to the strong trot should be fluid and effortless; asking for somewhat more animation without forfeiting form. One of the major faults is a tendency to want speed instead of precision. A horse going fast, laying on the bit, strung out, forging now and then, and sometimes overstriding to a point of breaking is not a pretty sight and should be heavily penalized.

The strong trot should be balanced, animated, bold, and performed in effortless form. The horse should maintain free forward impulsion with sufficient speed to be ground covering, and enough collection to allow the horse to maintain the gait at some speed for an extended period of time. Form should never be sacrificed for speed, and excessive speed, at the expense of form or balance, is a definite no-no.

English Pleasure horse—good in front, but back is hollow and hocks are trailing out behind.

The horse should actually lengthen his stride and, in doing so, his speed will automatically increase accordingly. Each horse has a degree of impulsion needed to maintain form. Going beyond that point is as much an error as not reaching it.

The strong trot—also a two-beat gait but faster and stronger than the normal trot—should show a true lengthening, at a rate of speed that will vary between horses. Each horse should attain his own strong trot in harmony with his own maximum, natural stride. The horse must not be all strung out behind. He should show moderate collection without exaggerated high action in front. He must present a willing attitude and maintain form. The strong trot is done mannerly, cadenced and free moving. Posting is also required.

Exhibitors get in trouble at the strong trot by trying to copy someone else who may have been winning. They are, in reality, overshowing their horse, which is the most common failing seen at this gait. Often the rider's animation or overriding hinders the horse's natural motion and makes it look labored and forced instead of fluid and pleasant.

Naturally the strong trot looks better going down the rail on the straightaway, but it's probably even more important for the horse to maintain form on the turns. *Consistency of gait* is the key. As in the normal trot, some horses will have more elevation than others and this is fine if it's a natural elevation of the knee.

The strong trot is not the same as a let-down park-horse trot. It should be done with whatever motion the horse can achieve without force. When the horse goes beyond his balance point, he will either climb in front, string out behind, hollow his back or elevate his poll. Any one of these is enough to tell you he's gone beyond his form. Each horse has a form or frame in which he works best. He should be shown in his own best form, and judged individually, even though shown collectively. The key ingredients are form and motion.

The transition from the strong trot back to the normal trot or to the walk should be done with willing ease and dispatch. He should accept the aid without lugging on the bit or tossing his head. As soon as he reaches the walk, the horse should remain alert and responsive to his rider without dancing or fidgeting; showing a true softening of gait, sliding into it with willingness.

The canter is a three-beat gait, smooth, unhurried, with moderate collection, correct and straight on both leads. It should be asked for and performed with the slightest amount of effort. The canter, being one of the best gaits to ride, should give that comfortable appearance. It is a true gait, slow, relaxed, and rhythmic, and should be performed in form without the look of excessive restraint from the rider. The canter is a round motion, not vertical by nature. The speed with which the horse canters is again related to his physical attributes. The horse should appear light, not heavy moving, pounding, or grabbing the ground; maintaining a steady, consistent gait.

The head position can often cause a problem here if the horse is not truly in the bridle. When or if the horse starts to tire, this is the gait in which it will show up. He'll start to lose form, soften his back, put a hip to the side, raise the poll, or become overflexed. These are all defense mechanisms telling you he wants to escape the pressure. It also tells the judge that the horse is coming under duress. It usually starts with a flip of the nose, a pop of the tail, or pinned ears—all the horse's way of saying, "ease up."

The canter needs to be straight, meaning the horse's body should travel in a straight line from hip to shoulder. The mouth is a tattletale, simply telling what the rest of the body is doing. The judge and the rider can tell when the horse is falling out of form by simply observing or feeling the horse's head position. If the horse has the tendency to lock his jaw on the left side, for instance, this means the horse's right hip is escaping and he is not tracking straight. By the same token, if the horse has the appearance of locking his right jaw, the left hip is escaping the straight line.

The canter can also be done off or on the rail, depending on the horse's rate of movement or natural length of stride. A horse off the rail with a long stride may give the appearance of going too fast because he's passing everyone. In reality, he's going at the same rate of speed.

The top line at the canter is a good indication of balance. When the horse is in form, with the proper amount of collection and impulsion, the top line (where the rider sits) will be level. If it is not the horse is out of form. Amateurs get in trouble at the canter by not getting a position and keeping it. They have a tendency to speed up, then slow down, or wander about the arena trying to find a spot.

The canter should be done with suppleness, elastic freedom of motion, mobility, showing athleticism. Again, the problems seem to occur most in the transition period, especially if the rider is not sure the horse is on the correct lead. When a rider leans over to look at the lead, he is completely lost for that period and for all practical purposes, the horse is out of control for that instant. The body weight shifts, forcing the horse off balance and the rider to probably lean on the bridle reins. The rider not only creates trouble for himself but also for those around him. If the rider is on the wrong lead, he will either stop and start over or try to throw his horse back and forth hoping it will change to the proper lead (which rarely happens).

So, when approaching the canter command, it is necessary not only to put the horse in the proper position but to take notice of all other riders around you also. The canter comes from behind. When you see someone chasing their horse into it, you know they're in trouble from the start. The transition here is all important from the judge's viewpoint; it tells all about the horse's attitude—pleasurable, willing or not. Smooth transitions do not happen by accident and the results are long lasting in the judge's mind.

The hand gallop is performed with long, free ground-covering strides, always with control. The amount of ground covering may vary between horses due to size and length of stride. The hand gallop is not just a fast collected canter, but a true lengthening of stride, and is also correct and straight on both leads. Extreme speed is penalized.

The hand gallop can be summed up in several terms—a real gallop, 12 to 15 miles per hour, with intent and effort but without any indication of loss of form or manners. It is a true lengthening of stride, covering ground without appearing "chargy," not with the head thrown away but done with contact, in-hand, controlled, athletically moving forward; speed will take care of itself if the stride is lengthened.

It should not give the impression of being chased nor that the rider must keep urging the horse forward all the time. The horse should move freely beneath the rider, maintaining form and a level top line. Often the judge sees the two extremes: the rider hustling his horse around the arena, lapping everyone else, or the one who simply leans forward and never changes gait. The hand gallop should be a pretty motion, with the horse demonstrating the same pleasurable attitude witnessed at the other gait.

The transitions to all gaits should be done smoothly and without any sign of duress. The head carriage is important—accepting the bridle, not fighting it. He should perform with an elegance and style that's not forced or pulling. Manners are of utmost importance for a pleasure horse, along with his responding readily to all of his rider's requests.

In amateur and junior exhibitor classes manners are paramount and often overlooked by many judges. They need not be the same high-powered type of English horses needed to win an open championship. Motion has often overshadowed the manners portion. However, in amateur and junior exhibitor classes we're not looking for a lack of motion either. Many are critical of today's "higher-going" English pleasure types. While high motion should not be the criteria by which we judge, it should not be penalized when the true conformation of the horse allows it to travel with the knee breaking at a higher elevation. I like to see an amateur and junior exhibitor horse display presence and an attitude of cooperation, not conflict. Judges can always use conformation and quality to separate those that mechanically have done justice to the required gaits. The horse should not only go well, but look good doing it. Suitability to purpose.

COUNTRY ENGLISH PLEASURE

As time goes by and new styles or fads are introduced, there are periods of time when voids occur. This happened when the English pleasure horse's way-of-going was encountering a change. A debate surfaced and, rightly or wrongly (depending on your side of the fence), the "more motion'' endorsers won. The other type of English pleasure horse patriots regrouped and the Country English pleasure-horse division was born, creating another dilemma for those who show and judge.

All have agreed the class is needed and is in fact a godsend to those who want a true pleasure ride. Everyone concurred it must be different than the so-called modern English pleasure horse, but in what way? To many it was a place to show horses that couldn't be top ten in English pleasure; to others it was a way to show the ''natural motion'' of a horse without its being forced or overridden. To most judges, it became a burdensome task of sorting out several types of movers all going around at the same time but doing different things with their legs.

Time will sift things out, but confusion is now the focus. They are even calling it (tongue-in-cheek) ''City'' English pleasure when higher going horses win, and the ''Old Shep'' class when others do. The debate flares up once more as each judge interprets the letter of the rule without understanding the intent. The wording has been given a lot of thought, but to put all the concerns and desires of those deeply interested in the Country English pleasure horse down on paper is nearly impossible.

It may help to break the class into each category as there are some key phrases that indicate a definite direction for the class. The key words of the first rule: To be judged on attitude, manners, performance, quality and conformation—*in that order*. These last three words say it all. No other rule makes that firm a statement. In fact, attitude is not listed at all in most cases under the actual class specs. Attitude is further defined, as it is imperative the horse give the distinct appearance of being a pleasure to ride (a form of attitude). One of the points of emphasis relating to attitude (and spelled out) is a quiet, responsive mouth. This is easily seen by judges and spectators.

Horses showing duress or lack of responsiveness do it by showing disapproval in the ears, tail, and mouth. It's nearly impossible to put on paper all the various ear movements, but a horseman can tell when a horse is happy or not. The tail falls into the same category—whether they simply move it or are switching and wringing it can signal attitudinal changes. The mouth is easily described: gaping, jawing off, lugging, fighting the bit, or comfortable. The walk, relating back to attitude and manners, states it to be true,* flat-footed, and ground covering. Horses go as they are designed to go, so the restraints of conformation will hinder the horse's ability to cover ground without being forced. Hence the horse that moves to its own capacity should still be free, willing, happy, and content. These are all qualities easy to access if the horses are allowed to walk a little while (which some judges refuse to do, but should).

The normal trot specifies overall balance, being relaxed, easygoing,

---

*Meaning cadenced, a four-beat gait performed willingly and without interruption.

Country English pleasure horse—good, relaxed, happy attitude.

elastic, with freedom of movement. However, the physical action of the horse is still governed by its conformational qualities. It also states high action must be penalized. This action also encompasses production by force, duress, or any evidence of or extreme in driving the horse beyond his natural capabilities must be penalized. This is not usually the case in the normal trot.

The strong trot is where we see the variations occur in the use of the front and hind legs. The attitude and manners begin to surface in a greater degree because of the term "high action." Any action not deemed natural (for the horse's conformation) at the strong trot must be penalized. It is easily evidenced by the same tell-tales as before: ears, tail, and quiet responsive mouth. Pinned ears, popping tail, resentful mouth, hurried unbalanced cadence, trappy, one foot higher than the other, near pacing or hesitating behind, are all signs of unnatural movements. On the other hand, free moving with ease is a credit, and how this is accomplished is a direct result of conformation. It is important, however, for the judge, exhibitor, and spectator not to reward a lack of motion if the horse is a

Country English pleasure horse—head low, nose out, neck straight, no flexion at poll, ears back, has an unhappy expression.

bad mover and doesn't go very high. The points of attitude—happy, free, and relaxed motion—are the credits regardless of elevations.

The canter, being a three-beat gait, has the same basic requirements of the other English pleasure classes. But, by the absence of the words ''with moderate collection'' does not mean strung out or not in perfect balance. To be correct and straight on both leads there must be the adherence to the formula of collection plus impulsion equals balance. At the canter, attitude and manners again must be of primary importance— no charging or restraint, maintain a natural head position (near the vertical), be quiet in the mouth, and have a motion comfortable to the rider, level and smooth.

The hand gallop must show a true lengthening of stride while still maintaining three beats,* not too fast or too slow, or demonstrating any pressure at all from the rider. The ears should be working, tail quiet,

---

*At a point beyond 15 mph, the gallop in reality becomes four beats.

mouth responsive, top line level, moving at an increased speed without the appearance of hurrying. The horse should be controlled, content, and moving on.

Last and really relating back to the first words (attitude and manners), it is recommended that horses on the rail be asked to halt, stand quietly, back and walk off on a loose rein. These again are tests of attitude, responsiveness, and manners. Nervousness, resentfulness, or duress of any kind will surface during these tests. Naturally the degree of difficulty lies in *when* that command is given—from the walk, trot (normal or strong), canter, or hand gallop, at the middle or end of the class—and these are all decisions made by the judge. One word of caution when any command of this type is given is that consideration should be given to the depth of the competition, the conditions of the arena, surrounding distractions, and what you are trying to accomplish. It is always better not to try to trap horses and riders in a situation by calling the command at an inopportune time and reverting to a fault-and-out method. It is always better for the judge to allow all the horses to perform to their best and pick the winner based on the specifications of the class and Country English pleasure is no exception to that premise.

HUNTER PLEASURE

The steady growth of the hunter pleasure classes in certain areas of the country gives that opportunity to those riders who choose not to ride western, saddle seat, or go over fences. The good hunter pleasure horse will demonstrate more than just three gaits and will be able to show balance and the ability to "shift gears" in smooth transitions with willingness, control, and balance. He should be an outstanding example, possessing those qualities that make an Arabian horse distinct from other breeds. He *should not* be judged nor should he be expected to emulate the Thoroughbred in movement.

The head carriage should be neither too high nor "dumped over." The nose should be slightly ahead of the vertical and the horse should not be behind the bit. He should be properly set up in the bridle and not allowed to become "strung out" with some elevation of the neck and a slight break at the poll without looking braced or rigid.

The walk should be flat-footed and free moving with a clean stride. The trot should be smooth, relaxed, and give the overall effect of a good pleasure ride. The mouth must remain light and the horse must demonstrate a complete acceptance of control without resistance. Horses should not be penalized for *slight* errors. The canter should be smooth, comfortable, and effecting both leads with a definite three-beat cadence. Transitions must be clean and effortless, without anticipation on the part of the horse. The hand gallop should show a true lengthening of stride without the loss of form. Extreme speed shall be penalized.

A good Arabian hunter pleasure horse should be able to show smooth transitions from one gait to another along with standing quietly and backing readily. They are judged on manners first, then performance and, most important, suitability as a hunter, even though not expected to jump.

THE PARK HORSE

One of the most popular classes at the show, and also one of the most controversial, is the park horse class. Over the years, rules along with ideas or concepts of what a park horse is supposed to do have changed many times.

Looking at the class from the judge's standpoint, the horses enter the ring at the trot, which most judges consider to be the most important gait of the class. However, the rule book does not make this distinction. It states that it is a three-gait class: Walk, trot, and canter. But the trot does command most of the attention.

The park trot is extremely bold and brilliant, characterized by free shoulder action. It should be animated, natural, cadenced, with impulsion and power from behind, and light and airy in front. The horse should

A park horse trot.

have leg flexion and extension (foreleg extending fully forward at full stretch, with floating motion combined with hock action that is powerful and well raised, the hind leg being brought forward with a driving stride), and loss of form due to excessive speed shall be penalized.

From the judge's own likes and dislikes, he must decide how much credit to give or take away when the horse performs correctly some of the time but not all of the time (as we see more often than not in the ring). Many horses are overridden at the trot—in-and-outers. They "hit a lick" for maybe one-fourth of the way around the ring then break, hitch, or do something to take away from the overall picture of rhythm and grace. There are all kinds of exaggerated mechanical ways-of-going (unnatural to the way they are built); these too must be considered and penalized.

The park trot is not only light and airy in front with elevation and extension, but of equal importance (and often overlooked) is the hock action, which in reality is what allows the front to work. The place in which the horse demonstrates that he is running out of gas is from behind. The hock action becomes less and less, and so does the impulsion. Many times this manifests itself into pacing behind because the rider is still trying to keep forward motion to a maximum. The horse, if inclined to be weak behind and then is put in a vice by the rider, quickly becomes unsteady and unable to maintain the gait for any period of time. The front end must be controlled by the hands and the hindquarter by the rider's leg if the horse is to be balanced. Most often you'll see a snatch and grab, spur and release type of tug-of-war going on between rider and horse, and the judge must be able to see through the maneuver.

The other gaits, as called for, include the walk, which too is perhaps a distortion of the truth. A true walk is a four-beat gait and most horses do not walk a four-beat gait in the park horse class. Many judges only use the walk as a transition gait from the trot to the canter or to reverse direction. However, the walk definitely needs to be judged in the overall performance but not given the percentage of credit the trot deserves. The walk should show animation and brilliance, be brisk and vigorous. It must show control and collection, be true and straight, not prancing all over the arena like a powder keg ready to explode. If a horse is good and balanced and controlled at the trot, he will most likely be the same at the walk. If the trot is unsteady and wandering out of control, then in all probability the walk will be similar. The walk also allows the rider to get into position and organized for the next gait that is called.

The canter should of course be true, collected, animated, smooth, unhurried, and balanced. The movement should be light and airy, with more elevation than in the pleasure division. The horse must be supple and mobile, and, it goes without saying, he must be on the proper lead both front and hind. Don't confuse collection, balance, and unhurried-with-elevation to mean simply cantering in place or jumping up and down. Impulsion is a basic need here also.

The horse should not fuss with his head, fight the bridle, pin his ears, switch his tail, or otherwise show duress. He should have more action than a pleasure horse, but it should not be artificial. He should have a definite athletic look about him and wear his ears properly, looking right through the bridle. The horse in general should be regal in appearance, happy, content, level, with tail carried up and quiet, legs moving with shoulder action, and a rounding of the shoulder to allow the extension at the right place, not a flipping of the feet out in front without the knee doing its share.

All horses do not make park horses, so the judge must be willing to overlook some mechanical difficulties to get the best-moving horse. In this class, the judge shouldn't try to make a marathon out of the class. Because of the motions required, it places a strain on the horse to hold the gait for any length of time. The judge usually makes transitions to protect the class, even if it means going back and repeating one gait or another. In this class the rider and judge must act (not react) to the way the horses are going and help the class to show. By the same token, if all the horses are going properly and strong, it makes it the crowd pleaser it is designed to be.

In certain classes such as open, maiden, novice, limit, stallions, mares, and geldings, the rules place the percentages on brilliant performance, presence, quality, manners, and conformation. But in the junior class they are to be judged on quality, brilliant performance, and manners. The amateur, ladies, and junior exhibitor classes are judged on brilliant performance, manners, quality, and suitability of horse to rider. What is meant by these different sequences of words is where the emphasis lies. In classes for young horses, for instance, quality moves to the front whereby in the ladies, amateur, etc., manners changes place in order of preference. So, the judge must separate what is meant by the words and put them in their proper perspective. The accepted perspective we all take for granted is as follows, in order of importance: trot, canter, and walk. Therefore, the park-class gaits in reality are on a relative value scale of: walk—5 percent; trot—60 percent; canter—25 percent; conformation—10 percent. If everyone knows this is how it breaks down, and we actually give credit for natural action and penalize heavily those who perform artificially, the class will not be so controversial to watch or to judge.

Judges are expected to separate and put in order: (1) Those horses who do not maintain a trot, but when they are trotting, are great; (2) those who maintain the gait but show no action and are better suited in the pleasure division. The dilemma: How much do you forgive a horse that has good action as opposed to the credit given to the mechanical horse performing the gaits with little or no action? Naturally the answer depends on the degree of the infractions and the lack of action the mechanical horse possesses. But, as a rule of thumb, the class specs list performance and brilliance first in the order of priorities, which allows for quite a bit of discretion on the judge's part. Forgiveness has become a major part of the park horse class.

A horse that has park action (mainly at the trot) and breaks occasionally can still be placed over a horse with a more pleasure-horse go, even though he has not made any so-called mistakes. However, horses that have false action (for example, flailing legs in front and racking or pacing behind) should be heavily penalized. Many judges, though, seem to either not be familiar with a rack or pace, or choose to ignore it. The park horse must trot at the diagonal two-beat gait. The forgiveness simply comes from breaking gait occasionally while performing with elevated action—"coming off the ground on both ends," as it is said, using the hocks for impulsion, driving up under the horse in true trotting form. Balance will always be the key to performance. In the park class, the "credit" method, rather than demerit usage, is essential—giving the horse

Shows a trot—front and hind legs working diagonally; and a pace—front and hind legs working laterally.

credits for good qualities instead of only penalties for slight errors.

Few, if any, park horses can maintain the animated trot for any length of time. Many use the corners as a letdown time to prepare for the pass on the long side of the ring. This leads to breaking. Those who don't let down somewhat and still try to make a pass usually break right when it counts most, in front of the judge.

Many horses in this class are not really in the bridle. Their mouths are abused, not cultivated, resulting in more and more breaking errors than those who can move up and down or forward and back with ease. The park horse's mouth must be soft and responsive, as this is the part that tells the rider what the hindquarter is doing. If the driving force is not engaged, no action can be achieved. Most riders defeat themselves and their horses by not remembering that basic.

Horse and rider engaged in combat—rider bent over, balancing on reins and horse's mouth; no leg contact; horse is strung out (hocks trailing behind).

For a park horse to perform at his best, his body must be in a straight line. Watch the horse perform. When he's going to break or cheat, he usually locks his jaw on one side or the other, bracing for the jerk or pull as he falls out of sync. Again, if the horse locks his jaw on the left side, it simply means his right hip is escaping, a preamble to breaking. The rider should be able to feel this and move the shoulder and hip back into the needed straight line—not by just pulling on the right rein, but also by engaging the right leg to move the body. When the alignment is accomplished, the horse's jaw will unlock and the horse will again be true and cadenced. If the horse locks his jaw on the right side, just the opposite takes place.

The park horse can't perform with a hollow back. Many, simply to

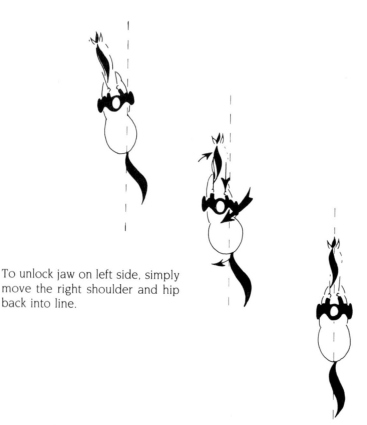

To unlock jaw on left side, simply move the right shoulder and hip back into line.

escape the pressure, raise the poll, lock the jaw, and invert the back, causing a heavy motion with the hocks trailing behind and not working. There is a true art to showing a park horse. "Reading" what he is doing is half the battle; the other, being able to make the needed adjustments, which requires a knowledge of the individual horse, of how long it can sustain at each gait, and a true understanding of its physical capabilities.

Most horses perform with more elevation if you remember another simple basic: To release the front end and engage the hindquarter, you must move the center of gravity back. The amount depends on the conformation of the individual horse.

The ideal park-horse type is one that has well-formed, substantial feet; clean flat-boned legs; a short back with smooth loin; a compact body deep through the heart; and a barrel ribbed close to the hips, which should be well-muscled with full quarters and have a big level croup with the tail coming out high. The neck should be nicely arched onto the head with a fine throatlatch. The neck should flow into the shoulder where the withers are fine, not beefy. This is coupled with "heart" or desire, the unseen portion of the horse that makes him want to work.

Oftentimes the enthusiasm of the crowd destroys the class—the cheering for the horse with the most motion sometimes forces the rider to ask for more and more, instead of simply steadying the horse. As the horse tires or runs out of gas (air usually), he needs to be steadied, not crowded. The judge sees all of this unfolding as well as the horse's actual movements. The horse, if distracted, reacts by breaking gait—a normal reaction.

If a judge sees a park horse begin to fall out of frame, weave and wander at the trot, pick up speed at the canter, or hitch behind at the walk, it's a sure sign the horse will not perform the gaits well enough to win, unless of course everyone else is doing the same thing, which happens more often that not. The words steady, true, cadence, and balance coupled with elevated action are what it takes to win this event.

DRIVING

I've broken down the driving portion of showing the Arabian horse into categories. The first we'll discuss is the pleasure driving, which, as the name implies, should be looked at as a horse that is a true pleasure to drive. He is shown in light show harness hitched to a two- or four-wheeled vehicle suitable to the horse. The pleasure driving horse enters the ring at a normal trot, is shown at the strong trot, and must be able to pull the cart at the walk. They perform these gaits both ways of the ring and then are brought to the center and lined up. They must be able to back readily and stand quietly—two important factors of a good driving horse.

The horse's head position controls his balance in this class as in all others. This is, however, one of the only classes where you can set his head with more than just your hands or other aids. The head can be positioned with the use of the bridle and overcheck. If the horse is hitched with his head too high or low, he will not move in balance. Take the time to find out how to hitch your horse properly, as many horses are beaten before they ever get to the show because of improper hitching.

Manners and temperament go hand in hand as the most required ingredients for a pleasure driving horse. The horse should appear to the judge as if he is enjoying his job. A horse that lugs or is high strung will not make it in this division. Type gives the horse appeal and good conformation provides the overall symmetry to finish the picture. Correct conformation can also make the judging job easier.

Pleasure driving should depict just that—a pleasure. The class should not be strenuous or demanding, as the judge is not looking for extreme speed or action. The horse should be capable, sensible, reliable, and consistent. He should carry himself in a collected, proud, alert manner, accepting his check while the driver gives an easy effortless appearance while driving.

The horse's normal trot should be easy and with style, never looking

Good pleasure driving horse.

Pleasure driving horse faults—ears back, nose out, no flexion at poll, landing on heels, hocks trailing, low tail carriage.

Pleasure driving faults—ears back; winging with front feet; toeing out and going wide behind; hocks strung out, not under horse.

like he is pulling the cart with his mouth or pulling the driver's arms out of their sockets. The transition from the normal trot to the strong trot should be fluid. Seeing how fast a horse can trot is not the primary purpose of the strong trot, it is, rather, a willingness of the animal to respond to the driver's request to move into a more animated trot and the precision in which he performs it.

When asked to walk, the horse should respond to the driver's request without a fight and settle down to an alert, ground-covering flat-footed walk. While walking, the horse should not be twisting and turning his head to get away from the check, or bobbing his head off the check. A well-bitted horse wearing his check properly should perform the walk in the same manner as he performed his other gaits. It is important for the judge to inspect every entry in the line, giving each horse the same amount of attention whether it's the first-place horse or one that is out of the ribbons. When backing, make sure your horse is lined up straight to begin with and allow enough room on either side for the judge to pass safely. Horses should not run backward in a cart. Three or four steps are sufficient.

Equipment requirements should be considered. A complete harness consists of a bridle with blinkers, overcheck (with separate overcheck bit) and/or sidecheck, martingale, cavesson, and snaffle bit (straight or jointed).

Harnesses are sold complete with the above items because they are the safety features on the harness. Each one serves an important function and should be considered a requirement for the driving class, not an option.

1. Blinkers direct the horse's vision to the front and prevent him from seeing horses coming up behind as well as other distractions.
2. The overcheck prevents the horse from dropping his head between his front legs and kicking out at the cart or the driver, causing injury to the driver or damage to an expensive piece of equipment.
3. The martingale serves to control straightness as well as prevent the horse from throwing his head into the air and running away. The leverage of the martingale offers better control also with the snaffle bit.
4. The cavesson is adjusted to keep the horse's mouth shut and allow the snaffle to do its job properly. It should not be so low that it pinches the horse's mouth when the snaffle is in use. Should a runaway occur, the cavesson helps to keep the horse's mouth shut, preventing the bit from being pulled through the mouth.

The harness has its function and should be fitted properly. Blinkers should not irritate the horse by pressing against his eye, as it could cause him to turn his head to one side. The cavesson should be under the overcheck. If the overcheck bit is used properly, it helps to keep the head straight and allows the snaffle to guide the horse.

The saddle portion of the harness should fit in a way that does not interfere with the horse's shoulder movement or length of stride. The breast collar should be just above the point of the shoulder. When hitched properly, the horse should be far enough forward to have a free stride without hitting the shafts or the front of the cart.

Quality and performance are the other important factors in judging a driving horse. Look to see if he is alert, stylish, willing, and performing with ease and confidence. These are a few things to ask yourself before the final, overall picture is complete.

The driver should learn to use the ring to his best advantage by always planning ahead and trying to stay on the rail. Having to constantly pass or cross the ring is not showing the horse to its best advantage. It interferes with the smoothness and consistency of the horse's gait and also other drivers. Being too fast can create a problem as much as being too slow and forcing others to keep passing you. By always planning ahead, drivers should have a reverse-of-direction in mind. Usually, it should be across the ring to the opposite wall. Take time and make sure the direction you are heading is clear and that it places you in a good position again on the rail.

Remember that each horse has to travel according to his size and length of stride. Don't expect a smaller horse to keep up with a larger horse without losing form. The object is to create a pretty picture with the hocks well under the horse, while maintaining speed and elevation. However, the horse should always have collection at all three gaits. Sacrificing collection for speed does not reward you with a blue ribbon. You want to have speed and animation, but "always in form."

Many of the horses I see in the show ring are checked up too high. This causes them to stick their noses out and to lose cadence behind. Remember, very few Arabian horses are built with their necks rising perpendicular out of their withers, like Saddlebreds. Most have their necks set on somewhat lower. When they are checked too high, they are very uncomfortable. This makes them hollow their backs, toss their heads or swing them from side to side, and lose their back ends. When you see a driving horse that is hitching behind, it's probably because he is checked up too high. If he is hitched with his head too low, he is forced to lean on the harness and pull only with his front end. The most important thing the overcheck does is teach the horse to raise his front end, allowing him to drive off his hindquarters, and putting his hocks well under him.

We need to remember that horses naturally carry 65 percent of their body weight on the forehand. In order for the driving horse not to appear heavy on the forehand he must learn collection, to travel forward with lots of impulsion from behind, and to be light and airy with good elevation and extension in front. The overcheck is a great way to help him learn to do this.

Good example of a formal driving horse—good balanced action, square trot, animated, expressive ears, and head well set.

The formal driving horse should simulate the same relationship to the park horse as the pleasure driving horse does to the pleasure horse. The formal driving horse is only asked to walk and trot. However, the walk should be brisk and animated, with a brilliance that is not demonstrated by the pleasure horse's relaxed gait. The trot is also animated and brilliant with a natural high grace, performed with impulsion; light and airy, reaching in front, and with good hock action behind. The horse should be cadenced, controlled, and balanced.

The formal driving horse is high-headed, bold, has good balanced action, collection, and a square trot. He looks through the bridle with animation and presence, with a well set head and his ears forward for a proud look. A formal driving horse should not be hurried to give the impression of racing, as speed is not a good substitute for lack of action.

A formal driving horse should be reasonably "upstanding" and possess a moderately long neck set high on a well-laid-back shoulder that

No hock action—this gives an unbalanced trot to this formal driving horse.

Formal driving horse faults—ears back; sour expression; nose out, lugging on bit; mouth open; low tail carriage.

This formal driving horse has its ears back and is pointing.

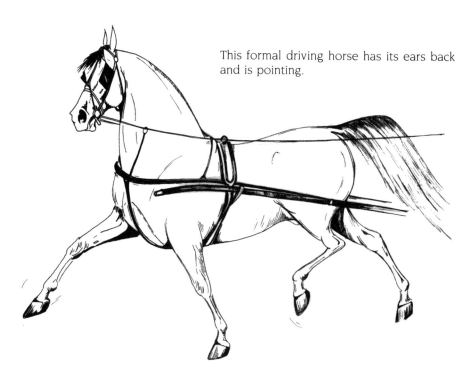

105

allows the front end to work freely. Good hocks, working well under the horse with balance and impulsion, give the impression of pride and self assurance. Beauty alone does not produce presence; the horse must have a willing attitude with brilliance, animation, and balance. Improper conformation for a harness horse is the most common fault in this division.

Again, the way the horse is hitched is extremely important to allow the horse the freedom to perform in harness. While the pleasure driving horse can perform in either a two- or four-wheeled vehicle, the formal driving horse must be shown with a four-wheel show vehicle.

Many problems can and do occur in the driving classes. Often these can be directly attributed to a lack of experience of the driver or the horse, and in all too many cases it's a combination of both. Judges pay particular attention to the driving horses as they enter the arena, and they communicate with the ringmaster to watch closely as the horses move into the extended gaits. When a horse continues to break into a canter, becomes fussy, or gives the appearance of wanting to "run off," judges should bring the class to a more orderly gait and excuse the driver who is losing control.

There is another problem area besides the horse that breaks continually or speeds up uncontrollably, disturbing others, and it is the horse that sulls up and refuses to go forward. He is even more of a danger because of a predisposition to rear or flip over, landing in the cart.

Because of these situations, safety becomes one of the most pressing duties of a judge when there are a number of driving horses in the arena at one time. The size, shape, and general condition of the ring are important in driving classes. Small arenas can accommodate only a few horses. In those classes that have amateur and junior drivers, the judge should limit the number of horses and buggies to a safe amount, and he should hold sections with a finals instead of filling an arena with too many entries, realizing that the safety of the horses and drivers is paramount.

When a horse sets his jaw and the rider is pulling on the lines with no apparent response, judges should anticipate a problem and act accordingly by returning to the walk. When the horse quits, the judge should dispatch the ringmaster to lead the horse forward until he is ready to untrack and regain forward motion.

The reverse portion of the class is also important and should be handled with great care. If there are only a few entries, the judge may simply ask for the drivers to reverse (which should only be executed at the walk) and allow enough time for everyone to accomplish it without feeling hurried. If there are a number of horses, the judge should allow the ringmaster to reverse them one at a time on the diagonal of the arena.

During the lineup, headers should be allowed in the arena as soon as the horses approach the center. Caution and safety cannot be overemphasized by everyone involved in the driving classes.

MOTION

Everyone who shows a horse desires a good mover. Motion is in every backgate discussion, even though it differs with each class. Everyone talks about it, most see it, some cultivate it, but few can describe it. Why? Because what we want keeps changing. As soon as we define a particular way-of-going, up jumps a horse with a little different style or "athletic ability," and our whole direction changes. We continually hear the well-worn cliches—like scopey, mows the grass, daisy cutter, folds well, soft, level, smooth, trappy, thrashy, or pounds—describing good and bad. Hunters are scored on their way-of-going, using symbols to depict motion: GM—good mover, FM—fair mover, BM—bad mover, and FAS—find another sport!

Desired motion is not only different in every class but in every breed with the same class title. Arabian park horses have motion different from the Morgan division, which is again different from its counterpart, the three-gaited saddle horse. Nowhere have we seen a greater change in movement than in the pleasure divisions, both English and Western. Horses in these classes bear little resemblance to those of a few years ago. English pleasure, for example, has been emphasizing more and higher motion with impulsion. Well received or not, that's how it is.

The Arabian hunter under saddle classes are growing in popularity because of the "more motion trend" in the English pleasure classes. They must be careful though not to simply create a place for those not able to place in today's English pleasure division, to put on different clothes and show. The motion is different in hunter under saddle than in English pleasure.

With all the commotion about pleasure horses today, we're undoubtedly going to see some changes come about in what we refer to as good movers. Maybe there are a lot of people who don't fully understand what ingredients make up a horse's movement or why horses go as they are designed to go. I say this because the mechanics of how a horse moves are really quite simple. Most think of motion as only leg movement—a fallacy, at best. That's why we see weighted shoes, unnatural hoof angles, rubberbands, shackles, developers, exercisers, running-Ws, chains, rattles, hock hobbles, and, in many instances, irritants, all with the sole purpose of changing leg movement. Maybe, if we look at what makes the horse move, a clearer understanding will emerge.

Motion in the horse comes from several sources and mostly from a combination of sources. The hindquarters are the horse's motor, the back is the transmission, and the forelegs constitute the suspension system. Contrary to some beliefs, the forelegs have no necessary function in moving the horse forward. The horse is propelled forward from behind, and his back (spine) governs the type of movement his legs will make.

Taken as a whole, the spine (from poll to tail) is a many jointed and therefore flexible portion of the horse's body. The movements which each portion of the horse's back can make and the positions each can maintain are determined by the shapes of the articular surfaces between the individual vertebrae. The joints between the neck vertebrae permit free movement in any plane.

At the risk of becoming technical, the largest muscle in the horse's body lies along either side of the spine. Many believe it's there to hold up the spine. The horse's back is not held up by any muscle. It is held up by the "dorsal," the horse's single longest ligament. It runs in sections from the poll to the withers; the withers to the middle of the synsacrum (front of the croup about at the hip); the middle of the synsacrum to the tip of the tail; and the middle of the synsacrum in another branch reaching to the hock. The back functions like a cantilever bridge. Muscles work by contracting, not when they are stretched. Normally when a muscle is stretched, it's relaxed. Ligaments are just the opposite. They work like cables, only when they are stretched.

Angles are the key to a horse's motion. Angles in shoulders, quarters, and pasterns greatly determine the horse's action and freedom of motion. If the shoulder is too steep, it puts the horse's front legs too far under, cramping his stride and making him restricted in reach. A good horse should be able to reach out well past his nose with his front feet. How many classes do we see today where the horses can't or don't do this? A horse with a long, sloping shoulder has more room for a better length of muscle. A horse with an upright shoulder and similar angle in the quarters is cramped in his leg action and the gaits lack elasticity. The horse moves up and down, virtually in one place. The way the horse moves and his ability to move in balance are a direct result of the angles. If they are the same or similar, the horse will move with more rhythm. The steeper they are, the more up and down, less ground-covering type of motion will result. The more sloping the angles, the more level, reaching, and ground covering the gait will be. Mismatched angles* will create conflicting movement and a tendency toward mixed-gaitedness or not being able to maintain form for any length of time.

The conformation of the "humerus bone" (upper arm) of the foreleg is critical to the presence of natural high motion. Technically speaking, motion is the product of three components:

1. Rotation of the scapula (shoulder blade)
2. Unfolding at the scapulo-humeral joint (where upper arm and shoulder connect)
3. Folding at the elbow and carpus (knee)

Longer scapulas are capable of a greater arc of rotation. Sloping

---

*Mismatched angles relate back to the trapezoid in the chapter on conformation.

scapulas will spend most of that arc going up. A lever system is needed to increase the range through which the carpus can be moved. The humerus is that lever. Therefore, horses with the longest, steepest humeri will have the highest natural motion. If a horse has a long, sloping shoulder but a short, horizontal humerus, it can be taught to fold tightly at the elbow and carpus, but will be unable to raise the carpus above the level of the elbow.

Summarily, the horse with the longest humerus has the most scope. It follows that you can predict the style of movement a horse will have just by looking at the bony conformation. Example: Horses with long, steep humeri have spectacular motion which is both scopey and high. Horses with short, steep humeri have high motion also, but it is short and choppy. Horses with long, horizontal humeri have a "mow the grass" type of action.

Relating this to the Arabian, we find that only one in a hundred Arabians has a humerus proportionally as long as the average thoroughbred or American saddlebred. Most Arabians have a moderately to very-steep humerus. Hackney horses and ponies, however, have the longest steep humeri of any breed.

So, even when the functional back is truly short, the Arabian horse seems to stand over too much ground. It's because the short humeri place the elbow and, thus, the rest of the foreleg too far forward. This is the reason why Arabian classes should look different from the saddlebred classes. Most saddlebreds have more scope and can therefore fold higher and lighter.

When heavy shoes are applied to the Arabian with a long, horizontal humerus, the leg folds to the level of the elbow. The weight drags the foreleg out and forward instead of straight down as the limb unfolds, thus depicting "pointing." When heavy shoes are placed on the horse with a short, steep humerus, the motion is short and stamping, and the horse may learn to roll and twist from side to side, "shrugging" its shoulders to gain more carpus height.

Horses that are able to extend, use their motion and good sloping angles to their advantage (to be fluid), actually lengthen their stride, not just go faster in an up-and-down restricted manner. Desired motion will change continually as we find more horses capable of being athletes. "Good movers" will be tagged onto those horses that go closest to the style determined to be "in" at the moment in any given class. It should always be the quality of motion rather than mechanical motion itself that separates the good movers from the bad.

CHAPTER
~ 4 ~

Western Performance

WESTERN PLEASURE HORSE

Probably the most asked question of a judge in any discussion of horse shows, is "How in the world do you judge those pleasure classes when there are thirty to forty horses in the arena at the same time and all are going well?" Well, it isn't easy, so let's delve into this division known as the Western pleasure horse.

The word "pleasure" looks and sounds quite simple. Perhaps the reason is because the whole division is limited by performance requirements. Horses perform only at the walk, jog, lope, and hand gallop, or other extended gaits, with perhaps a few variations thrown in, such as the halt or back-up. The simplicity is, however, only in the form of the required test. To the judge and to the experienced showman, this is truly one of the most difficult divisions to judge or perform in.

From the judge's standpoint, and most definitely depending on where he stands in the arena, the view he gets or the angle he focuses on plays a major role in the overall outcome of the class. Regardless of the type of horse, the animal must be seen in order to be judged. If a judge stands in the corner and looks at three-quarters of the ring, he sees quite a bit more than a judge who looks at one spot on the wall and sees a horse only for a split second as it passes by. Most spectators see the class from yet another angle than either judge, all of which affects what is seen and by whom.

The walk, for instance, is the most basic of all gaits. When looked at from various angles, it appears not to be the same for all horses. Some walk fast, some plod along barely able to keep going, some are always on the verge of breaking into another gait and must be checked continually, some travel crooked or downhill, some appear to be walking on eggs. How then do we judge the walk?

First, judges should look at the entire horse as it is walking along, making certain he travels true and is not stepping all over himself or stumbling. Walking along free and easy, the winner need not necessarily be the fastest-walking horse in the ring but, more important, should be one that can speed up or slow down on command without resistance. Also to be considered is what the horse does when another horse comes close. Does he pin his ears and want to bite? Crowd him over? Or does he ignore the other horse and listen only to his rider? The latter reaction, of course, is the ideal. The pleasure walk is depicted as ground-covering, flat-footed, and displaying a good attitude. We could go on then to say the walk should be free-moving, not restricted or forced, but in a form that allows the horse to travel correct, straight, and balanced.

The rules also say, "special emphasis on the walk." One might conclude from that statement that the walk should be studied and the horse allowed to walk for a distance in order to display his qualifications at that gait; it should not be used simply as a transition to get from one gait to another. The duration a horse should walk is up to an individual judge. He knows when he has seen enough to be able to make a judgment; no gait should be a marathon, but last long enough to be considered. At the same time you are judging the horse at the walk, you have the opportunity to decide how well you really like the horse as a whole.

Some judges don't spend a lot of time walking the pleasure horse around the ring, but proceed rather rapidly into the jog, which gives a better indication of how he actually travels from a mechanical standpoint. Horses do all kinds of things at the jog. They forge, wing, drag a toe, cross over, and they even limp. Some swing their heads and bodies from side to side, some charge, and some could jog in the shadow of a picket fence.

What should you as a judge look for when all the horses in the ring seem to be doing the same thing? One of the most essential qualities at the jog is a smooth top line. Many people overlook the fact that, regardless of what the horse does with the rest of his body, he must have a level top-line movement simply in order to be a true pleasure to ride. We've all seen horses that jog so hard the rider's teeth rattle and his smile becomes so forced it looks like he is in pain. Instead, the jogging horse should move in cadence, as if he's marching. He should travel square and true, and be flexible enough when he hits the ground not to shake the rider out of the saddle. He should be completely fluid from the head, down the neck, and over the back to the croup. He must also be able to slow down or move out on command, as at the walk, and not show any reluctance to making whatever transition is asked (transitions are one of the most important parts of any class).

The next gait that is called for is the lope, which may be done from the jog or from the walk. It too has its own peculiarities with reference to each horse. Nevertheless, all horses must be on the proper lead and be able to stay on it to win a prize. But what are the differences between horses at this gait?

A judge who stands in the corner sees a horse not only from the side view but also coming straight toward him and going straight away. A loping horse looks different from the side than from head on. When the animal is coming toward you, it is obvious if his head is straight or cocked off to one side, or if he shoulders in or shoulders out, or if he rolls his back or puts a hip to the inside, or how he carries himself when passing another horse or what he does when another passes him. The horse's top line at the lope is just as important as at any other gait, for basically the horse must be a pleasure to ride—smooth, rhythmic, and comfortable.

At the hand gallop, the judge has the opportunity to see a horse move along with more freedom than at the other gaits. This gait should be a true gallop, not just an extended lope. A horse should move right out but not stampede or run off; it's not a race, just simply another transition (more horses blow up at the hand gallop than any other gait, mainly because they are not listening or paying attention to their riders). The true hand gallop must be under control. If the horse is not attentive to the rider, especially around turns, chances are that he will lose his arc and change leads to keep his balance.

At this point in the class, a judge goes into his own "druthers"—head position, speed, color, size, type—whatever his own preferences may be along these lines. All people do not like the same things in a horse. Perhaps a better way to say it is that all people put emphasis on different qualities they consider important.

After the horses have worked both directions of the ring and at whatever gaits the judge has called for, they are lined up for further inspection. This is the place where the judge's preferences are really brought to the fore. Conformation and appointments are looked at, studied, and then compared to what was seen on the rail. This is the time when, if you have several horses equal, you can use your preferences to help make the decision.

The final inspection is the time to ask all the contestants to back up. This important phase of the class is often the deciding factor between two horses. Imagine two or more spectacular horses that mechanically did everything asked of them from the moment they entered the arena. When inspected for conformation and appointments they remained neck and neck. When asked to back, one throws his head in the air and opens his mouth but still backs up readily, while the other gives to the bridle with a little flex at the poll and marches backward as if to say, "Is this what you want?" Naturally, any judge's prayers are answered, and the class ties itself.

Headset, or head position, is a much overrated evaluation. Some people, even judges, place their total emphasis in a Western pleasure class on the horse's head position when, in fact, it should be one of the least-counted evaluation points. In every division and with every horse, the headset is, and should be, different, depending on the job and the horse's conformation.

We have many obvious abuses of headset, and some not so obvious but just as dangerous. Headset can be described in three basic ways.

1. The correct headset (for a given horse)
2. Not enough headset
3. Too much headset (overflexed)

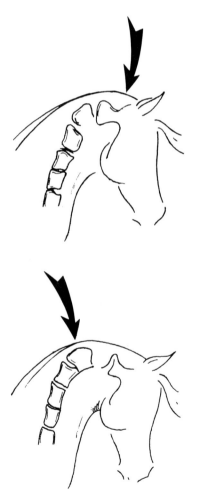

Analyzing headset. (top) Correct—flexing at the poll. (bottom) Incorrect—flexing behind the poll at the fifth vertebra.

Horse flexing at the fifth vertebra.

Naturally an extreme of not enough or too much is easily detected and must be related to by the degree. The abuses come from too much headset (overflexed) coupled with the desire of some trainers to have the poll carried lower than the withers at the jog or lope. The horse needs to look where he's going, but when the horse is overflexed, behind the bit, poll low, and eyes looking at the ground, all he's going to see is the ground. In this instance, it would be more desirable to have less headset. I don't mean for the horse's head to be up in the air looking at the stars, but the nose carried slightly less than vertical, at least allowing the horse to see where he's going, not put in a mechanical vice.

The poll is the key issue here. If the poll is too high, the back becomes hollow and a loss of action results. But worse yet is the poll that is lower than the withers, which effects heavy, downhill, and out of form.

In the Western pleasure division you will see a wide variety of headsets (or lack thereof). That is exactly as it should be. Horses will go as they are designed to go. We hear this over and over, and it's true. Whatever position, the head and neck are still the counterbalance that allows the horse to function mechanically. The three ways the horse does not function at his best are:

1. In an overflexed position (the easiest way for any horse to block a rider, run away, or stampede is to put his chin on his chest and take charge)
2. With his poll lower than his withers (at other gaits than perhaps the walk)
3. The head-in-the-air syndrome

Horse in overflexed position with his poll lower than the withers.

All defeat the purpose of the assembly of the horse's parts to make him an athlete.

It always makes me wonder when I see all of the gyrations we put our horses through why we are so intent on taking the world's greatest natural athlete and putting so many mechanical restrictions or encouraging man-made unnatural gaits on him that we lose the natural beauty of movement of the horse. Headset, one of the most important of all aids in helping a horse to perform, has become a tool of hinderance to that performance. We should be evaluating horses on how they move, how smooth they travel, how willingly they respond, and most of all how balanced they are.

Every horse requires a little different ingredient to aid balance. Balance relates back to the symmetrical arrangement of his parts. Different gaits require different degrees of collection and impulsion, but balance should be one of the main sources of evaluation. Balance is a direct relationship of collection and impulsion. The headset takes on a meaning related directly to the particular horse and his balance-position requirements.

Horses that have necks that come out high from the withers or are put on with a natural arch should carry their heads in the near-vertical position, depending on length of neck and cleanliness of the throatlatch. A neck that comes out a little lower will carry a somewhat lower poll, again depending on length and shape of neck and throatlatch. Ewe-necked horses are at a loss before they start. It's almost impossible to give them any type of headset that will last. Every horse's head position will either aid or hinder his movement. We should see what fits the particular horse at his natural best and cultivate that position.

The pleasure horse division, while one of the largest at any show, is far from being the easiest from the judging standpoint. What we're really trying to find is the horse that looks and acts as if it would be a pleasure both to own and ride, not the one that makes the fewest mistakes. That statement, "that horse acts like it would be a pleasure to ride," carries more significance than most people think. The indefinable quality that produces champions goes beyond the mechanical. If we wanted to label the quality, we would have to call it *attitude*. "Attitude," in the pleasure horse division, is the most desired characteristic. It goes beyond the connotation of manners because although manners can be taught, attitude is an inherent factor that is easily distinguished but hard to put your finger on. Attitude, whether good or bad, is seen throughout an entire performance, whether the horse is making a transition or merely showing along in a good position. The horse will give you an indication of his true attitude (that is, if you will take the time to notice) by what he does with his head, eyes, ears, and tail. It is more noticeable during a transition period, but is not limited to that particular time. How the horse reacts to *any* situation, from the time he enters the ring until the last award is handed out, is what denotes his attitude. When crowded or by himself, when asked to do something or left alone, when moving into the lineup or already there, a good attitude is of prime importance in this class.

To a horseman, head position is an ingredient that is a direct result of the horse being "in the bridle" or, more simply said, the way he adjusts to the bit or whatever he is controlled by. Being "in the bridle," however, is often confused by a horse being flexed or overflexed at the poll. A horse can be in the bridle in many different ways, depending on the way his head and neck are set on his body. This is as it should be, because the way the horse carries his head affects the way he moves, his balance point, his mental reaction, and his overall muscular control. In order to be a true pleasure to ride, a horse must carry his head in a position that is comfortable for him and allows him to demonstrate his athletic ability. Depending on the horse's conformation and balance point, his head must be carried in a manner to allow maximum use of rotation movement and balance. Overflexed and underflexed are both going beyond the point of balance.

If, for instance, a horse has his head and nose up as if he's trying to look the rider in the eye, he must, in order to get it up there, drop his back and become strung out. This affects everything he does and, consequently, reduces his athletic ability. When the horse puts his head in this position, he is usually trying to get away from some form of duress

A Western pleasure horse with a good head position—comfortable, allowing him to demonstrate his athletic ability.

where the bit or hackamore is concerned, and he is definitely not in the bridle. This can happen whether the horse is at the walk, trot, lope, or merely standing still.

At the other end of the yardstick is the horse that puts his head on his chest and bulls his way along. This, too, causes a change in the way the horse travels and, in turn, changes his balance and mental attitude; he is also resisting whatever he is being asked to do. The head-in-the-air problem usually stems from not enough of whatever it takes to get the particular horse to respond, while this overflexed position relates to too much of whatever was being done. Some horses, because of their conformation, will carry a more vertical head position and require a little more collection in order to be balanced and go in rhythm. Horses with a naturally lower neck carriage, that flex more at the neck than at the poll, will carry a lower head and will require less in the way of collection to move in balance. Any movement overdone, such as take back, pick at, check, or bump only accomplishes making a horse become overflexed; an overbridled horse soon will become sour-eared and switchy-tailed because of constant duress. By the same token, the loose-reined rider who throws all away puts his horse off balance by allowing more weight to be on the forehand. The horse will start to wollow and roll his body.

Accept the head position that allows your horse to move properly, that is, smooth on top and offering the apparent ability to be a pleasure to ride. It takes some time and experimentation to find that spot but that is what headset is all about.

Today, Western horses often begin their show careers in "snaffle bit" classes. Judges and exhibitors alike must keep in mind that these classes are designed to allow horses to be shown in a manner suitable for the first years of training. Movement should be relaxed and natural, and there should be light contact with the snaffle bit or the bosal. Snaffle bit pleasure classes were developed not only to showcase the products of today's performance horse breeding programs but also to generate solid individuals for the junior, senior, youth, and nonpro pleasure classes.

There are some specific things a judge can do to help the exhibitor keep a young horse's interest fresh and preserve his good attitude and movement. In fact, the way that the snaffle bit classes are conducted can contribute to the longevity of the pleasure horse, which will in turn be of benefit to everyone.

This is not to say that a judge should think like a trainer while officiating in the ring. The judge's role is to report what actually happened during a class, not what could have been easily fixed by the rider. Although the personal experience of riding pleasure horses can give a judge the insight to spot a shoulder that is falling to the inside on a corner. For example, it is not in his or her job description to make "what if" assessments on the horse's performance, such as: "If the rider had just picked up on the inside rein . . . ," or "If the footing had been better . . ." (all horses in the class are dealing with the same footing), or "If the horse hadn't been shown so hard last week . . ." The judge does not need to be occupied with such thoughts. They are the responsibility of the horse trainer.

What a judge can do, though, is to conduct the class in a positive manner and from the standpoint of a horseman. Rather than just waiting for these young horses to make a mistake and then penalizing them heavily for the error, the judge should spend his or her time looking for the superior horse and then reward that excellence.

At the same time a judge is enforcing the rules, he or she can also run the class in a way that helps to prevent sourness and allows the exhibitors to show their horses to the best advantage. From the moment the young horses enter the ring until they leave, every detail of the class routine can affect the future attitude and performance of an individual horse and the way the class contributes to the breed as a whole.

If the judge sees raw skin or detects bloodiness, the horse can be disqualified, or perhaps allowed to change equipment. For example, if the bosal horse shows rawness on the chin or nose but not on the corners of the lips, he can be shown in a snaffle bit. Conversely, a snaffle bit horse that shows rawness on the lips but not on the chin or nose can be shown in a bosal.

Headstalls must be dropped so that the judge can make a thorough check. By using a bit gauge, the judge will determine whether the bit is the legal minimum of three-eighths of an inch in diameter one inch from the cheek. The mouthpiece must be smooth and jointed and must taper gradually from the cheek to the center of the snaffle. Rings must be at least two inches in diameter and no larger than four inches. A curb strap is optional, but if used, it must be attached to the bit below the reins.

A bosal must be of braided leather or rawhide and no larger than three-fourths of an inch in diameter at the cheek. No metal is allowed under the jaw or at the noseband; the judge will check when the bridle is off the horse by using a magnet. When the bosal is properly fitted on the horse, there must be a minimum of approximately one-and-a-half inches between the bosal and the nose.

The class routine is at the judge's discretion. Since the judge can start the class either direction of the ring, working the horses clockwise first will add a little variety to the young horse's show-ring experience.

The horses are walked in the first direction. Two-year-olds, especially early in the season, should be given a long time to walk, maybe one to one-and-a-half times around the ring. The walk, which is *very* important, should be a flat and pure four-beat gait. Although the horse's topline should be steady, it should not be rigid; artificial stiffness makes a horse more tired and less fluid. The young horse should show evidence of suppleness and responsiveness to the bridle.

The horses are jogged in the first direction for a good length of time. A judge often spots what will likely be the first place horse during the first jog. The top horse will move in a consistent frame, flat, and level, not swinging the nose from side to side or nodding the head up and down. The horse should not rush at the jog nor should he "tippy-toe" with short mincing steps.

The pretty jogger flattens his knee and suspends his front leg in the air for just an instant while the rest of his body "catches up" with the motion. This results in a horse that moves slowly and naturally, yet with impulsion. A horse like this is not only great to look at but good to ride.

The horses are brought back down to a walk for about half the arena and then asked to lope in the first direction. Early in the year, and especially with two-year-olds, the judge may actually look at the ground for a few moments while everyone gets started. It is fine and actually recommended if, in order to find a position on the rail and to prevent anticipation in the young horse, a rider pauses for a few seconds before loping. But excessive pauses are undesirable and can cause a chain reaction that results in the whole class "waiting."

Although correct lead departures are essential, what is just as important is the quality of the horse's movement and his cooperation with the rider. Of course, the top horse will be a superior mover.

If the obvious top horse misses a lead but then calmly listens to the rider and picks up the correct lead and lopes off easily and pretty, he still deserves to win the class. Quite often, the horse that was the best mover at the jog is also the best loper.

The lope must be natural, and each horse should travel the way he is built to travel. Due to the nature of the gait and the design of the horse's body, in order for the lope to be performed with suppleness and balance, "something has to give." In order for the hindquarters to swing well under the horse, the underline of the horse contracts and the topline arches very slightly in two areas. One place that rounds is at the loin. With each reaching-under stride of the hindquarters, the relaxed back of the top-notch pleasure horse flexes. A horse that has a long or tense, hollow back travels strung out behind and can never be a pretty loper.

To compensate for the driving under from behind, the front end must reciprocate with a very slight elevation, with the neck or poll raising slightly. Such a frame allows a horse to lope slowly and with collection because his weight is settled on his hindquarters, where it should be. Depending on a horse's individual conformation, he may lope in a slow rhythm and still cover more ground than the other horses in a class. Passing is perfectly fine if the horse is traveling the way he is built to travel and not running off.

Before changing directions in the ring, horses are generally brought down to a walk for one-half to one full time around the arena. However, three-year-olds may be asked for a lope-to-trot transition in order to separate a group of top horses. Since style of movement is such a subjective matter, transitions can often be helpful in making a more objective assessment of a horse's physical ability.

The horses usually reverse away from the rail. They should stop and reverse quietly and responsively. A one- to two-second pause is fine after the turn to teach a young horse patience, but a ten-second pause is an unnecessary exaggeration.

The work in the second direction is similar to that of the first. After the walk, jog, and lope, in the three-year-old class, the judge may ask the horses to stop on the rail, back, and just stand quietly. The horse that becomes sullen when asked to stop or back is moved down or out of the placings. The pleasure horse should never say "NO" to a reasonable command.

Two- and three-year-olds should always be brought into the lineup at a walk, to prevent a sourness that makes a horse want to duck into the center when on the rail. Once in the lineup, if not having been asked previously, the exhibitors may be asked to back their horses. For variation, the three-year-olds might be asked to first walk forward a few steps and then back. As mentioned before, if a horse locks up with resistance, it can hurt his placing or eliminate him. The horses are then checked for any bloodiness that may have occurred during the class.

It should be remembered that when more than one judge officiates in a class, there are likely to be some differences of opinion due to individual preferences for style of movement. Also, due to the different vantage points of the judges, one may have seen a real wreck that greatly alters his placings, while the other judge(s) may not have seen the problem.

When there are several go-rounds before the finals, it is important for both the judges and exhibitors to clearly understand what method of placing is being used in the finals—a "composite" or clean slate.

With the composite system, the final placing of each horse is determined by the total of his scores in the finals plus the go-rounds. In the clean-slate system, the go-rounds are used to determine which horses will show in the finals, but each horse enters the ring for the finals with an equal chance to win because the previous scores are erased.

The top-notch pleasure horse is a tremendous athlete who is fresh and in good physical condition. He performs with perfect poise and ideal body position at all times. The pleasure horse has a calm and willing disposition, which is evident by his responsiveness and cooperation.

The poorly conformed horse or the lazy or overtired horse cannot hold a correct and consistent position on the rail—it is simply too much of a physical strain. It is virtually impossible for a horse that is built heavy on the forehand or has been trained to move in that manner to perform in a balanced and collected fashion. When it is physically difficult for a horse to do what is asked of him, he responds with resistance and irritation—poor movement, head up, switching tail. The key, then, to success with a pleasure horse is to choose one that is made for the job.

Some breeders are aware that we are well into the age of specialization; to win in pleasure, you have to breed for pleasure. Trainers dislike forcing a horse into a frame that he is not suited for to simply compete in an event. And judges dislike placing such horses. But often in the past that's all there was to choose from.

When you as a judge see an outstanding good mover, give him recognition and you'll encourage breeders to produce more premier pleasure horses.

TRAIL HORSE

The trail class may be the only event where a person can take nearly any type of Arabian horse, teach it to go over obstacles, and have a chance of winning or doing well in the majority of shows today. Many of the better trail horses have been so-called "backyard" horses. Some people who have raised their own horse and taken their time have had good luck with this event. Such a horse is often not pretty enough to "go on the rail" or lacks the talent to be a stock horse. Usually trail horses improve with age and the greater number of obstacles they encounter.

There are criteria a judge uses, such as that a trail horse should have some personality, and be prompt through the obstacle course. He should give the appearance of being careful but willing. Basic control is often displayed as the courses become more intricate and challenging. Trail horses should move right along without giving the impression of rushing. It really turns a judge off to watch someone spend five minutes going over four poles on the ground, ten minutes to back through an "L," and another five minutes to walk twenty feet.

A trail horse class should be interesting to both exhibitors and judges, not a class where you go to eat lunch.

I often hear, "What in the *#@%!? is that doing in a trail horse class?" "If I ever saw a thing like that on a trail ride, I'd take a different route." "Whoever dreamed up this trail course must have stayed awake nights to come up with obstacles like these." Comments such as these are common among participants, spectators, and even judges from time to time. Just what should a good trail horse be expected to do?

As an example, I can quote the following from one of the rule books: "Trail horses must work over and through obstacles, without losing control; rider should open a gate, pass through it and close it. Other tests which may be required are: carrying objects from one part of the arena to another; riding through water, over logs or simulated brush; riding down into and up out of a ditch without lunging or jumping; crossing a bridge; backing through obstacles; mounting and dismounting from either side and performing over any natural conditions encountered on the trail." The last catch-all phrase, "any natural conditions encountered on the trail," enables the course dreamer-upper to contrive almost anything, from elephants in a ladies' class to trained bears in the championship, and any or everything in between.

Some trail-course builders have one thing in mind: to stampede the contestants and see who survives. It is obvious to the judge and to the trainers and riders whether the course designer ever rode on the trail (or in the arena for that matter). Some designers get downright sadistic in what they expect you to do. Good trail courses should be given a lot of thought, keeping in mind the material at hand or what may be available to use. The object of the class is not to see how many horses or riders can be maimed, but instead, be a true test of the horse's ability over simulated trail-ride obstacles.

Several standard types of obstacles can and should be used, such as a gate that allows many methods of opening and closing—push away, pull toward, back through, etc. Walking over logs shows a horse's willingness and ability to pick his way through or over a maze of something in his path without panicking or fretting. Logs give a judge the opportunity to see whether a horse will look where he's going or merely stumble along, as well as to see if he is coordinated enough to control his feet with what he sees. Logs can be set in many ways: raised, crossed, spaced even or uneven.

For a little change of pace, several types of bridges are used readily and make a good obstacle. I've seen the back-through type of obstacle

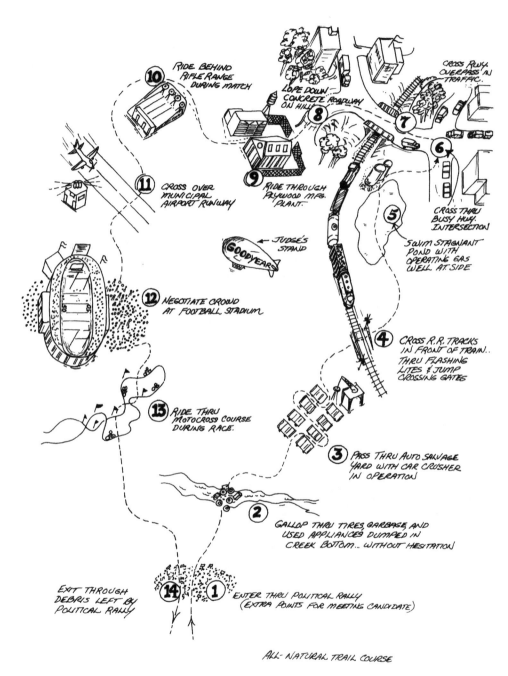

Trail course ''à la naturale''—the Purple Heart is awarded if you survive this course!

Walking over logs shows a trail horse's willingness and ability to pick his way through a maze.

set in many fashions, but all to show the flexibility of the horse in a situation from which he might have to back out. The judge, with obstacles, should watch more than just the horse's feet, as the horse's attitude is most important. If he shows duress by switching his tail, sulling up, or charging, then these traits should also be taken into consideration and scored accordingly. The "jump" type of obstacle is used often to allow for the similar type found on the trail: a large log, a pile of brush, or whatever. It is not simply enough for the horse to jump over it clean, it's the way in which the horse navigates and handles the situation. These are only a few of the standard obstacles found along with tires, water, slickers, side-pass, and a mailbox. All these are good and useful if placed correctly to allow the horse to show his ability. It is possible to set up a pretty course that is safe and navigable, and the judge should see that this is done.

It is almost impossible for trainers or the do-it-yourself type exhibitor to build at home every type of obstacle that they might find in the arena or on the trail, but as a judge's basic rule of thumb, the trail horse should do what is asked, whatever it is. He must listen to the rider and act only on command, not just blindly go along. There is much time on the actual trail ride when the horse just goes along on his own—this is the portion in between each obstacle when the horse walks, jogs, or lopes. During the obstacle tests, the horse must be in hand, doing no more or no less than the rider is asking.

The trail horse must show three major attributes: calmness, agility, and control. Calmness is a trait inherent with certain horses, and a prospective trail horse should be selected first on the basis of a good disposition and even temperament. Highstrung, nervous horses never succeed in this division. The obstacles in trail classes, which judges generally associate with disposition and call "calmness" obstacles, as we discussed before, consist of such things as going through water, boxes or holes; ground-tying, hobbling, crossing bridges, tarps, or plastic sheets; carrying items such as a sack of cans, a shovel; putting on a slicker; working in the proximity of domestic animals such as goats, pigs, chickens, ducks, or anything that can be somewhat spooky. (I don't really expect horses to put up with freshly skinned hides, as the blood odor is a natural fear-inducer, but many shows have these in their classes and they must be dealt with.) Most horses, in the beginning, object to water if they can't see the bottom. A horse will go through a clear stream, but distrusts the mudhole, because he can't tell how deep it is. Bridges can be approached in the same manner.

Agility is basically an inherent trait, too. However, many horses will seem clumsy and awkward because they don't understand what is to be done. The "agility" obstacles consist, for the most part, of walk-overs of

Boy, is this ground-tieing boring . . . mind if I step out for a little action?

varying heights, widths and shapes, and steep banks. As walk-overs come in all sizes, widths, shapes, and descriptions, horses successful at these obstacles are the naturally agile ones. Unfortunately, many never learn to be clever, or they lack the visual depth perception to distinguish heights and distances. Sometimes a horse will look up toward the grandstand while walking over a series of elements without touching a thing, but a good judge should watch more than the feet and would mark this horse down for lack of style. A horse should drop his head slightly through these obstacles, not "drag it on the ground" because it is a fad, but he should look where he is going. Riders who keep a tight rein and hold their horse's head up usually incur many walk-over faults such as rubbing or knocking over poles.

Control is most important. Without control, everyone would fail to negotiate a good majority of the obstacles. I categorize "control" obstacles as the gate, side-passes, back-throughs, and corners, as well as turns on the forehand and the hindquarters. To accomplish any and all of these maneuvers requires a basic preparation before attempting any of them. Most horses have been taught to steer from the reins. This is fine as long as the horses are moving forward, but when they start to move diagonally, sideways, or to the rear, you bring a new force into play—the rider's legs.

The theoretical goal for the rider is to control all directional movement ahead of the cinch (the horse's shoulders) with the rider's hands (reins) and all directional movements behind the cinch (the hindquarters) with the rider's legs. A simple push-away gate becomes a series of combination control signals: side-pass to the latch for position to open; back-up to clear the horse's head of the gatepost; push the gate away; ride through until the rider's knee next to the gate has cleared). The leg next to the gate then moves the horse's hindquarter away and gives room to close the gate; then the leg away from the gate passes the horse back to the gate's "closed" position. All other gate maneuvers—pull to you, back through, or push away—are simply applications of these same principles. Some people make them unnecessarily hard.

The side-pass is accomplished simply by forcing the shoulder and quarter in the same direction. Most mistakes that judges witness are rider error, caused by having the horse's front end on the poll due to the rider not really knowing where the center of his horse is. The center should be to the rear of the rider's leg, usually in the area of the flank cinch attachment.

Turns on the forehand and hindquarter are asked for frequently, an example being the tractor tire, or circle. Horses are asked to place their forelegs inside the tire and revolve the hindquarter around the outside. This is simply a matter of the rider immobilizing the horse's front end with the hand while moving the rear end around with the leg in the indicated direction. The reverse is true when the hindquarters are in the tire or circle. The rider's leg keeps the quarters immobile, while the hand moves the shoulder around in a slow-motion stock-horse spin.

I like to see a trail-horse course set so it can be negotiated in not more than 120 seconds comfortably. A good course should incorporate the jog and lope for a minimum of fifty feet, so I can easily determine how good a mover the horse is. The riders must understand the course the same way I do, so I always try to give explicit instructions: "The gate is a right hand, push away; take the gate in your right hand; you may move your hand anywhere along the top, but don't lose control; push the gate away from you, step your horse through it, and close it," etc. Questions should be asked by the exhibitors if they're in doubt and time should be allowed for this. The course is posted with enough time for the riders to study what's going to befall them in the trail arena.

There are two basic ways to judge trail horses: the plus or positive method, and the minus or take-away system. The first method, which I use, is giving points for each obstacle, such as 1 to 10. My reason for giving points or being positive is I personally place a great deal of importance on attitude. I judge a horse on how he approaches and departs, as well as actually negotiating, an obstacle. Example: A horse stepping off a bridge with one foot or all four would score in a range of 0 to 5 and would never get a 10; stepping out of a backthrough, 0 to 5, never a 10; losing control of gate, 0; stepping over side-pass once, twice, or more, 0 to 5, but never 5 to 10; knocking over obstacles, 0; refusing, 0; disregarding hobbles or ground tie (running off), 0; unnecessary delay (too much time), 5 to 10, but not 0, unless actual refusal occurred; ticking or touching poles, jumps, side-passes, etc., 2 to 6, not 0 or 10; wringing tail, gaping mouth, tossing head, etc., 2 to 5, not 0 or 10; off course, schooling, falling, lameness, bucking, and rearing all mean elimination.

The idea of credits rewards a horse for looking at obstacles that should be looked at and ignoring those that don't. Credit should also be given to a horse that responds to the aids as opposed to a dull response. Trail horses must be eager, but not hurried; fresh and alert, without stress or nervousness. Trail horses should give the judge an impression of gentleness and lightness. A partnership, if one exists, between rider and horse is readily seen by the judge. When the horse can negotiate the obstacles relaxed yet alert and responsive, credits pile up toward the top award. The rider is the guide, and the horse simply responds gladly to his bidding.

STOCK HORSE

Stock or reining horses today are some of the most sophisticated types of show horses. New and exciting working patterns crop up in the rule book to insure that the participants have an increasing test of difficulty that truly tests the agility of the reining horse. Judges, too, are finding the need to become more proficient as the number of entries multiplies. The basics, however, remain the same, no matter what part of the routine comes first or how many turn-arounds are requested.

Circles and figure-eights, for instance, are used to show balance and control. It's the quality of the circles as to size and shape that becomes important. If he executes the figure-eight correctly, the horse should be in the proper body arc (head to tail) with the hindquarters going in the same direction as the nose. A horse that has his head looking in one direction and his tail going in the other is not in a proper body arc. The horse needs to demonstrate flexibility in the rib cage to perform proper circles and direction changes.

The lead changes should be executed in the same place each time. The horse must change leads both in front and behind or he will be greatly penalized. The pattern should be deliberate, and the horse must change his body arc as he changes leads. Often this change is very slight to the untrained eye, but the arc should change nevertheless. While doing so, the horse should not show duress or resentment such as tail switching, jumping through the change, tossing his head, or gaping his mouth. He should be fluid and demonstrate control and position. A common fault that should not be overlooked is a horse that "shoots through" or stampedes at the change point, which breaks up the form and continuity of the figure-eight.

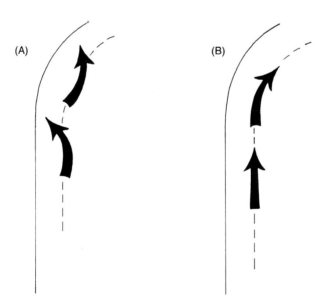

Horse should be in proper body arc (head to tail). (A) Incorrect—head looking one way, tail going the other. (B) Proper arc.

So the eight, which seems a rather simple test, can demonstrate many things to the judge, who must then place a value on each item. For example: Is it worse to drift around or miss a lead change for a couple of strides? Is an open mouth worse than popping the tail? Is head throwing a greater evil than bouncing off the wall? The judge must relate his own knowledge in assigning penalties to each of these faults.

A question that often arises, when old style patterns are used, is how the horse should get from the eight to the starting point of the first run-down if the pattern is not specific. Under these circumstances, it's best for an exhibitor to ask the judge and clear up any misunderstanding. The same goes for closing or not closing up the eight or circling first.

Many people think the run-down is only a means of getting to the place to slide or turn around. Not true. The run-down, an extremely important factor in the overall picture, shows the horse's willingness to do what is asked.

Some also interpret the run-down to mean "how fast he can go." Speed may work for some exhibitors, but only if the horse can handle it in form or if it's requested, for instance, in a championship class. It should never be a factor in a green, snaffle bit, hackamore, or similar classes. Horses should perform at their own level and never sacrifice form for speed.

The run should be smooth and even. The horse should be penalized heavily if he starts slow and continues slow three-quarters of the way down, but then stampedes the last two or three strides and is pulled to a stop. The horse must run all the way into the stop and not shut off part way down or back off at the end. He should run steady and straight all the way to where he is asked to go to the ground.

The point in the testing that gets the "oohs" and "aahs" from the crowd is the sliding stop. Many times, reining or stock horse classes become sliding contests, even though that's not the way they were designed. The judge must then look at the stop in more ways than how long the slide lasts.

Position, attitude, and execution are the most important factors in judging this phase. Position must come first, for if the horse is not in position, the rest will not follow. In short, "he just can't stop." Position is the horse's overall picture, from the way he holds his head when pulled to how the body arc remains and the legs stay together well under the horse. Position also includes how the horse handles the ground: Does he "pop out" of the stop, walk out, stop crooked, throw his head, gape his mouth, stop on his front end, or elevate too high in front? All of these faults show the judge that the horse is off balance.

Proper balance, which is the result of proper position, becomes evident, as does how hard the horse must be pulled when asked to stop. Position of the rider has a great deal to do with the overall picture. The rider can pile up minus points if he simply leans way back, pulls, and

Incorrect stopping position—horse under duress, head up, mouth open, front end elevated. Rider simply pulled on the reins to stop.

hollers "whoa." If he bounces out of the saddle or falls on the neck, the picture becomes distorted, giving an illusion that the horse is not really able to perform.

After the stop has been executed, then comes whatever turning maneuver is called for. It may be a simple half-turn, rollback, turn-and-a-half, two-and-a-half, or half one way, full the other. Again, position is the key word. If a horse "kicks out of gear" on the turn, lunges forward, hangs up, arcs one way and turns the other, wanders, jumps around or swaps ends, he would be heavily penalized for being out of position.

The severity of the penalty is at the discretion of the judge, who also uses this discretion when interpreting speed at the turn. Flexibility and handiness are what are wanted. The horse should use his pivot foot properly and drive off his hocks with impulsion while turning around. This also must be done without any signs of duress or resentment.

The same type of stop and turn-around is executed at the other end of the arena (the opposite way). If the first end happens to be spectacular, the judge will be looking for the same promptness, smoothness of form, and continuity at the second end.

By the final part of the routine, in the center of the arena, the horse sometimes becomes less willing. But now is when the horse must not back off. The run to the center of the arena should be done the same way as at the two ends, not just a lope for a stride or two and then a stop. A strong finish is impressive.

Position of rider important—he is too far out of saddle, hence out of balance.

Here is where promptness is most visible: in a strong center run and stop, a well-cadenced back-up to illustrate a willingness to respond, and in aggressive offsets or whatever is asked for.

A judge must then relate all these items to the overall routine of each horse in the class, use his druthers when it comes to speed and handiness (depending on the type of class or what a particular horse can handle and still maintain position), compare one performance to the other, and pick a winner.

The best stock or reining horse should be willfully guided or controlled with little or no apparent resistance and dictated to completely. Any movement by the horse on his own must be considered lack of control. All deviations from the exact written pattern must be considered a lack of or a temporary loss of control and, therefore, a fault that must be marked down according to severity of deviation. After deducting all faults against execution of the pattern and the horse's overall performance, credit should be given for smoothness, finesse, attitude, quickness, and authority of performing various maneuvers.

There are some basic ideas as to how the class is judged. The basis of scoring is from 60 to 80, with 70 denoting an average performance, and after each horse works, the score is announced. Any ties for first place are worked off, using the same pattern and order of go as was used during the event.

According to the rule book, any type of bit that is free of mechanical devices may be used. Curb chains are permissible provided they are at least one-half inch in width; free of barbs, wire and/or twists; and lay flat against the horse's jaw. The following will result in no score:

1. More than one finger between the reins on split reins
2. Changing hands
3. Fingers between reins with romal reins
4. Two hands on reins
5. Wire bits, bosals, or curb chains on mouth piece
6. Use of tack collars, tie downs, nose bands
7. Electric shockers, whips, or bats
8. Using reins or romal as a whip
9. Failure to drop bridle for judge or steward
10. Willful abuse of an animal while showing

Any rider may untangle excess rein where it may prevent the rider from continuing the pattern, providing it can be straightened without affecting the performance of the horse and at an appropriate time in the pattern. A rider's free hand may be used to hold the romal in the normal fashion, provided the use of the free hand is not in violation of the rules. The following will result in a score of 60:

1. Failure to complete pattern as written
2. Performing the maneuvers not specified
3. The inclusion of maneuvers not specified
4. Equipment failure that delays completion of pattern
5. Balking or refusal of command where pattern is delayed
6. Running away or failing to guide where it becomes impossible to discern whether entry is on pattern
7. Jogging in excess of one-half circle or one-half the length of the arena while starting a circle, circling, or executing a rollback
8. Overspins of more than a quarter turn

The following will result in a reduction of 5 points:

1. Freezing up in spins or rollbacks
2. Spurring in front of cinch
3. Use of free hand to instill fear
4. Touching saddle with free hand
5. Fall to the ground by horse or rider
6. Break of gait

Starting circle or eights on incorrect lead, delayed change of leads or eights on incorrect lead will be judged as follows: Delayed change of lead by one stride will be penalized $\frac{1}{2}$ point. From the start to quarter circle, deduct 1 point. From the start to one-half circle, deduct 2 points. From start to three-quarter circle, deduct 3 points. For the complete circle, deduct 4 points.

Deduct $\frac{1}{2}$ point for over or under spinning up to one-eighth of a turn; deduct 1 point for over or under spinning up to one-quarter of a turn.

Where a change of lead is specified immediately prior to a run to the end of the arena, failure to change lead will be penalized as follows: 1 point if lead is picked up within two strides; 2 points if lead is corrected prior to stop; 3 points if lead is not corrected. In patterns where the horse is required to go around the end of the arena, the horse must be on the correct lead when rounding the end of the arena. Failure to be on the correct lead will be penalized 2 to 4 points, depending on the distance traveled on the incorrect lead, with 4 denoting a complete failure to be on the specified lead.

Deduct 2 points for failure to go beyond markers when making "run-downs."

The judge has the authority to remove any contestant from a show he is judging, should the exhibitor show any disrespect or misconduct as to render himself or the show in an unprofessional manner.

All riders must drop the bridle immediately after the performance. They must be checked by the designated judge in the arena or the steward at the gate. Those riders not complying receive a "no score."

"Run-downs" are made from one end of the arena to the other or to the center. They can be executed in the middle or along the side of the arena, depending on the pattern. They are the lead-in to a stop and turning maneuver or rollback, a stop and back, or a stop. The horse should demonstrate a relaxed, fluid attitude when starting a run-down and, throughout the maneuver, a controlled speed consistent with the size of the arena and ground conditions. All runs should be executed in a straight line.

Credits should always be given when deserved such as running in a straight line; guiding with a minimum of rider commands; using controlled speed; and maintaining an even, natural stride throughout the maneuver. Faults are also considered such as: resisting rider commands in any way; indication of a reluctant attitude (gaping mouth, wringing tail); jumping into a maneuver; failure to maintain a distance of twenty feet from the walls, run in the center of the arena, or to run in a straight line; anticipation of the rider's commands.

Circles are a controlled maneuver at the lope in a designated area of the arena. They must be made in the appropriate geographic area of the arena, and right and left circles must have a common center line in the middle of the arena. The horse must begin on the correct lead from a walk, and show a clearly defined difference in the speed and size of each small (slow) and large (fast) circle. Also the slow right circles must match the slow left circles and the fast right and left should be identical. The horse must lope in an even, fluid manner with a minimum of rider contact and/or commands. The transition of size and speed from large to small, or the reverse, must be accomplished in an even fashion with a minimum amount of contact from the rider and no visible resistance from the horse.

Again, credits are:

- Speed and size of circles relative right and left
- Controlled, fluid motion by the horse
- Clear definition of speed and size between large and small circles
- Transitions made in the center of the arena
- Minimum of contact between the horse and rider

The faults are:

- Any resistance to rider's aids on the part of the horse
- Excessive or prolonged contact between the rider and horse
- Resistance to commands from rider by the horse as indicated by gaping mouth, tail wringing, overflexing, or a change in size or speed of a circle that indicates rider is not in control
- Any indication that the horse is reluctant to complete the maneuver (during transitions, head out of position, tail wringing, gaping mouth, ears pinned, etc.)
- Uneven strides or overflexing that detract from the fluid nature of the lope
- Unclear definitions of speed and size
- Speed and size of circles not relative left and right
- Failure to have a common line between right and left circle in the center of arena
- Jogging into the lope

Lead changes are the act of changing the propelling side of the horse's body when changing the direction traveled at a lope. The lead change must be executed at a lope, with no change of gait or speed and at the exact location dictated in the pattern description, and in one stride. A horse should be considered out of lead if both front and rear leads are not changed within one stride. It is desirable that, when running around the ends of the arena, the horse be on the correct lead when starting to turn the corner.

Credits are:

- Maintaining a fluid motion and constant speed through the lead change
- Minimal contact between horse and rider
- Executing the change in the exact position in the arena dictated by the pattern
- Demonstrating a willingness by the horse to be guided through the lead change and into the correct position for the next maneuver

Faults are:

- Any indication of resistance to the rider's commands
- Excessive contact or application of commands by the rider

- Any change in speed or temporary loss of the rider's ability to control speed and direction
- Anticipation of lead change by the horse

Spins are one or more 360 degree turns executed with the inside hindquarter (pivot) remaining stationary. When spinning, the horse's propulsion is from the front legs, and continuous contact should be made with the ground and one front leg. The location of the hindquarters should be fixed at the start of the spin and maintained throughout the spins. The spins should be executed at the exact position in the arena indicated in the pattern description.

Credits are:

- The use of controlled speed while maintaining correct positioning
- Starting and stopping the spins without excessively altering the position of the hindquarters
- Fluid, consistent motion
- Light contact and commands by the rider
- Consistency in positioning, speed, and rider commands in left and right spins

Faults are:

- Failure to maintain the position of the hindquarters
- Any resistance to rider's commands or the necessity of the rider to use excessive commands or contact
- Both front legs leaving the ground (hopping)
- Overextension causing the horse to move ahead and alter hindquarter position

Rollbacks are a maneuver that combine a stop, a turn over the hindquarters, and an exit in one fluid motion. They must be executed with no more than a slight hesitation after the stop, and the horse should not step ahead or back up prior to the turn. The horse should be in a position to lope off in a straight line when exiting a rollback.

Credits are:

- Fluid motion with fixed hindquarters
- Light contact and commands from rider
- Exiting turn in the correct position for the next maneuver

Faults are:

- Resistance to the rider's commands
- Excessive contact or commands by the rider
- Failure to maintain position of hindquarter
- Stepping out of stop or backing up prior to rollback
- Exiting turn other than in a position to begin the next maneuver (over or under turning)

Stops are the act of slowing the horse from a lope to a stop position by bringing the hind feet and hocks under the horse in a locked position and sliding on the rear shoes. The horse should enter the stop position by bending the back, bringing the rear legs and hocks further under the body while maintaining forward motion and ground contact with the front legs. Throughout the stop the horse should continue in a straight line and the position of the hocks and rear feet should not vary relative to each other. The rear feet should remain in a constant position once entering into the stop, and the horse should not pick up one or both hind feet nor should the back position be altered causing the horse to stand up. The head and neck should be in a slightly flexed position consistent with the arch of the back.

The credits are:

- Distance traveled in a smooth fashion
- Entering into the stop on command of the rider, but without excessive contact or commands by the rider
- Stopping in a straight line
- Maintaining an even rhythm through loose and fluid contact with the ground and the front legs
- Use of light contact only by the rider

The faults are:

- Picking up either and/or both hind feet
- Leaving the stop position (standing up) at any time throughout the stop
- Failure to enter into the stop as soon as dictated by the rider
- Sliding in a crooked fashion
- Resisting the commands of the rider or excessive contact by the rider (head up, gaping, tail wringing)
- Walking ahead and out of the stop
- Backing-up at the end of the stop, except as dictated in the pattern description or as necessary to maintain balance
- Excessive lifting of front legs from ground

The back-up is the horse moving in a reverse motion in a straight line a required distance. The horse should begin the back-up in a controlled manner, without hesitation, until directed to stop by the rider.

Credits are:

- Use of speed while retaining a relaxed attitude
- Lightness of contact and commands from rider

Faults are:

- Hesitation in starting or during the course of the back-up
- Failure to back-up the distance required in the pattern
- Resistance to the rider's commands or the use of excessive contact or commands by the rider (tail wringing, mouth open)
- Failure to back-up in a straight line

While it is generally accepted that some experienced judges have developed their own systems for scoring a stock horse, it is however desirable to have an official standardization system. Each horse begins with a score of 70 and, as each maneuver is completed, the judge adds or subtracts from the composite score depending on the level of performance. Each maneuver is scored as follows: minus 1/very poor; minus ½/poor; 0/average; plus ½/good; plus 1/very good. A judge may at his/her discretion add or subtract an additional ½ point for truly exceptional performances, good and poor. At the conclusion of the pattern, the judge will add to the composite score a mark between minus 1 and plus 1 as an assessment of the overall pattern (definition of the pattern, smoothness, way of going, general appearance). When a penalty is applied under this system, the maneuver is graded independently. For example: If a horse has a good right spin but incurs an overspin, the spin will be credited (plus ½) and the overspin will be deducted (minus 1) from the composite score. It's a good idea for judges to try and keep a running composite score mentally and alter this score mentally as each maneuver is completed.

A SCORING EXAMPLE:

PATTERN #3		70.0
1st maneuver	Spins right good	+.5/70.5
2nd maneuver	Spins left average	0/70.5
3rd maneuver	Circles right and lead change average	0/70.5
4th maneuver	Circles left and lead change average	0/70.5
5th maneuver	Run around end of arena, rundown, stop and rollback good	+.5/71.0
6th maneuver	Run around end of arena, rundown, stop and rollback good	+.5/71.5
7th maneuver	Rundown, stop and back average but backed crooked	−2/69.5
Overall	High head and tail wringing—very poor	−1/68.5
Composite of Run		68.5

WORKING COW HORSE

For those who made a living actually working cattle on a ranch (and theoretically everything we do in the horse show arena is supposed to simulate the "conditions" found in that atmosphere), a good, finished cow horse was a cowboy's "right hand." They were supposed to outfigure, outsmart, outdodge and out-think even the cleverest of cattle. Speed, cat-

like agility, flexibility, strength, and balance were the sought-after qualities. "Cow savvy," it was called. The horse was supposed to run hard
one way (after the cow), head the cow, duck, squat, turn, and come out
of it so fast that many an ol' cow, I'm sure, thought there were two horses
after him instead of just one.

In arena conditions, the size and evenness of the cattle, the layout
of the ring, and the footing are variables that at times interfere with a
working cow horse class. Arenas that have gazebos or judge's stands in
the center are extremely difficult both to show and judge in. Cattle that
have been used for roping and cutting, or otherwise soured from previous
outings, are another cause of alarm. Not having enough cattle to be able

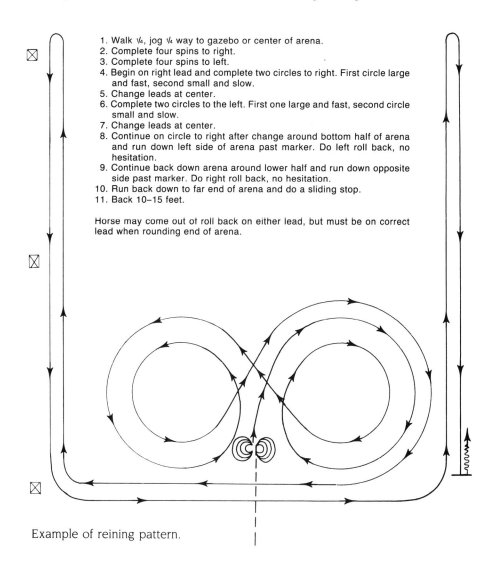

1. Walk ¼, jog ¼ way to gazebo or center of arena.
2. Complete four spins to right.
3. Complete four spins to left.
4. Begin on right lead and complete two circles to right. First circle large and fast, second small and slow.
5. Change leads at center.
6. Complete two circles to the left. First one large and fast, second circle small and slow.
7. Change leads at center.
8. Continue on circle to right after change around bottom half of arena and run down left side of arena past marker. Do left roll back, no hesitation.
9. Continue back down arena around lower half and run down opposite side past marker. Do right roll back, no hesitation.
10. Run back down to far end of arena and do a sliding stop.
11. Back 10–15 feet.

Horse may come out of roll back on either lead, but must be on correct lead when rounding end of arena.

Example of reining pattern.

to work another cow if your first draw is unworkable is a common problem for judges and showmen alike.

At present, horses are to be judged on a basis of 60 to 80 points, which may be expanded from 0 to infinity in the future. Most judges give the following type of cow-working instructions: "After you call for your cow and it enters the arena, box it or hold it at the end of the arena for a time, then let it out down the fence, make a turn or two each way on the fence, and then bring it to the center of the arena and circle each way." When the judge has seen enough, he'll announce or whistle for the contest to end.

When the cow enters the arena, the judge watches both horse and cow as they size each other up. It is perfectly permissible for the rider to rein the horse throughout the routine, as this is a reined-cow-horse type of class. What the cow does as she comes in will establish what the horse will do. A slow, old cow that saunters in and stands in one spot will require a different type of control from the one that comes in on the run and tries to charge right through the horse and the fence. Various tactics must be employed and, by the same token, different values placed on each by the judge. If a horse can make a slow cow look as if it's turning inside out, so much the better, and if the horse can hold on to the one that looks like a freight train and make it give in and settle, points also add up. Judges must take into consideration what kind of cow the horse is asked to handle.

Working the cow.

Sometimes a slow steer will really come apart when the rider lets it move down the fence, and it should be obvious to the judge that the rider is letting the cow down the fence and hasn't lost it somewhere at the end by overworking it or not doing enough to control it. When the cow is let down the fence, the horse must show enough speed to get to the head and make the turnback. Some horses want to run shoulder to shoulder with the cow and let the arena corner do the turning, or at least help in that direction.

It really stands out in the judge's mind when the rider controls his horse's speed; sends it to the head for the turnback; then, as the horse drops in on the cow, he follows it around, regaining control when coming out of the turn; and then he handles the cow along the fence for the turn the other way. What usually happens is that, when the cow ducks back, the horse is not fast enough in the turn to head it again. The cow hangs up and crosses the arena to the opposite side, making the rider follow it around instead of taking charge and making it go where he's directed.

There are many theories on cow work, such as staying away from the cow and shutting her off at the right angle, or following her and intimidating her into the turns. But what we're really looking for in this part of the work is the true cow horse who reads the cow's every move and is ready when the moment arrives. As all horses do not react the same—nor do all cows—it must be a combination of how hard the cow is to work (some won't work no matter how great the horse is, while some you could work on a pogo stick) and how capable the horse is with the type of cow he has drawn.

After the holding at the end and the two or more turns on the fence—left and right—it comes time to "wrap up" or finish the cow off. Here is where a great deal of experience pays off, not only for the horse but for the rider as well. It is a time of judgment—when to do it—so the cow is still fresh enough to make the rider look good, but not so fresh he's going to lose the cow in the center. When the rider makes the commitment, it must be done. The horse is asked to shoulder the cow or handle it in a close, tight circle each way, without the aid of the fence. The cow must be just right and the horse must have the conditioning, with enough left to handle the chore without following the cow around in a circle, puffing and gasping for air.

Cow work is truly an art. It can be spectacular, particularly if fresh cattle are used. The show management should provide enough fresh cattle so the same one won't have to be worked over and over, and a rider can be given another (at the judge's discretion) if he draws a bad cow.

Judges look for and score accordingly the following: Most bad equine manners such as biting, striking, or running over a cow are assessed a 3-point penalty. If the horse only nuzzles a cow with his nose or lips while working or circling, no penalty will be given. However, if the horse while circling the cow runs over the cow, causing the fall of horse and rider, or is out of control and crosses the path of the cow (thus endangering the rider and horse), the work is terminated at that point and a score of 60 is awarded. Horses that run past the cow are penalized 1 point for every horse length past the cow. Any horse failing to show sufficient control of the cow while circling receives a 2-point penalty. Horses that hang up on the fence, exhaust the cow before circling, or fail to hold the cow on the end of the arena during boxing are assessed a 3-point penalty.

Other faults that judges consider are:

- Switching the tail (which illustrates duress or resentment to what is being asked)
- Nervous throwing of the head or lugging on the bridle (also signs of unwillingness)
- Halting or hesitating while being shown (which indicates anticipation of the next command before it is given, a trait usually found in overtrained horses)

By contrast, the characteristics of a good working horse are:

- Good manners
- Willingness to do what is asked
- Being "shifty," smooth, and having his feet under him at all times to demonstrate complete balance and body control
- When stopping, having his hind feet well under him
- A light mouth that responds to a light rein, especially when turning
- A natural head position (whatever it is for that particular horse)
- Being able to work at a reasonable speed and still be under control of the rider

Each contestant is expected to be in total control of the cow, the basic ingredient of the class winner.

WESTERN RIDING

Western Riding is often thought of as the Western equivalent of dressage. It's an event that challenges a horse with a combination of maneuvers that have been modified from the pleasure, reining, and trail classes. To do well in Western Riding, a horse must be alert and tuned in to the rider. He must express no physical resistance, especially in the mouth and rib cage, and must have a good mind that will accept the rider's commands willingly, without charging or anticipation.

The horse's conformation dictates to a large part its natural head carriage. Remember, an individual horse's way of going and his head position will be determined by such things as length of neck and where the neck comes out of the shoulder. A horse should not be penalized throughout a pattern because he is a little more high-headed than a judge personally prefers. If the horse is an otherwise fine performer, he should be awarded positively for his athletic ability, rather than picked on because of his conformation.

Although the ideal pattern is precise, it is not desirable to aim for crispness of movement at the expense of smoothness and form. A horse that is bunched up and tense but is precise in lead-change location should not be placed over the smoother, more natural mover that changes leads in an acceptable way but is slightly off the exact spot each time. Speed should be consistent throughout the pattern with no increased speed through the lead changes or loping down the center.

The judge should be a horseman and view each horse's overall performance, judging positively rather than trying to catch horses committing small infractions. Rather than basing an evaluation on penalties, emphasize the talent and cooperation of the horse and rider.

Scoring today requires reasoning behind the scores. So, to be able to provide consistent reasons, a judge needs to have some kind of a system to refer back to. The score sheet is divided into seven specific components. In each, the judge can assign positive points and penalty assessments. At the end of the pattern, an overall or composite score can be added as a final means of evaluating the work.

Using score sheets makes details of the class accessible to spectators and exhibitors. A posted score card helps an exhibitor to see where the judge liked his horse and where the mistakes occurred. Knowledgeable opinion always has and still will enter in the evaluation of a horse's performance. Some judges like a fresher horse, allowing it to look around a bit as long as it stays in proper form. Other judges place more emphasis on a strict business-like attitude. With this system, such variation in opinion can be reflected in the composite score.

Also, judges have slight differences in penalty assessments. For example, failing to change a lead behind has a variable penalty depending on the distance the error is prolonged. Assessing such an error will boil down to a combination of a judge's ability to make an accurate observation and the occasional need to make a judgment call.

The Western Riding pattern may begin with the gate, but it is optional and often is not used in order to save time. The pattern most often begins with the contestant moving toward the log at a walk. As a courtesy, the exhibitor should be in position, ready to move, as the judge takes the final look at the previous rider. The horse is required to walk calmly over the log without hitting it or rushing. The rider should not use unnecessary arm or body theatrics as the horse passes the log. Often, a signal of this type shows the judge that the horse has been trained to put its head down as an affectation, not as a means to honestly inspect the obstacle.

Allowing the horse a few steps of walk without penalty after crossing the log before beginning the jog helps guard against anticipation. A rider should use the arena to his benefit, moving farther away from certain cones when necessary, and riding deep into the corners to aid position-ing. When the horse begins to lope, riding deep into the corner for the turn will set the horse up for the approach to the first lead change. This helps to line the horse up so he approaches the line of five pylons with his body straight. A horse cannot change leads if his body is bent.

If a horse is going to miss a lead change, it usually tends to be the first change because the rider has not taken advantage of the arena, thus allowing the horse to approach the first change out of alignment. A horse should move forward on a lead change, not up, down, and then forward. If a rider makes the first change late, he ends up pushing the next cone, and by the time he reaches the fifth pylon, the cumulative effect of his initial error has put the last change of the first line way out of position. Changing slightly early on the first cone would safeguard the rest of the pattern and should be taken into consideration by a judge.

The speed down the middle of the arena should be consistent with the rest of the pattern. Excess speed is sometimes used to cover up the lead changes that may not have gone so well. Excess speed is not nec-essary or desired of the horse in Western Riding and should be penalized. As the rider prepares for a soft, quiet stop, he should plan his signals so that the horse ends up 10 feet beyond the center of the arena (marked by the log). This will allow him to correctly end the pattern by backing to the center of the arena. There is no added point advantage in showing off by backing up fast, and it could earn you penalties for loss of control and form.

The scoring system allows the horse to enter the ring with a 70. The pattern is divided into the following seven segments:

1. Attentive walk and crossing of log
2. Jog, lope
3. Five-cone line with four flying lead changes
4. First two crossovers with lead changes
5. Lope over log
6. Next two crossovers with lead changes
7. Lope down the center, stop, back

Each component is evaluated using the following scale:

Plus 1½—extremely good
Plus 1—very good
Plus ½—good
0—average
Minus ½—poor
Minus 1—very poor
Minus 1½—extremely poor

A composite score of from plus 1 to minus 1 can be used to evaluate the horse's overall performance—guiding, use of arena, consistency and appropriateness of speed, manners, and disposition.

The following can be penalized:

Use of hand to instill fear
Losing control of gate
Early trot before log
Hitting log at walk
Moving log at walk
Breaking to a walk before lope
Early lope
Incorrect lead when beginning lope
Change over in front and not behind to correct wrong lead
Failure to lope
Failure to change lead behind
No lead change front or hind
Extra changes
Simple change (break gait)
Jog over log instead of lope
Change lead over log (extra change)
Hitting log at lope
Rolling log at lope

Disqualifications result from knocking down cone, failure to stop/back, off pattern (pass on wrong side of pylon, etc.), missing log, and adding or omitting maneuvers.

The judge must remember that Western Riding is neither a stunt nor a race, and should be performed with reasonable speed. The horse will be judged on quality of gaits, change of leads, response to the rider, manners, disposition, and intelligence. Credit is to be given for and emphasis placed on smoothness, even cadence of gaits (starting and finishing pattern with the same cadence), and the horse's ability to change leads precisely and easily (front and rear) at the center point between the markers. The horse should have a relaxed head carriage, showing response to the rider's hands with moderate flexion at the poll, and negotiate the pattern in an easy fashion, neither diving into nor rushing through the markers. By the same token, the horse should cross the log at both the walk and the lope, without breaking gait or radically changing stride.

Let's take a look at the following pattern and routine as prescribed:

1. The short, double line represents a swinging gate at which the horse must put the rider in a position to open, pass through, and close without dismounting. It may be located in any part of the arena and should be one that will not endanger horse or rider.

2. The eight small X's represent markers (barrels, kegs, or standards recommended). These should be separated by a uniform *measured* distance of not less than thirty nor more than fifty feet on the side

with five markers (see diagram). The judge is responsible for correctness of the pattern.

3. The rectangle represents an obstacle (one small log), a minimum of eight feet in length.

4. The long and sometimes twisting line indicates the direction of travel and the gaits at which the horse is to move. The dotted line (· · ·) indicates walk, the dash line (–––) jog, and the solid line (——) lope.

Except for junior horses shown with a hackamore or snaffle bit, only one hand of the rider may be used on the reins, and hands must not be changed. It is permissible to change hands when opening the gate if the gate is in such a position as to justify the change of hands on the reins. The following characteristics are also considered as faults and should be judged accordingly:

1. Opening mouth excessively or raising head on maneuvers
2. Anticipating signals or early lead changes
3. Stumbling
4. Losing stirrup or holding on
5. Any unnecessary aid given by the rider, such as talking, petting, spurring, quirting, or jerking the reins

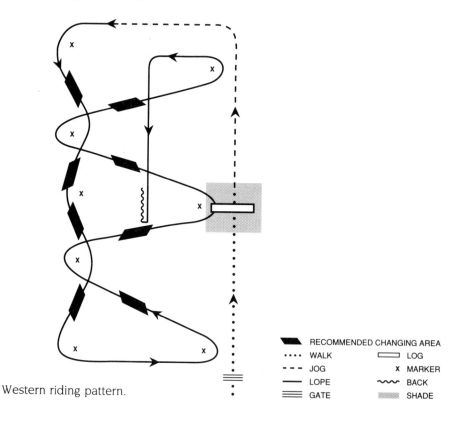

Western riding pattern.

RECOMMENDED CHANGING AREA
···· WALK   ☐ LOG
– – – JOG   x MARKER
—— LOPE   ∿ BACK
· ≡ GATE   ▓ SHADE

CHAPTER
~5~

Equitation

INNER THOUGHTS

Bending the Rules

Over the years, judges have resolved many quandaries. But one dilemma, with a good track record, has become quite persistent: What do you do with an equitation rider who doesn't quite conform? Some are obviously not properly attired or lack the correct appointments as spelled out. These riders are easy to distinguish. But what about those who bend the rules or some small infraction thereof? Going by the rules, are they to be penalized only a small percentage if they don't have a tie or scarf, rope or riata, hobbles, clothes of the proper color, or disqualified? We also encounter the rule circumventors who continually try to catch the judge's eye with insignias, odd colors, or unorthodox pieces of equipment not identified as legal.

The decision becomes easy when it's based on mistakes that have been made in forgetting things or rules that say *shall* and not *should*, *must* and not *may*. The exhibitors understand these rules. The dilemma worsens, however, when rule-benders are involved. They attempt to project individuality, but succeed only in vexation, as the judge tries to sort out legal from illegal, proper from improper, penalty from disqualification, all taking time away from finding the best horse or rider.

Consider the following. Hunter seat equitation rules state traditional appointments. A rider enters the arena on a good horse with a Navajo saddle blanket cut down to English saddle size (not rounded or shaped,

147

but a small Western-type pad) instead of the normal hunter-type pad. If the horse wins, a fad is created and several marketeers drift with the tide and a raft of Navajo pads show up in the hunter division. Not quite what was intended by the rule writers. Use of solid, conservative colors is another area often challenged. If pinstripes are so subtle you need a magnifying glass to detect them, are they solid colors? To wear matching jackets and jodhpurs or not (in season) depends on how seasonally oriented the judge is and in tune with Mother Nature. What about wearing more than the rules allow? What about the required attire plus a sweater over the whole ensemble? Okay in winter? What about insignias, chaps, saddles, or sweaters, all emblazoned with legal forms of advertising? What if its the best horse in the class, and a rider slips a forbidden finger between the reins as he or she is asked to back. Do you pretend not to see? Do you ignore it? Or, do you throw the perpetrator out? These are all dilemmas for the judge.

There are judges, unfortunately, who actually look and hope for an infraction. "Aha! caught that one," is their attitude. This habit backfires more often than not. Consider the following case in point. Fifteen horses are in a stock seat equitation class. Twelve of them are from one stable, all with hobbles fastened on either side across the saddle; of the others, two horses were on wrong leads and one was lame. A judge's (wrong) decision was to eliminate all in the group of twelve whose hobbles lay across the saddle. First and second prize went to those on the wrong lead and the lame horse was third. The judge even announced publicly that the reason for the disqualifications was illegal equipment. It was pointed out later to the judge, who barely made it out of town without the discoloration of fruit stains, that the rule book described (at that time) that hobbles were to be carried below the cantle and fastened on the near side. The disputed hobbles were, in fact, below the cantle and fastened on the near side, but fastened on the off side as well.

Clothes are always a topic of what's appropriate. To a colorblind person, anything goes; to the person whose closet contains one color, all else should be frowned on; to the one whose wardrobe rivals a Christmas tree, gaudy is best. Those in a quest to be different are rarely aware of the problems they cause. From formal attire at 8 AM, to jingle bells on the cinch, or tape on the curb chain, the list is endless. Individuality always has merit but should be within the realm of taste, for good and bad also reflects a matter of opinion. Exhibitors who don't want to actually conform should question their plan in the same way the judge must. What will this do to the direction of the industry if this degree of unorthodoxy prevails? If I place this rider on top with unconventional attire or appointments (even though technically legal) will it create a monster we'll have to live with until those who placed below get the rules rewritten?

Exhibitors and judges have obligations to the horse-show world to direct and create destiny. Change, just for the sake of change, can often be detrimental to the overall good. Creativity, on the other hand, is always welcome as long as it doesn't interfere with tradition, the key word. Tradition is testing by the annals of time, and gimmicks or novelty have always been short lived. Probably no other sport has as much tradition or history to fall back on, and simple elegance has invariably been the direction. Whether English or Western, history gives us prime examples to follow. Understanding each piece of equipment and attire, why it was created, and how it works will have a bearing on change.

Judges are more impressed with the proper traditional appointments. Most are horsemen who appreciate well-tailored attire, well-groomed horses and riders, tack that fits the horse and is well cared for, hats that are shaped, chaps or jodhpurs of the proper length, neat and contained hair, tasteful earrings (if worn), and polished and fitted boots. The "hey-look-at-me" type of exhibitor, bending tradition, borderline legal, is generally frowned upon by the judiciary. Of course in a *horse*-only class, the best horse should win. But, it's still hard to give the blue to someone whose hat looks as if it's been sat on, whose spurs are on upside-down, whose crop is stuck in the boot tops, whose mouth is chomping gum, or who is responsible for any other antic designed to create individual attention on purpose or by accident.

Judges would much rather have the exhibitor show the horse to the horse's best advantage and let the judge do the judging. It takes away from the judge's concentration when a class comes into the arena, begins to perform, and one of the best riders shows something questionable in the judge's mind—a Western horse with the reins dangling (thrown away) when everyone else has light contact, an English horse with a polo mouthpiece bit, a legal but twisted half-inch curb chain.

Whether tack or clothes, the mental gymnastics and rule-book searching (by the judge or steward) as to the legality of the entry makes the class more difficult to separate. A red ribbon in the tail used to mean that the horse kicks. Now when we find a red ribbon in some classes, does it mean he does kick? Does green mean he doesn't? Or is it just decoration? The easier the exhibitor makes it for the judge, the more the showman conforms to the accepted practices of showing, the more traditionally proper the entry is presented, then the more blue ribbons will grace the wall.

The Right Proportions

The equitation division is divided into three distinct sections: Western, or stock seat; hunter seat; and saddle seat. A judge must remember in equitation classes that only the rider is being judged, therefore any horse that is suitable for a particular style of riding and is capable of performing the required routine is acceptable. The judge cannot afford the luxury of his own preference as to color, type, or age as long as the horse is suitable to the rider.

Using the stock seat section as an example and realizing that it is to be judged on seat and hands as the basics (with equal emphasis on each), we can then break this system down further on a relative value basis.

The seat should be close to the saddle, which is impossible if a rider is not communicating with the horse using the aids. The hands, of equal value with the seat, must be the "telegraph line" between the rider's desires and the horse's mouth. Let's say that hands coupled with seat equal 100 percent.

Riders are judged on the rail at the walk, jog trot, and lope, both ways of the ring. A rider's body should appear relaxed, comfortable, and flexible, which is the ideal, or 100 percent of that phase.

I always advocate a positive system of judging, that is, finding the best rider in the class and not the least lousy. From that standpoint, starting at the walk, let's examine a class and its perspectives, using the idea of percentages to establish value.

Although the walk should be a relatively easy gait to perform, judges too often overlook it and use it only as a means to get from one gait to another. The walk has special emphasis in its relationship to the jog and the lope, and should receive 30 percent of the total. For example, if a rider can execute the walk by being relaxed and comfortable in motion with the horse, he achieves the full assigned value. But on the other hand, if he must continually check back, or drop behind the motion, or wiggle his legs back and forth to make the horse move, the value becomes less.

You as the judge must take into consideration what a rider does to get his horse to walk properly. If a horse breaks for a step or two and the rider does what is needed to get the horse to resume the walk, he would not be penalized. If this action became excessive or frequent, however, he would be heavily penalized because of lack of control.

The jog trot comes next as it relates to the other gaits. It must be judged during the transition period as well. In fact, the most important part of the job is when the rider gives the aid—too much, too little, or just right—adding up to 20 percent of the total judging picture. Horsemen know the jog is probably the easiest gait to perform after this transition, so the major percentage should be assigned to the transition and not to the rider's form as he jogs around.

The lope, like the walk, has special emphasis, and it should receive the largest share, or 40 percent. But this emphasis is on getting into the lope on the correct lead, then maintaining the lope in position, along with speed of gait and control.

Therefore, rail work should be looked at as a possible 30 percent for the walk, 20 percent for the jog trot, and 40 percent for the lope, using the percentages to demonstrate the relative difficulty of performing each gait. The remaining 10 percent is for the back-up and the rider's attire, to a total of 100 percent if all is perfect in an equitation class performed on the rail only.

The degree of difficulty is the basis for the relative values, no matter what is asked for by the judge. If individual tests are called for, the value of these tests related to the rest of the work should be established at the outset.

In the Medal Class, for instance, where riders work the rail and perform a stock horse type of routine, the rail work gets its share and the stock horse portion its share, too. This would be broken down according to degree of difficulty, or a ratio of 60 percent individual and 40 percent rail work (or, work as the entire class as a group) as follows: The figure-eight, which requires positioning of horse and rider as the lead changes are made, is 15 percent; first run-down, stop and turn-around is 15 percent; second run-down, stop and turn-around is 15 percent; and center run-down, stop back and offsets are 15 percent. The total is 60 percent. As for rail work, the walk is 12 percent, the jog 7 percent, the lope 18 percent and 3 percent for the rider's attire. The total is 40 percent of the entire judging picture or a ratio of individual performance of 60 percent and group performance of 40 percent. This is the proper difficulty factor ratio in this type of class.

This same system of judging should be applied to the saddle seat class, where a group performance is followed by individual testing. You could take the rule book and list the tests and assign a percentage of difficulty to each one and relate it to the overall judging practice, thus eliminating the chance that the whole class is judged on one item.

Classes judged entirely on individual performance become more readily adjustable, because, for example, each fence jumped in Hunter Seat Equitation is a separate item and can be viewed as such.*

There is a narrow line, though, in not getting into the predicament of "not seeing the forest for the trees." Nor am I advocating that the judge keep a running numerical total on each phase the rider performs. Rather, the judge, trainer, parent, and exhibitor should place the same emphasis on the same parts of the class, using the overall picture to determine the winner.

We all need to look at a performance with the same perspective, but how can we do that until we establish what that perspective is and agree to follow it?

---

*Any system that you use should establish the fact that the ability of the rider is what is being judged, not the cost or capability of the horse.

STOCK SEAT EQUITATION

Equitation is an advanced form of communication. It is showing the judge which rider is capable of having his horse perform any task requested using invisible aids. It sounds simple, but in reality stock seat equitation, as defined by the rule book, is to be judged as follows: "Riders will be judged on seat, hands, performance of the horse, appointments of horse and rider, and suitability of horse to rider. Results as shown by the performance of the horse are *not* to be considered more important than the method used in obtaining them."

On the basis of the limits of the criteria, stock seat equitation can be a controversial subject. Even with the basics being the same, there are as many different styles of riding as there are trainers and teachers. Style seems to go with the part of the country in which you happen to be competing. It is *style*, then, that leads to controversy, not the equitation itself.

Several years ago, equitation was based on sending a rider into the arena on a robot-type "push-button" horse. He was told to stay in one position; not to move or do anything but stay on the rail, walk, jog, lope, and if he made all the leads, he'd come out on top. This is not equitation today. What judges are now looking for is the best rider, with the best (suitable) horse, working together as one. "Best suitable horse" means the one that fits the rider best, making him or her look good, not the best halter or conformation horse. While the horse is not being judged *per se*, it is the vehicle used to show off the rider's talents whatever they may be.

As the rider enters the ring, he presents a composite picture to the judge, coordinating all body parts to make a free, natural, quiet picture. A rider should never look stiff, but should be straight, square, and graceful.

There are basic equitation positions to which one must adhere:

HEAD. The rider's head should be alert, lifted in line and in balance with the body. It should never be carried up, turned, or tipped down. Eyes should focus in front and 30 to 40 feet ahead of the horse, with the freedom to look around, and even with some eye contact with the judge.

SHOULDERS. Shoulders should be square, with one hand holding the reins over the horn and the other hand resting on the thigh. There is a decided tendency to carry the shoulder of the hand holding the reins forward, but this can be eliminated by a slight turn at the waist to line up the shoulders. Shoulders should never be carried back or hunched.

ARMS. The upper arms should fall freely down the shoulders toward the hip bones. Never let arms be tight against the body nor allow them to fly with the horse's motion. The forearm, holding the reins, should be parallel to the ground. All handling should be done with hand, wrist and by bending the elbow. The bend in the elbow is of paramount importance

A rider should never look stiff, but should be straight, square, and graceful, presenting a composite picture to the judge.

as this provides a cushion for the horse's mouth. The off forearm should be bent to conform with the angle of the upper body and thigh.

HANDS. There are two ways of holding the reins, depending on whether split or romal reins are used. Split reins are held running across the palm of the hand from the index finger to the little finger. One finger may be between the reins. The end of the reins are left hanging on the rear side of the horse. The position of the hand not holding the reins is optional. If the finger is not between the reins, the rein end must be on the off side. Romal reins are characterized by the hand being carried in a loose fist, with the reins running from the little finger out over the thumb. The second knuckles of the fingers are pointed toward the horse's ears with the thumb up and folded on the knuckles. The reins then run across the body and are gripped by the off hand, which is held on the thigh.

BACK. The back should be straight, not stiff, and preferably with no arch or slump.

HIPS. Hips should be directly under the shoulders and the hipbone should be tilted slightly forward. The motion of the hips should never be from side to side. This kind of motion is found at the jog, causes the saddle to move on the horse's back, and can produce soreness in the horse's loin area.

SEAT. The seat should be deep and always in the center of the

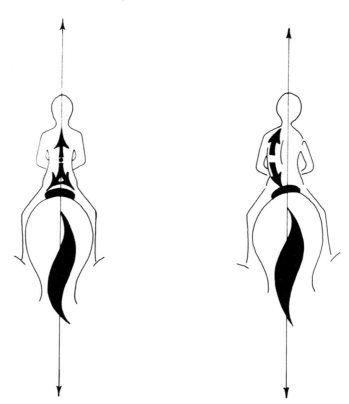

Correct position—rider in center of saddle with rider's and horse's spines in alignment.

Rider leaning off center—crooked back, out of balance with horse.

saddle. The rider should never sit on his or her tail bone. The rider's spine should always be in line with the horse's spine.

THIGHS. Thighs should be kept firmly against the saddle. Relaxed contact, but no rolling or rigid gripping. The thigh angle should be more downward than forward.

LOWER LEGS. The lower leg placement is extremely important to the balance of the entire body. The legs should hang down straight below the knee from a side view. From a front view, they should hang naturally away from the horse. The lower leg should never dangle, be spraddled wide, or thrust forward. Too great of an effort to hold legs too close to the horse results in faulty turned ankles, incorrectly placed foot pressure, loss of knee contact, and looseness of thighs.

FEET. The ball of the foot should make contact with the stirrup with the entire width of the boot sole. Pressure should not be put on the ball of the foot, but rather on the heel, so the heel will be down. Feet should be held naturally, neither extremely turned in or out.

RIDER'S MOTION AND POSITION AT GAITS. The walk may be the most important gait executed during a class. Remember, first impressions are important when entering a show ring. Any motion or equitation fault evident at the walk will be much more pronounced at any of the faster gaits. At the jog trot, keep a slight up and down motion to overcome the side-to-side tendency produced by the diagonal two-beat gait. When loping, a rider must deal with the problem of the thrust from the hindquarters of the horse. The body must be kept with the horse's motion. If this is not done, the rider will tend to bump back and forth with the upper body. There is a natural tendency for the inside leg to drift forward and put the rider off center in the saddle.

USE OF AIDS. The proper use of aids (hands, body, legs, and feet) cannot be overemphasized. Each aid must be used subtly, but effectively. The hands must be quiet, with no jerky motions, yet must be solid with flexibility. The hand should remain above the horn as much as possible. The hands should always appear light, relaxed, and quiet. The only motion with the legs should be to apply slight calf pressure, when necessary, to promote impulsion. The feet should be used behind the cinch only. By keeping the leg no farther forward than the cinch is to shorten the distance the foot must travel to apply pressure to the horse. The heel should not be raised when using the foot as an aid. The body weight should be distributed properly to be in balance with the horse. Weight distribution should be adjusted gracefully and lightly.

These elements of position are all basic and fairly well accepted as uniform. But style is something else. Each rider is different and each horse equally individual, therefore they must be treated differently. A six-foot tall, slender rider will not be mounted in exactly the same position as a four-foot tall, chubby rider and they in turn will not be in the same exact position on different horses. In equitation, the basics must be taken and put together in a way that makes rider and horse one unit symmetrically. This is what the judge looks for as each rider enters the arena. It's a style, or perhaps it should be called an unstyle, that works for the individual rider being judged.

The judge addresses the class as it enters the ring and takes an overall look as each rider passes by the first time. Does the rider look presentable? Does the saddle fit? Is the attire correct and fitted? Are horse and rider a unit? If yes, these things will be conspicuous at first look and, by the same token, the sloppily dressed, overtacked, under or overmounted rider will present the negative answer.

When it comes to show-ring attire, think about the whole picture with neatness and simplicity being the basics. Fit is mandatory for clothes, but don't confuse fit with expensiveness, for a dart, tuck, or letting-out can do wonders. Chaps should fit properly and be neither too long nor too short. The hat should be shaped and kept clean. Boots should fit and be polished. Riders should also know the proper way to wear or carry their accoutrements.

Fit is not limited to clothes. The bridle should fit the horse and the bit should fit in the mouth and be adjusted properly. The saddle should fit the rider and the horse, and be cleaned regularly. All of these simple, often unthought-of items separate the ne'er-do-well from the true showman. It's difficult for a judge to award the blue ribbon to someone who, for the whole class, has had his hat on backwards; or his spurs on upside down; or his rope or riata wadded up like a clothesline; or his number whittled down in size so it's illegible; or no number at all. If the rider takes the time to coordinate the attire and tack to complement the horse and not overshadow him, the judge will take note.

After all riders have walked and the judge has given them the once-over, it's normal to proceed into the jog. This period between any two gaits, called the "transition period," is the most important period of showing in equitation. We'll assume the appearance is perfect, the horse is turned out equally as well, and the judge really took notice of the overall picture. This transition period is where the rider must show his abilities. If he over-aids the horse, such as using too much leg or spur, or if he doesn't aid enough, it all comes to light during the transition periods.

After the horse is into the jog, then it's easy for the rider to get back in the basic position I talked about before. But, for that instant, during the change from the walk to the jog, the real test of how the rider and horse work together becomes apparent. The horse also either helps or hinders effectiveness. If he tends to fight the rider, it looks rough; if he cooperates with the rider, it looks smooth.

Another factor becomes evident as the class proceeds around the ring. Is the rider in front of the motion, behind it, or right with it? Naturally, to be in balance with the horse, the rider should be in motion with it. As I said before, all horses do not go alike and you, as the judge, must take this into consideration. A heavy-going horse with his head down can't be ridden the same as a high-headed, wandering type of horse. The rider must find the balance point of any given horse and ride the horse accordingly, keeping with that horse's particular motion or balance.

Getting into or keeping out of trouble also shows up during the transition period. If a rider is truly riding his horse as it relates to equitation, the judge must take into consideration his ability to adjust his position in the ring if he is in a crowd. Does he got out of the crowd? If he's by himself, does he stay there?

The next transition will be into the lope, or back to the walk and then into the lope; whichever, it is a transition nevertheless and good points and bad are again put to test.

There is one other very important ingredient for the successful equitation rider, and that is "attitude." After everything else is taken care of, this single attribute will be the deciding factor. Attitude is that indefin-

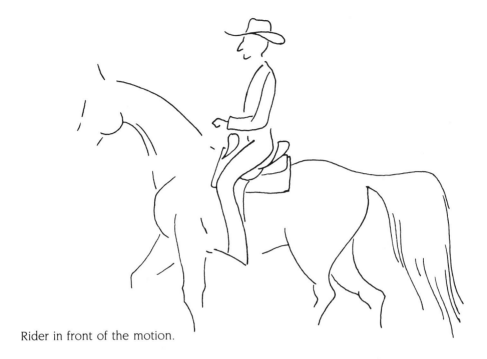

Rider in front of the motion.

Fair position but hands are cocked and leg is forward—no aid.

Sloppy position—Rider is slouched, legs loose, head forward, behind the motion.

able quality that surfaces, both good and bad. The right attitude, you might say, is the basic ingredient of a champion. There is a big difference between being knowledgeable about a sport and winning in that sport.

The Medal Class requires a stock-horse routine where equitation again follows the basics as outlined. The tests required for this work are a series of figure-eights, three run-downs, square stops, turn backs, backing maneuvers, and offsets or pivots (as described in chapter 4 on Western classes).

When executing the figure-eight, the rider should keep a good pattern, using hand and leg aids to make the change of leads. The leads must be changed both front and hind, preferably at the same time. The rider should not look down to see what is taking place but use his head as the focal point of balance, looking slightly in the direction he is going. The rider should be tight in the saddle, not twisting or wiggling when the change is made; he should flow with the horse through the change, not pump or bump to keep the horse going. If the horse does not change leads, the rider should continue to try to accomplish the change, not merely give up and stay on the wrong lead or cross-lope, so that the judge knows that the rider is trying to correct the horse's mistake.

In the run-down, the rider should keep the same balance and posture as if he were on the rail, without flopping his arms and legs to make the horse run. He should squeeze and drive the horse into the stop. The rider who lopes very slowly three-fourths of the way on the run-down and then charges full speed the last three strides and pulls to a stop should be penalized. The run-down should be long and graceful with the rider in control, not just a passenger along for the ride. When the rider reaches the end of his run-down he should appear to know where he intends to stop his horse.

When asking the horse to stop, the rider should drop his weight down in the saddle and grip with his thighs and knees, but avoid bracing his legs in the stirrups. However, the rider must maintain enough pressure in the stirrups to keep from losing them. The rider's head should be kept up in the stop, and not lean forward or backward. The rider should *never* lean over backward, put his feet on the dashboard, and pull. Hands should be light and supple. The rider should follow the horse through as the animal goes to the ground, then hold it there until the stop is completed before relaxing hand or leg aids.

To execute the turn back, whether it's a half turn or a full spin at the arena end or a center offset, the rider must maintain his balance with the horse. If he is turning his horse to the right, his body should be with the horse, not leaning off to the other side. The rider should use the aids and turn with a slight forward inclination toward the horse. If the horse refuses to turn or "hangs up," the rider should exert greater pressure with the leg aids to show the judge he knows what to do. Remember though, over-aiding should be penalized as much as not enough aid. The hands must be light and supple, using a short pull-and-release method, a very slight movement, almost imperceptible. This is where it is obvious if there is communication between horse and rider.

All of these maneuvers should be made in the same tracks away from the rail, not wandering all over the ring. The judge should reward precision and position over a wild runaway performance: A horse should work with some speed, but the rider must always give the impression of being in complete control. Showing in this phase of equitation should be accomplished with promptness, dispatch, and a true knowledge of how the horse reacts and what it takes to get him to perform. The object is to have the horse do the routine perfectly while the rider looks good doing it, which, along with a few other ingredients like self-discipline, confidence, determination, and poise, will be the winning recipe.

SADDLE SEAT EQUITATION

I often refer to saddle seat equitation as an art, the art of effective and easy control of a horse in a horse-show environment. The performance of a skillful rider is as graceful as a ballet dancer, as precise as a quarterback. It is the uniting of rider and horse to become as one, in demonstration of grace and dexterity. Equitation is a training level for riders from which both open and amateur riders come. For this reason I feel saddle seat equitation should be taught and judged to reflect that every position of a rider's body has a reason, and for every horse's reaction there is an action or course.

The position of the seat is the basis of it all. Improper position of the seat will not allow the legs or upper body to function correctly. A rider must sit evenly in the middle of his saddle, with his pelvis forward and seat bones resting on the saddle. A well-fitted saddle is imperative; the length of the rider's thigh bone, for the most part, determines the proper length of saddle. If a saddle is too short, the rider's knees will be in front of the stirrup leathers, and the opposite will hold true if the saddle is too long.

Since the foundation of balance is the seat, or where the rider's body touches the saddle, the seat bones should support his weight evenly on either side of the saddle. This contact alone, however, will not be enough.

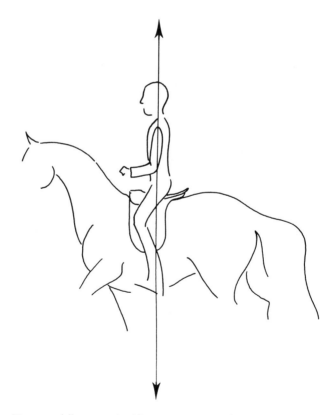

Correct position—saddle seat. A rider must sit evenly in middle of saddle, pelvis forward and seat bones resting on saddle.

The next point of balance is the inside of the thighs. To determine whether the rider is sitting correctly, if the back part of his thighs are gripping the saddle, he will find himself resting behind his seat bones. Resting too much on the inside of his thighs means that his seat bones will not touch the saddle. When seated properly, the ball and socket joint of the hip will be in line with the heel.

The rider's knees should rest well down on the sides of the saddle, the knee joint resting easily against the saddle. Squeezing the knee should never be encouraged; it will limit leg use and also tighten thigh and buttock muscles, which will lift the rider's seat out of the saddle.

The rider's back is the link between the legs, seat, and hands. The straight-as-a-poker torso gives the impression of a rider who is afraid even to turn his head if necessary, or to yield his body to the motion of the horse; each gait has slight differences in motion transferred from horse to rider, and the rider needs to re-adjust to these changes only as much as is necessary to coordinate himself with the horse. Sitting too straight

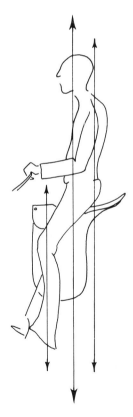

Incorrect position—feet forward, rider hunched, sitting on tailbone, not in center of gravity.

is usually a fault found in novice and beginner classes where young riders try so hard to stay in form, looking "just right" without losing basic position. The only thing faulty here is the apparent loss of body influences over the horse's performance. Too rigid a form fails to inspire the horse; instead of looking assured and confident, both horse and rider produce indecisiveness, lack of spirit, and purpose.

The rider's hands and arms should work independently from the rest of his body. Hands should be carried in an upward, relaxed position. How high to carry the hands above the withers is dictated by the way the horse carries his head. The hands should be carried wide enough to allow a direct line of contact to each side of the horse's mouth. A steady contact with the horse's mouth should be maintained; the amount of pressure may vary, but the horse should not be allowed to fall behind the bridle. A lazy horse has a tendency to be bad-mouthed in order to be light in the bridle, but the horse must be made lively and pushed forward by the rider's legs and seat, rather than pulled into position by the reins.

Studying the reactions of the horse will indicate whether the rider's aids are being correctly used and having the desired effect. A horse diving into the bridle when it stops, throwing its head, and trying to kick at the rider's leg pressure, or being heavy in the bridle, are all indications that the aids are not being used properly. In order to respond to the aids, a horse must be collected and listening to his rider. The rider who must

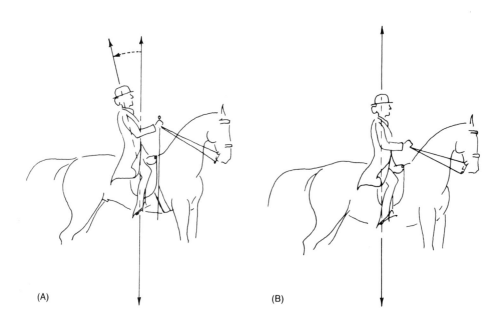

(A)   (B)

A common distortion in saddle seat equitation (A). Correct position (B).

insist on a lively and willing response is not just baggage to be transported about, but an active participant with the horse in a series of movements suited to and accomplished by the specific horse. When the natural aids (legs, hands, voice, and body-weight distribution) are smoothly applied, the horse confidently goes about his work. This is what separates the skilled horseman from the ordinary rider.

Equitation, in the whole sense of the word, means a great deal more than looking great on a horse. If one were to consider the most neglected aspect of riding skills, it would be the lack of finesse between the work of the hands and legs. A horse that is worked from the hands alone has his mind on his mouth. He will tend to lean on the bridle, stiffen his jaw, poll, neck, and shoulders. Sensitive, responsive rein pressures, coupled with clever, almost invisible rein adjustments, plus subtle leg aids are a must for the equitation rider. In conjunction with subtly applied rein signals and corresponding leg aids, the rider must be sure to keep his seat well down, his thighs softly closed in, and his upper body erect, perfectly balanced and tuned to the horse's movements.

Ring generalship often makes the difference between a position designated as "blue ribbon caliber" and those of another color. When two or more riders exhibit the same good basic position, can secure the gaits similarly, and show their horse in an effective and easy manner, to decide which one will be the top winner of a class the judge must look for another asset to make it possible—a "something" that makes one rider stand out from others. This "something" is a positive approach to the entire job, riding as beautifully as possible, and securing from that particular horse all the performance that he can possibly produce.

This extra "something" also calls for expert maneuverability in a ring filled with other riders, some of whom are not entirely sure as to where or how they are going. The rider who adds self-assurance leaves the judge with no question in his mind as to what he has decided to do at all times, as he is in total command of his horse and the ring. The mark of a top-caliber rider—good basic horsemanship, plus an innermost positive approach of what must be done, without question or hesitance—is the result of hours of practice, hours of ring experience, plus a sharp mind tuned only to the job at hand.

Equitation classes demand the total picture—the ability to show a horse to its utmost capacity, and the ability of the rider to demonstrate various tests at which both horse and rider are in perfect form and accord. The more exacting tests require the rider to have a good sense of proportion, timing, and spacing.

The rider is required to view the scene and consider quickly the space needed for each movement, selecting the exact points or spots for the beginning and conclusion of each. When riders fail to make such mental notes, the patterns tend to become untrue.

HUNTER SEAT EQUITATION

The elements of judging hunter seat equitation start with the rider's fundamental position while working on the flat and, then, moving into the actual jumping phase.

The goal of a hunter seat equitation rider is to be flexible—to be able to hack a horse, hunt a horse cross country, and show a hunter or a jumper.

The general appearance of a hunter seat rider should be workmanlike—supple, light, and in complete control under any situation if an emergency should arise. With regard to the basic hunter seat position, there are three parts of the rider's body: the leg, the base, and the upper body.

THE LEG: The rider's leg is considered from the knee on down, *not* from the hip and below. His stirrups should be of a moderate length, long enough for security and short enough for the freedom of his horse. The ball of his foot should be placed firmly in the stirrup. Riding "home," with the boot all the way in the stirrup, makes it very difficult for the rider to flex his ankle and keep his heel down, and without flexion in the heel, there is a lack of security. The heel should be just behind the girth. A heel that is flexed in and down acts as a shock absorber as the horse lands, either in his gaits or over a jump.

Contact with the calf and the inner knee bone is very important. Many riders will pinch with just the knee, which forces their lower calf away from their horse's sides and acts as a swinging pivot from the knee-bone. The lower leg or calf is an aid, not a clinging, gripping support and riders who grip with only their lower leg or calf and no knee are really gripping with a driving aid. Contact should be evenly distributed between the calf and the inner knee bone.

THE BASE: The base of support includes the rider's thighs and seat. To be seated properly, the rider's thighs should be flat and the seat bones in contact with the horse's back through the saddle.

Two-point contact, used when galloping or jumping, occurs when the rider has no weight in his seat at all. The two points of contact are his two legs (in three-point contact, the rider's two legs and his seat make contact with the horse). Riders should be able to be very much in control of a horse in any given situation in either contact, two or three point.

THE UPPER BODY: The hands and arms, which are a part of the upper body, should form a straight line from the rider's elbow to the horse's mouth. Hands should be held over and in front of the withers, several inches apart. The thumbs should be halfway between the horizontal (a flat hand) and the vertical (a straight up-and-down hand); this halfway point provides the softest, most elastic connection with the horse's mouth. Elbows should rest by the rider's sides. The rider's chest should be raised, and not be allowed to sag or cave in. This position also carries the rider's back, giving him more control and strength.

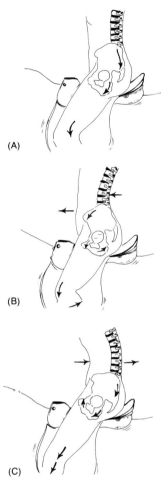

The base. (A) Correct position in saddle. (B) Pelvis tilted too far forward, allowing leg to swing back to counterbalance. (C) Pelvis tilted back placing weight on tailbone—makes leg swing forward (out of balance).

The small of the back is one of the most important connecting links with the horse. It should be relaxed and supple, following the horse's movement. In no way should the rider consciously think of moving the small of the back back and forth. If the rider is relaxed and sitting on his horse properly, a light, relaxed movement can be seen there, and it shows that the rider is in harmony with the horse's gait.

The rider's head should be held erect and straight, in a natural, proud position. The shoulders should be back, but relaxed, carried as the chest and the back are carried, in an elegant and positive position. "Elegance" is a good word in defining the best rider. For a rider to be elegant and graceful, he should not hunch or slouch.

The rider's eyes are of utmost importance. They should be up, looking straight ahead and preceding all turns and movements. The more a rider can look ahead and *feel* what he is doing, instead of looking down

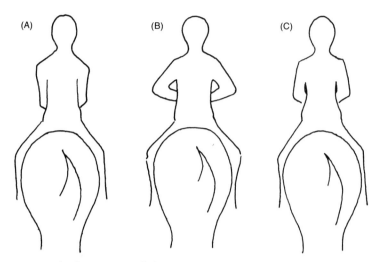

Elbows. (A) Pinched in, pressed downward from shoulder—stiffens entire back, neck, shoulders. (B) Out—causes balance to come from arms; stiffens shoulders, neck, and hands brace on horse's mouth. (C) Natural—relaxed, comfortable, resting easily at rider's side.

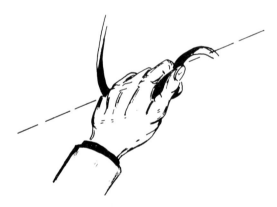

Correct hand position—halfway between the horizontal and the vertical (top view, looking down).

to *see* what he is doing, the better off he is as far as his balance is concerned. Whenever adjusting position, the rider should feel that position adjustment without looking down. Above all, a rider should never look down to find or confirm a lead or diagonal and those who do should be penalized.

Upper body position varies with the different gaits. The upper body at the halt should be vertical. At the walk, it should be slightly in front of the vertical, at the slow sitting trot, slightly more forward than at the walk. At the ordinary posting trot, the rider should be inclined forward in order to be with the motion of the trot. At the canter, the rider should return his upper body to the position that he maintained at the slow sitting trot. The position of the upper body at the hand gallop is the same as the posting trot, but it stays out of the saddle in the two-point contact. The speeds within the different gaits coordinate with the upper body's forward inclination so that the rider stays in balance, or "with the motion" of the horse, not in front of or behind the motion.

To be with the horse, the rider's center of gravity coincides directly with the horse's center of gravity. In other words, as the horse's pace increases, the animal's center of gravity moves farther forward, and the rider's body moves forward so that his center of gravity is directly over that of the horse.

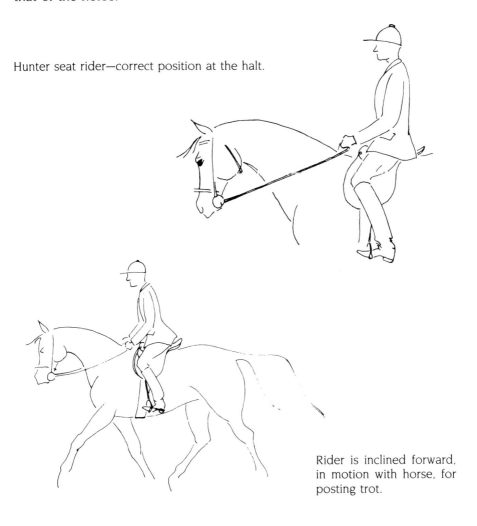

Hunter seat rider—correct position at the halt.

Rider is inclined forward, in motion with horse, for posting trot.

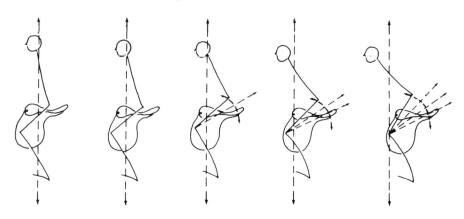

Upper body positions as they vary with the different gaits.

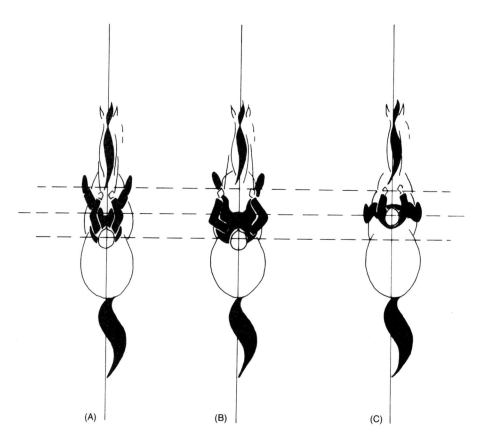

Both (A) and (B) show rider behind center of gravity, feet forward, working against horse. (C) Depicts rider in balance—correct center of gravity. (D) Three-point con-

Hunter seat equitation demonstrates that a rider has learned to execute hunter performances over certain types of courses with smoothness, accuracy, and control. He should be able to handle any emergency, should it arise, have style and form, and be strong, yet considerate of his horse.

OVER FENCE CLASSES

Now that we understand the basic positions and what is required on the flat, we'll go right on into the various degrees of showing over fences and the methods used.

We have discussed posting with the motion versus posting behind the motion, and how the same feeling on the approach to the jump is had when the rider posts with the motion of the trot. Remember, the

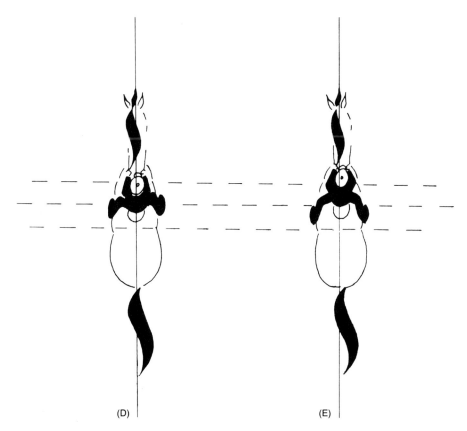

(D)   (E)

tact, inclined slightly forward. (E) Two-point contact, upper body inclined more forward.

center of gravity is inclined forward and the upper body is inclined forward. The rider is up rather than on his buttocks. His heels should be flexed down to absorb the shock of landing over the jump the same as they are to absorb the shock of landing on each stride of the posting trot. The weight should be distributed between the heels, the thighs, and the inner kneebone, rather than the seat. This is the first important aspect we must notice in judging—whether the rider is with the motion of the horse, inclined forward, in balance.

In judging some major faults with beginners, the first technical aspect of jumping is the release. "Release" means giving the horse his head. It is as simple as that. For the very beginner, the first stage of release may be to grab the mane halfway up the horse's crest, not below the crest. As soon as the rider releases the horse below the crest, he falls and loses his balance and collapses as he lands over the jump. Resting on the crest gives added support.

The next point of technique would be the rider's eyes. The rider's eyes must precede every turn. In other words, when he turns a corner to come into a jump, his eyes must turn the corner before the horse has turned the corner. As he turns the corner, he looks over the jump at a focal point thirty to forty feet beyond the jump. He rides into the jump looking at the focal point. We call this eye work—getting, holding and stopping on a line. It is absolutely imperative for a rider to learn this eye technique.

The next step of utmost importance would be heel control. As I have mentioned before, flexion in the heels is most important as a shock absorber. It absorbs the shock of landing over the jump. Instead of jarring the rider loosely out of the saddle, it absorbs smoothly and securely in his flexed ankles and heels. There is no violent upheaval as he lands on the ground after the jump if his heels are flexed down. His heels also act as a brace and a vicelike security and also grip against a horse that's pulling. When the heel is driven down against a pulling horse, he has much more chance of holding and stopping the horse than if he lets his heels slip up and loosely fly back into the horse's ribs. So, we have heels as a technique following posting with the motion, release of the horse's mouth, and eyes to control the line he rides over the jump.

Holding the two-point and three-point contact: For equitation and hunter riding, the rider should be in a two-point contact out of his saddle so he can smoothly follow the horse. A rider who is out of the saddle eliminates ducking and throwing the body trying to catch up with the horse—which three-point contact will produce if the rider isn't ready to jump the fence. When the rider has sufficiently learned to hold the two-point contact, he can allow the horse to arc his body over the fence. In other words, the rider doesn't jump the fence with his body, he lets the horse do the jumping. The horse closes his stride and gathers. The rider does not consciously think of jumping the fence with his upper body. If the rider is in two-point contact, he should follow his horse without throwing his body, allowing his horse to close his upper-body angulations. If he is in three-point contact he's deep in the saddle with a vertical upper-body position ready to ride open jumpers, green horses, balkers, and hesitant horses. He shouldn't anticipate with his body when trotting to a fence—a leg, a cluck, or a release will signal the horse to jump. By squeezing the horse with the legs—a cluck or a release for the take-off point—the horse will jump the fence. If the rider throws the upper body or over-aids by diving out in order to get the horse to leave the ground for the fence, it is a fault of his equitation.

Judges are basically responsible for the course and knowing the distances. It's best to keep them around 24 feet, which is a normal one stride; 36 feet is a normal two strides; 48 feet is a normal three strides. Anything below these distances would be tight; anything above and beyond these distances would be long and the horse would need more pace for the long distances and less pace for the short distances. Pace in relation to distances for combinations is of paramount importance. A rider cannot ride combinations with any accuracy unless he knows the pace, and this must be maintained and established to get into and out of the combination.

The rider also must use the upper body on turns. Either in the deep-seated three-point contact or in the light, forward two-point contact.

The judge must analyze that a rider's upper body must open up and straighten up a little bit around his turns. The rider must move a little bit behind his straight-line upper-body angulation because of the collection and the balance required for turning. The rider opens up slightly for his turn. If he is just in front of the vertical on a straight line, he should be on the vertical for the turn. If he is inclined forward on a straight line, he should be just in front of the vertical for his turn.

When riding a course, it is important that the rider execute a proper circle before heading for the first fence. In an equitation class, this gives a good first impression. There are many ways to make an accurate, disciplined, and controlled-looking circle before starting the course, all of which means that the pace should be established a considerable distance before the first jump.

The rider's eyes and the course's lines must be considered in riding the course. In other words, when a rider is at the stage that he is ready to ride a course, he considers eyes and pace. He shouldn't have to think of heels, hands, upper body, or any technical exercises over a course. He should concentrate on his pace and lines of direction—his eyes and his pace, lining up his lines, eyes for his turns, and pace control for each line and each turn.

When angling fences and jumping narrow or spooky fences, to eliminate the possibility of a run-out or refusal, the rider should use a combination of the leg and rein aid. In other words, if the horse starts to run out to the left, a right rein aid and left leg (shoulder to hip) should be used to correct the deviation. A judge also must take into consideration how a rider handles any adversities.

A judge should recognize a hunter versus a jumper. As I have said, for hunter work the light forward position shows off the horse to its best advantage. It makes the rider and the horse one unit, smoother, more flexible, and fluid for a smooth, unified hunter picture. This is the two-point work.

The three-point work is deeper, more controlled and it's more balanced toward the rear. It is used primarily for jumper work and very green horses. Horses that are almost too green to be shown, that are learning to negotiate jumps, are ridden with a very deep seat. The best advantage for an equitation rider, when smoothness counts, is in the two-point contact.

A judge must remember pace differences. For a green horse, the pace could be considerably slower than it is for a seasoned jumper. We want a smoother, more fluid, balanced ride for hunter seat equitation tests. Hunter seat equitation is used to show a judge that a rider has learned to execute hunter performances over certain types of courses with smoothness, accuracy, and control. He should be able to handle any emergency, should it arise. He should have style and form. He should be strong yet considerate of his horse. He should not be rough or erratic. He should be a polished, finished, workmanlike example of a fine horse-man or -woman. A judge takes all of this into consideration before placing the best rider in the class on top.

Most exhibitors and, most assuredly, all beginning show riders, wonder what mistakes, if any, the judge looks for as the class is in progress. Nearly all of the judges I know have more or less the same viewpoint. Today, we try to find the best rider in the class, not the one who makes the fewest mistakes. But all judges have their own "pet peeves" and place different values on different types of errors made during the course. There are many common errors that can be categorized and placed into levels of competence by the judge.

Over fence classes tend to be the ones with the most questions and probably, from the judge's standpoint, the easiest to explain. Hunter seat equitation over fences produces approximately eight obstacles that must be jumped and the horse must be well ridden between fences also. The beginning rider makes obvious mistakes that will, in most cases, keep him or her out of the ribbons.

One of my pet peeves is what is depicted as "H.O.N." on my score sheet, meaning "hands on neck," and I score very heavily against this mistake. I expect a rider, in order to win this type of class in front of me, to be able to ride the horse off the ground and give him the support he needs when he needs it, not gallop down to the fence in good cadence and, three strides away, pitch the reins and grab a handful of mane and hope everything comes out all right.

Instead, I want the equitation rider to feel his horse all the way and let him jump out of his hand giving with him as he rises to the center of the arc and keeping in balance at the takeoff and the landing—a smooth, subtle release in rhythm, not a dive and hang-on impression that is readily seen by all. The more experienced equitation riders keep the motion fluid with their hands—not a jerk, grab, or rate back and spur, but a true feel of the horse's mouth through the reins, which shows the judge a definite communication with the horse.

Another common error committed, again especially by beginning riders, is looking down or off to one side as the horse leaves the ground. The picture of true balance of horse and rider over the fence is distorted if the horse jumps square into the middle of the fence and the rider appears to want to dismount in mid-air. There is no need to look down at the fence after you've left the ground nor to turn your head sideways or close your eyes or do anything but look between your horse's ears until you begin your search for the next fence.

You not only appear to be out of balance if you look anywhere but straight ahead but, in fact, your head controls your balance point and you do put more weight on one side or the other if you put your head there. The more advanced rider will always line up his fences in advance and know where he is going, not take pot luck. By doing his looking in advance he has no need to look anywhere but where he is going.

This brings to mind another area where major mistakes are made—flexibility. For the novice to keep his head straight may result in a stiffness or rigid appearance, which again is not desired. To look where you're going and not lean on the neck doesn't mean to be stiff, posed, and robot-like. Good, experienced riders who win are flexible and able to adjust and do whatever is necessary to make their fences smooth and appealing. The judge can readily determine which rider is flexible and able to cope with any situation and which one is braced against the horse (either with the leg stiff and forward or the back rigid or with the arms and hands stiff and unyielding as the fence is executed).

A lesser mistake (not minor by any means but less visible to the layman) would be the ability of the rider to remain in motion with the horse, not way in front nor behind. Many riders, who seem to have a pretty good go for most of the course, often roll out at a fence—which means to chase the horse off the ground instead of wait for him. This usually means a disruption of balance and makes the horse "chip in" or get in too close before he jumps.

On the same premise, a rider can be too far behind the motion and get left in the rumble seat when the horse leaves the ground, especially if he happens to stand off a ways from the fence and the rider is not quite ready. Mistakes like that are common and must be related to the rest of the performance as those mistakes made with the legs are numerous.

Too many riders try to show in equitation over fence classes with no leg contact at all. They simply let their legs hang loose.

Continuous movement through the stomach region also results in a movement in the seat and destroys the tight contact with the buttocks that is desired. A movement or pumping motion, or what appears to be a wiggle or twist as the rider approaches the fence, bears a direct correlation to the leg. The pumping, twisting, wiggling rider is trying to keep a secure leg but drive the horse with his torso because he can feel the horse backing off on the approach to the fence. While this is a false way of driving the horse forward, it does appear quite often and is marked as a mistake.

Not all errors are committed while actually jumping the fences, nor at only three strides away on the approach. Many are committed after the arc has been completed and the horse is on the landing side. Many riders anticipate the landing and sit up too soon, giving the impression of leaning back as the horse lands; they cannot stop their forward motion and drop over again after the horse lands, not being able to keep their balance.

Some riders push their feet forward to the "dashboard," bracing against the landing, which makes for the stiffness and rigidity seen in many riders. Form should be maintained throughout the approach, take-off, arc, landing, and moving-off phases of jumping. Form, in this instance, means balance and coordination between horse and rider.

Mistakes all too often occur the moment the rider enters the arena. They are not sure of the course, the direction to circle, or whether to circle at all. Indecision such as this is obvious to the judge who scores it accordingly. If you enter the ring, know the course, and circle the correct way, you may think that should suffice; but it doesn't. The picture is distorted if you're not on the proper lead when circling or cross-cantering, which is a more common error.

The rider should be on the proper lead even in classes over fences, not only in the opening circle, but around the corners as well, or at any time there is a reversal of direction. The correct lead has an influence on the next fence. While being on the correct lead doesn't always insure the next fence will be correct, changing leads or cross-cantering to the fence usually insures it won't be. You really handicap your horse if you gallop around the turn on the wrong lead and make him adjust at the last moment in order to leave the ground. And, if you cross-canter all the way around the turn, you can be sure your horse will not be balanced to execute a pretty fence.

Wrong leads are not the only area between fences that stand out in equitation. The horse (although he is not judged in an equitation class) is still the vehicle by which the rider demonstrates his ability to negotiate a course of fences in form and balance. If you're fighting with your horse all the way around the turn, this certainly isn't the way to demonstrate any good abilities you may have. The hunter seat equitation classes over fences are judged from the time you enter the arena until you leave and, as I stated at the start, the judge wants to find the best rider and pin him first, the second best and pin him second, and so on down the line.

The reason that mistakes are mentioned here is to give you an idea of what is seen by the judge, who must then evaluate rider error or horse error and the severity of each. The top equitation riders are the ones with the well-balanced attitude—aggressive, but not eager; confident, but not conceited; self-disciplined and knowledgeable. If a slight mistake is made, either by horse or rider, their calm, capable method of handling it will, in most instances, outweigh the actual slight error.

Of course, major faults will always preclude anyone from winning if others in the same class have not created faults of the same severity. In all classes, however, everything is relative in judging—rider-created errors or horse-created errors. Often it becomes a matter of judgment. The main purpose of the judge is to pick the best rider in a particular class based on the performance of both horse and rider as it relates to the equitation guidelines.

TESTS

Equitation, being a unique division with special problems, is in need of judges who have special qualifications. To most who are active in training, teaching, and showing, equitation is a science and should, they insist, be thought of in that light.

The major area of concern is that some judges don't seem to put enough emphasis on the class. Some show managers don't either, and actually try to prohibit the judge from "taking too long" by not allowing individual work (as suggested by the rule book). On the other hand, some breed organizations require individual tests first.

Further concern is expressed regarding the type of tests given. Many feel they are not representative of what should be occurring to truly test the ability of the rider to show his horse.

Many judges do not have any reason for the particular test that they give. They choose the test only because they've "seen others do it and it seemed to work okay," which may be easy but it's hardly logical.

Speaking of logic and good sense, in far too many instances we have made the equitation division a "coached" class instead of a "thinking" class. In so doing, we've affected a disservice to exhibitors when people around the ring, in the warm-up area, and even at home, tell a rider everything he must do as he goes around the ring. We should instead be cultivating the thought process, or allowing better communications (rider to horse), which is what equitation is really all about.

The basics of equitation should be to teach a rider to think and understand how a horse works mechanically and mentally, then demonstrate this knowledge in a testing procedure under some pressure.

The test that the judges come up with should require a demonstration of these basics. The test should allow the rider to show that he knows how his horse works the best. The rider should know that going from the walk to the trot, the trot to the lope, or the walk to the canter, are transitions that require impulsion; that coming from the canter to the walk, or the lope back to the trot, are recessive, or softening, movements that require less impulsion. Hence, the invisible use of the aids (leg for impulsion, hand for softening) should be evident if tests are properly thought out and executed.

The rider should understand and be able to demonstrate the balance of the horse he is showing, acknowledging that collection plus impulsion equals balance, with this becoming only a matter of degree as the gaits are performed.

The basics have always been the same: good seat and hands. Seat—meaning naturally close to the horse and staying in the saddle—should, however, go to the next dimension. When equitation is being demonstrated, engagement of the seat bones, not the leg, is the first aid for impulsion. When the horse is asked to go forward, the seat bones are engaged, then the leg, which telegraphs the impulse to the horse for forward motion.

A simple test—such as from a standstill, loping, or cantering forward on the left lead—allows the rider to engage the seat, a leg, and clearly show the judge he knows that, when the horse lopes off on the left lead, the first thing that happens is that the horse stretches or tightens his right back muscle, which is felt through the rider's seat. If this doesn't happen, the horse is not in position to pick up the left lead. The lope or canter requires impulsion. How much depends on the particular horse's responsiveness.

The stop, after the lope or canter, is the hand taking back. Even though it requires impulsion, it requires more from the hand, which must at all times be sympathetic, asking for the transition while maintaining the balance needed. Hence, hands and seat work together as basic aids.

A test should be one that allows the rider an opportunity to show his skill at feeling his horse. He should know his needs before it happens, acting instead of reacting to the fact the horse needs an adjustment of some sort. This is felt through the seat bones and the hand as the horse's muscles expand and contract.

The horse's mouth is simply a tattletale that reveals what the rest of its body is doing. If the rider is truly in communication as the horse backs up, when the hindquarters start to drift to one side or the other, the hands and seat should feel the direction. The rider simply engages the proper aid and the horse continues to back, straight and willingly.

Another maneuver that allows the rider to demonstrate his ability to ride for himself, and not just be a good listener, is simple turns where the horse has to be handled using hand, seat, and leg in conjunction with each other. The main criterion, though, is for the judge to have a reason for the test he gives. He should have some established basis from which he derived the test so everyone will know.

Tests to avoid are the ones that only prove the rider can count or listen to coaching, such as "canter six steps, stop, back four steps, stop, walk five steps, stop," and so on. A test should not take much time, not more than twenty to thirty seconds.

It doesn't prove anything, for instance, in stock seat equitation, to give a test that encompasses the whole reining or stock-horse pattern, which are already provided for in the Medal Classes. Nor should a judge work the hunter seat rider through a series of maneuvers that are not representative of what he must do when he meets the over-fence challenge. Nor, to simply have the saddle seat rider count strides as he changes diagonals or leads.

Equitation, or horsemanship, is truly an art, and should be thought of that way by the judges, who, by the way, must know more than the riders about how horses go. Otherwise, the tests won't mean a thing.

I happen to think simple tests are more difficult to execute than the more memory-linked, rehearseable kind and that's what I use. All the tests that I ask for have a definite purpose. I think them all out well in advance, using such criteria as layout of arena, depth of rider's ability, and level of competition (novice, 11 and under, or championship). I often use variations of the same basic test or principle to allow riders to demonstrate to me as judge their ability to understand how the horse works.

Example: In the lineup, I simply ask the rider to back until I tell him to stop, lope, or canter forward to the rail on a given lead (left or right, depending on the degree of difficulty I desire), stop and stand facing the rail. Sounds simple, but let me relate how it separates the riders for me. The back-up is an easy maneuver that every rider should be able to perform regardless of age or experience. It allows me to observe the light hands I'm looking for as well as a feel of the horse's mouth. Asking a rider to back until I say stop, allows me to see who truly understands the mouth. Any horse will back a few steps (usually three or four because of training). After that, a feel of the mouth is needed, and some adjustment must be made because the mouth has been pulled on and used up. At this point the horse either hangs up (stops) or starts to back crooked, thus requiring a leg-aid adjustment as well as the rein portion. The rider who understands his horse's mouth accomplishes this adjustment with invisible aids seen only by the judge (a horseman) who is looking for them.

Rider working against horse when backing up—no leg aid, rider out of balance with horse, and mouth has been pulled on and used up.

Next I ask for the lope or canter forward on the left lead. When I tell the rider to stop his back-up, I can do it so the horse is in position to lope or canter forward on the left lead. Or, I can stop him out of position that would require an adjustment if the left lead is to be achieved (another degree of difficulty). The same criteria would hold true if the right lead was asked for.

The rider must demonstrate that loping or cantering forward from a standstill requires the aid for impulsion. In addition, the judge knows that if the horse is to lope (canter) on the left lead, the first muscle he engages is his right back muscle. So, the rider must show he also knows this by engaging his seat bones first. If the rider raises out of the saddle instead of snuggling down, a major error is committed, even if he was lucky enough to obtain the requested lead.

Riders should know the key to all horse's movements is impulsion. How much impulsion is needed to execute the lope (or canter) is different in every horse. The rider must know and feel what it takes for his horse to be smooth.

The next degree of difficulty comes into play depending on where I, the judge, stand in relationship to the other horses in the line. If I stand a distance away, the space between me and the next horse is great, hence the easier to navigate through. If, however, I stand close, the opening narrows and a steadier, more impulsive aid would be necessary to smoothly pass through. Another trouble spot occurs after the rider is on the proper lead. If he coasts, he will find his horse quitting or backing off as he passes the other horses in line.

If I'm standing off the horse's right shoulder and I've asked for the left lead, the rider engages his right leg, which tends to push the horse toward the other entries. If I request the right lead, the rider uses his left leg aid, pushing the horse toward me. So, where I stand is extremely important.

Next, as the rider approaches the rail, the horse focuses on activity there, and again backs off, thus requiring continued impulsion all the way to the end. A rider cannot coast or be coached through this test, and the rider who truly understands how his horse works and can execute the maneuver with soft invisible aids usually comes out way on top. As I've said, tests whenever given should have a reason, the meaning of which both judge and rider comprehend, and should be used to let the rider demonstrate his ability without outside interference.

CHAPTER
~6~

Hunter and Jumper

THE WORKING HUNTER

In Arabian show-ring competition, there are few, if any, classes less understood—or more misunderstood—than the working hunter. A working hunter is, ideally, a horse that could be ridden through fields and woods, over brush and fence, following hounds chasing a fox. To do so requires a bold, athletic horse that responds willingly and obediently to its rider, one that uses its ears, meets each fence or obstacle squarely, and jumps with sufficient impulsion for a perfect takeoff, arc, and landing. The horse's forearms should be tucked in front of its chest and held parallel (or slightly higher) to its body. The horse should move with the proper rhythm, pace, and cadence suitable to the course.

This is the ideal, but few horses or rounds are ideal. The rules specify faulting a horse for certain infractions—refusals, runouts, knockdowns—but beyond this, little is said. Which, then, is worse? A horse that twists, or one that hangs a leg? A horse that jumps inverted or one that shifts its hindquarters to one side? In all cases, the more dangerous faults should incur the heaviest penalties. Understand the event, know the criteria, and use logic, and you will find that scoring the rounds will fall into place.

While a judge is not necessarily a course designer, he is, however, responsible for the course, and must therefore know what obstacles are required and how they should be placed. After the course is designed and set, it is his responsibility to ensure that it is safe and correct. Because working hunter classes stem from fox hunting, the obstacles used are designed to look natural and conservative, the type that might be

181

A working hunter uses its ears, meets each fence squarely, has impulsion for a perfect takeoff, arc, and landing.

encountered in the hunt fields: gates, brush boxes that simulate hedges, brick and stone walls, coops, embankments (which are simulated by roll-top obstacles), and rails and logs, and picket or ladder fences. The course should be set to allow a horse to maintain an even pace, give a smooth ride, and jump cleanly, calmly, and safely.

Distances are measured on approximate twelve-foot strides, and the obstacles placed to allow the fluid, flowing pace and jumping arc that characterize a good hunter. The layout for a working hunter course should basically be simple, generally little more than two diagonal lines crossing in the middle, with another line around the outside. This figure-eight inside a circle provides the required change of direction and, therefore, of leads. Besides the obvious necessity of having the course conform to AHSA rules, however, there are a few other considerations necessary for designing a suitable course. These are the size of the arena, the location of the entrance and exit, and an estimate of the horses' and riders' abilities (whether it's a five-entry amateur class in the outback or the finals of a working hunter championship). A course should fit the arena. A beautiful course that works well in a large arena may, with turns that are too sharp and lines that are too close, trap horses in the cramped spacing of a smaller ring. The course should be laid out with flowing curves that allow an even, fluid stride, rather than tight turns that require shortening stride and breaking pace—and which are more difficult for a judge to score.

The rules require that each horse make eight jumps. With fewer than eight separate obstacles, a horse must repeat some of them to fulfill the required number of jumps. If an obstacle is to be jumped twice, and a horse knocks it down the first time, the jump must be rebuilt. The entry must stop while the jump crew resets the jump. If the entry is unaware the obstacle needs to be reset, the judge must blow his whistle to signal the entry to stop. Upon completion of the obstacle, the judge will again whistle to signal the entry that the course is ready. (The judge should always carry a whistle.)

There are a number of types of fences, but the single most common are simply rails placed horizontally between upright standards. The post and rails can be placed to create vertical or spread fences. Verticals may be truly vertical from top to bottom, or they may incline, or slope, slightly in the direction of travel, that is, with the fence sloping away from the approach, though not to the point of being a ramp. An in-and-out can be created by placing two vertical fences twenty-four or thirty-six feet apart to create a one- or two-stride combination. The rails used should be straight, either round or octagonal, and approximately four inches in diameter, with no more than a nine-inch gap between the hung poles. Rails may be painted solid white, gray, green, brown, rust, or blue, without stripes. Except for a simulated brick wall, red should not be used, as it does not commonly occur in the hunt field. Rustic, natural-looking obstacles are the most appropriate; birch and cedar rails make good, rustic jumps, and may be left natural, with the bark on. Other rustic-looking obstacles—such as boxes filled with shrubs or loose-cut fir branches, simulated brick and stone walls, and panels simulating gates, ladders, and picket fences—make excellent jumps and add variety to a course. The height of a gate can be raised by either placing a pole overhead, or by placing a box of shrubbery on the ground in front of the obstacle and raising the gate itself.

Hunter courses typically increase in complexity from start to finish. The last line of fences can be made more challenging than the first. Bear in mind, though, that a course designer may purposely create a problem that challenges expert riders on finished horses, yet he or she should not mistakenly trap amateur riders on green horses with short distances or tight curves. The last obstacle on a course for working hunters is usually a spread, which should be placed at the end of a line. As the name implies, spreads are relatively wide, up to three feet across, as measured from the front, or face, of the first element to the back of the second. The elements also should be measured from both ends, right to right and left to left, to ensure that the jumps are in line and parallel with each other.

Spread fences may be made of single-unit jumps such as coops and rolltops, or by placing two verticals together to create a double-bar spread known as an oxer. In hunter competition, neither triple bars nor square oxers are allowed. Oxers must ascend, with the front element three to six inches lower than the back. Safety is a prime consideration for courses and obstacles. Properly measured lines, with the distances to approximately twelve-foot strides, are most important (lines are measured from the back of one fence to the face of the next).

The aim of a working hunter class is to allow each horse to show to its best advantage. Unlike in jumpers, hunter fences should not, under any circumstances, be set at distances or angles that trap horses, but should instead be set to allow a steady, even hunter pace at the hand gallop of twelve to fifteen miles per hour. The horses should maintain the gait and pace that is required for distances between fences based on what is considered an average length of stride, or, in other words, multiples of twelve feet (twenty-four feet, thirty-six feet, forty-eight feet, etc.), even though a hunter should be able to shorten or lengthen its stride. When distances are correct, a given number of strides between fences, or between elements of an in-and-out, are considered proper. For example, forty-eight feet between fences theoretically requires the hunter to land, take three strides and then jump; landing and taking off are each comparable to a half stride. However, landing and taking off are usually not considered when counting strides, so that therefore, forty-eight feet is considered a three-stride spacing; thirty-six feet is a two-stride canter, and twenty-four feet a one-stride. Obviously, a 14.2-hand horse is going to have to take more strides than a larger 16-hand horse when covering fairly long distances, but a horse that moves well, has good form over fences and maintains a suitable pace for the size of obstacles should not be penalized for adding strides, unless he does so in a one- or two-stride combination or in close competition where elimination is otherwise impossible.

Distances are also related to rhythm and cadence. A hunter should sustain not only a steady pace, but should maintain a rhythmic cadence, moving freely, taking long, flowing strides, and stretching the forelegs for proper length, instead of taking short, choppy, or high strides. As a hunter comes into a fence, it should maintain its pace, and take off from the ground with the same rhythm with which it approached the obstacle.

The obstacles are designed to fall when struck by a horse or rider, but, ideally, only from a solid hit and not from a slight tick. Rails should be of the same diameter and weight. A fence that is top-heavy, with an extremely large pole placed over several thin ones, is deceiving. On the other hand, it is inappropriate to use lower poles of greater weight under a top pole so light that it is easily dislodged. The rails and panels are held in cups. Holes for the cup pins are drilled every three inches on the upright posts of the standards, which allows a jump to be raised or lowered in three-inch increments. Whenever possible, the pins, which extend all the way through the post, should be inserted on the side from which the horse approaches the obstacle. The only cups that should be on the standards are those that are holding the elements; any extra cups should be stored elsewhere; and, for that matter, extra poles should not be stored under a jump.

The single most important factor in constructing an obstacle is that it be solid-looking and well-defined so that the horse and rider can see and judge it properly. An airy jump, which does not touch the ground and has big open spaces between the rails, can be deceiving, as it may give a false perception of depth. Safety goes beyond mere looks and definition, however. Obstacles such as gates, picket fences, and ladders should have the boards spaced either two or eight inches apart. In the event that a horse hits the fence, a two-inch spacing prevents a horse from hanging a leg in the element, while an eight-inch spacing is sufficient to allow a horse's leg to safely go in and come back out. Although not required by the rules, standards with wings are highly recommended; they provide a more substantial outline and encourage a horse to go to the middle of a jump.

Ground lines, usually a pole placed on the ground about six inches in front of the fence, are necessary for any obstacles that do not touch the ground. If there are a sufficient number to make the fence look solid when lined up behind the ground pole, potted flowers and shrubs, loose cut greenery such as fir branches, or flowers, and shrubs in a box placed as a ground line not only make the jump look more substantial but also enhance the appearance of the course.

Course patterns must be posted at least one hour prior to the class. Although helpful, the types of obstacles and, except for in-and-outs, the distances between them do not have to be shown on the pattern. Fences should be numbered in the order that they are to be taken, with arrows pointing the direction of travel; the entrance and exit should also be marked. Though the pattern can be drawn on a piece of typing paper, it's better to use something larger, such as poster board. Place it high enough that someone standing at a distance or sitting on a horse can see the diagram. While it is not necessary to indicate distances on the pattern, the riders should be allowed to walk the course prior to the class to determine the number of strides and riding strategy. A warm-up area with schooling jumps should be provided.

Horses and riders should face a course that looks inviting. In theory, at least, if the first jumps are simple and relatively low, the entry gains the confidence to successfully complete the course. Horses tend to jump better when the first obstacle is placed so that it is approached and jumped while going toward the gate from which the horse entered.

In any case, dark or natural-colored fences must be kept out of dark or shadowed areas in indoor arenas, and an obstacle such as a white gate backdropped against a white arena wall should be avoided. Outdoor arenas, too, can have poor lighting, such as when trees or buildings cast dark shadows across bright sand, or when a horse and rider have to face directly into a rising or setting sun when taking a jump.

Prior to the class, a judge must examine and make sure that the obstacles and layout conform to the proper rules, and that all conditions are correct. Common errors are sloping verticals that are included in the wrong direction—toward, rather than away from, the approach; square or misaligned oxers; a lack of ground lines, or ground lines set too close or too far from the jump; and airy or improperly designed fences. Check the footing—don't have a jump where the barrel racers have churned up and deepened the sand, for instance, or where the line between jumps traverses a wet or muddy spot (which causes most horses to at least shorten stride, if indeed they don't try to jump it altogether). Finally, check the heights on each and every fence, and the distances between them, and check the direction that the fences and wings are facing. Make sure all the pins are in the correct position in the standards, with the ends coming out of the back, or landing side, and that all surplus cups and rails have been removed from the arena.

Though a judge may use any fair and equitable system he chooses, working hunters are usually judged on a basis of 0 to 100, rather than the more common 60 to 80 point system of many other classes. The wider scale allows an expert judge the freedom and scope to differentiate the abilities of accomplished horses. The horse's performance begins when he enters the ring, and ends when he leaves. If the class is outside and not in an arena, the start should be approximately fifty feet before the first fence and the finish about fifty feet beyond the last obstacle. The worst errors occur when a hunter endangers itself and/or its rider, particularly when it refuses or knocks down a jump, or leaves the ground too far from or too close to an obstacle and risks crashing into it. Refusals and front knockdowns are among the most dangerous of all faults, and under certain conditions, are grounds for elimination.

When describing major faults it holds true that a refusal is a willful disobedience, a mark of an unwilling, dishonest horse. Beyond that, a "stop" is also the sort of thing that can put a rider in the hospital: If a horse comes into an obstacle at a gallop and suddenly stops at the take-off point, with its rider already up and forward in a 2-point position preparatory to jumping, the rider could be thrown into the fence. A refusal occurs when a horse stops in front of an obstacle—whether or not the obstacle is knocked down or altered—unless the horse then immediately jumps the obstacle without backing even one step; but if the horse takes even one step backward, it is a refusal. If, however, the horse approaches a fence, stops, and then jumps the obstacle without backing, it is not a refusal.

A refusal counts as 8 faults, and three refusals require elimination. If a horse comes up to a fence, refuses and a rail falls down or the fence collapses, it is still a refusal, and not a knockdown. If a working hunter refuses while taking a combination, such as an in-and-out—in which faults committed at each obstacle are counted separately—the rider has the option of rejumping the whole combination or only the obstacle that he refused (as distinguished from jumper classes, where the horse must redo the entire combination).

If, after a refusal, the rider moves his horse forward to the fence without asking him to jump, the action constitutes showing an obstacle to a horse, and the entry is penalized an additional 8 faults. If the rider then circles the animal, asks it to jump and the horse again balks and steps back, that would be the third 8-point fault, and the entry would be "whistled out," or eliminated. Bolting, an evasion of control, and running out, an evasion of the jump, are expressions of disobedience similar to refusing, and both are assessed penalties of 8 faults, with the third occurrence eliminating the entry. Any combination of three refusals, bolting, runouts and/or showing a horse an obstacle, requires elimination.

An obstacle is considered knocked down when any part of it is hit by the horse or rider, a rail falls, or the top element is lowered, even if the pole that falls comes to rest on a different support or other part of the same obstacle. Fences in the hunt field are not designed to collapse when an animal brushes them. Because of the very real possibility of a horse catching its front legs and flipping heels over head on top of its rider, faults made with the front legs are more heavily penalized than faults made by the hindquarters, or behind the stifle. For example, a rear knockdown is penalized 4 faults, while a front knockdown is penalized twice as much, or 8 faults.

However, there are knockdowns and then there are elements that get knocked down. Ordinarily, a light tick by a front foot should not result in the collapse of a fence—indeed, light touches are not even considered except where competition is close and elimination difficult—but when the element does fall down, the judge must penalize the horse 8 faults. If the next horse slides in to a jump, crashes through and almost dumps the rider, it is still an 8-fault assessment. However, judgment, rather than mere scoring, is needed: The easy knockdown is not as severe as the bad refusal, and the first horse should place higher, all else being equal. If a horse runs through the fence and takes it chest high, it is 8 faults. If the next horse comes around the turn just as a balloon that falls in the ring spooks it into an easy runout, that horse is penalized the same 8 faults; the crash is nonetheless the more dangerous and logically results in a lower placing.

By the same token, hind knockdowns that are not the result of bad jumping should be scored comparatively to the performances of other horses—if one entry pulls down two top rails with a couple of light rubs by a hind hoof, another takes down two fences by twice catching the top rails at its stifle, and another knocks down an obstacle with its front legs, each receives 8 faults, but the judge must determine which errors were least dangerous and chancey, and place the horses accordingly. An entry is eliminated from competition if it jumps an obstacle before it is reset, bolts from the ring, fails to keep proper course, jumps an obstacle not included in the course, or if horse and/or rider falls.

There are of course other faults and errors besides disobediences, knockdowns, and touches that the judge must consider and that are not spelled out by specific rules. At first, a judge will not be able to distinguish all the many factors that come into play when a horse is jumping a fence, and will have to base his calls on only the more obvious and serious ones. As his eye improves, the judge will be able to differentiate between horses on the basis of more subtle infractions, such as errors that occur from improper takeoff and landing distances.

Generally speaking, a hunter should take off and land from equidistant points on both sides of the fence, with the points being approximately six feet for obstacles of three and one-half feet or higher, and about five feet for lower obstacles. When a horse leaves the ground too far from a jump, it may try to put its feet back down on the ground on the near side of the fence, and crash through it. Also, in an all-out effort to clear the jump, a horse may unfold its front legs and flail them in an effort to propel itself through the air, or it may stretch them far forward and try to dive over the obstacle. Diving, like the serious faults previously discussed, should keep a horse from placing in any class of depth and quality. A less risky, but still dangerous, form of diving is reaching, in which the horse leaves the ground somewhat closer to—but still too far from—a fence, unfolds its legs and reaches over it. Another maneuver often employed in this situation is cutting down, in which a horse clears the fence, immediately drops its front legs on the far side and lands at a point closer to the fence than that point from which it took off (the hind legs often catching a rail). Cutting down may be evidence of a lack of scope (i.e., jumping ability) since a more athletic horse in the same situation would leave from the longer distance, make its arc higher than necessary for the size of the fence (though appropriate to the distance), and land as far from the fence on the far side as it took off from on the near side. Assuming in both cases that no rail is dislodged, reaching should be penalized more heavily than cutting down because of the increased risk entailed by front-leg errors.

Faults result just as easily from taking off too close—propping and chipping-in—as they do from taking off from too far away. Propping generally occurs when a horse has approached an obstacle too fast, and it appears that if the horse is pushing away or setting back from the fence at the takeoff point, with its hind legs well up under itself and its front legs extended out, looking like a cow horse making a quick stop. A scopey, athletic horse can compensate for what is known as a deep, or close, spot and jump in otherwise good form by collecting itself, bringing its hocks well up under its body on takeoff stride, and rocking backward slightly so that its legs will clear the rails. Chipping-in is an extreme form of propping, occurring when a horse arrives at the jump with its strides off, and, in a split-second decision to adjust, throws in a short stride and often leaves the ground on one hind leg instead of two.

Hanging a leg or legs occurs when the horse drops or partially unfolds its legs from the elbow down. Almost as bad as a knockdown or a refusal, hanging a leg in front of the fence is a dangerous fault that can result in severe injury: If a horse in a hunt field hangs a leg and hits a fence, he is inviting a fall. Horses often hang legs when they come in too close to an obstacle and do not fold their legs to avoid knockdowns. A similar fault is dropping the shoulders, in which the shoulders and arms of the horse are lowered toward the ground, almost behind the center point of the horse, even though the forearm, knee and cannon bone may be correctly folded.

Rhythm, the desired smooth continuity of a hunter, is often affected by a horse's temperament. Getting quick, in which a horse's front feet quickly pat the ground immediately prior to takeoff, is a characteristic of high-strung or hot horses, and should be penalized like other actions and quirks of anxiety or nervousness. On the other hand, dwelling off the ground and dwelling in the air may denote a green or sluggish horse. Dwelling off the ground may be caused by a lack of momentum before takeoff, when the horse doesn't come into a jump with an easy, free-flowing stride. Dwelling can also happen when the horse arrives in good style and in stride, but is reluctant to come off the ground due to its own greenness, or a lack of impulsion signaled by the rider; or a fear of pushing off, of landing, or jumping into the rider's hands. Dwelling in the air is something of an illusion; it is akin to throwing a ball in the air and watching it hang for a split second at the apex of the toss. When a horse dwells in the air, he seems to hang momentarily over the fence, perhaps the result of jumping quick but with no forward impulsion, or of too slow a pace and a powerful takeoff.

A horse should approach the middle of a fence in a straight line, and jump in an even, smooth arc, without wavering or drifting to either side of the line. While traveling over the top of a fence, the horse should be attentive but relaxed, with its neck and back rounded. A flat, or inverted, top line is evidence of a lack of scope, or athletic ability, even though it may be only an habitual style of jumping. Drifting from the line occurs when a horse leaves the ground toward the middle of the jump, but then drifts to the side and lands off the center line. This can result in injury if the rider's leg catches a standard. Drifting may be a lateral evasion of the rider's aids, but it could also indicate poor schooling or a rider's habit of either leaning to one side or placing more weight in one iron, or stirrup. Less serious, but still to be penalized, is the horse that takes a jump straight, but not in the middle of the obstacle. However, jumping from an angle is permissible if it is necessary to maintain the flowing continuity of the course.

Overjumping occurs when the horse takes a fence higher or longer than necessary. Overjumping may be a mark of a green, nervous, or anxious horse, or it may be a result simply of exuberance. As a hunter goes over a fence, the horse should remain absolutely upright, without "laying on its side," an extremely dangerous trait that can throw the rider off balance to the down side (the horse may also not be able to land safely on its feet). Less dangerous, but still to be penalized, is twisting, in which an upright horse shifts its front end or its hindquarters to the side in order to clear the jump. A horse whose legs are not folded tightly displays loose form (which is not to be confused with the much more dangerous fault of hanging a leg from the elbow or shoulder), and, all else being equal, should be placed lower than an athletic horse that is a good mover and does fold properly. Other form faults include carrying the legs too close together so that the hooves cross, or so far apart that a wide expanse of chest is displayed. While neither fault is dangerous, both should result in scorecard placement below the horse that shows proper form.

Hand in hand with proper form are manners and way of going. Good manners and good moving don't guarantee proper form, but bad manners and/or poor movement almost certainly preclude it. A hunter should be ridden in hand, its placement and stride should be lightly guided by the rider's hands and legs, with subtle, sensitive movements that are essentially invisible to the observer. There are, however, different forms of hand riding. The term can be a negative description when it is used to describe a horse that is always under restraint and never allowed to move freely (in other words, held tightly in a frame under hard-handed restraint, continually set and never allowed to go naturally into a jump). By the same token, some horses need a lot of encouragement to go forward, but while the use of a crop is permitted, excessive use should be severely penalized.

Like all performance horses, a working hunter should be able to pick up the proper lead, preferably while going over a jump or coming into a turn. If a horse on the right lead comes around a right turn into a jump that will be followed by a left turn, the horse should respond to aids, or cues, while in the air and land on the left lead, or he should be able to make a flying lead change prior to entering the left turn. As far as leads alone are concerned, a horse that makes flying changes at the proper places is preferred to a horse that picks up the proper lead in front and then changes behind. That horse would be followed by a horse that counter-canters, while a horse that cross-canters (moves disunited on opposite leads in front and back) should be penalized most heavily since it poses the greatest risk to itself and its rider.

All in all, there is much more to judging working hunters than merely watching the competitors circle the course and counting the number of ticked and downed rails. Judges should emphasize unsafe jumping and bad form over fences, whether touched or untouched, as if assessing the type of horse that the judge himself would want to ride in a hunt field. For example, one horse in a class had a good round, but at one fence came in too fast and had to scramble to stay out of trouble—the kind of jump that puts one's heart in his throat. The next horse had an even, consistent go, but pulled down a rail on one fence with a light rub from a hind leg. Since an unsafe or dangerous jump, whether touched or not, can easily end the career of both horse and rider—all it takes is one unsafe or dangerous fence—the second horse should place above the first. But before a horse is penalized, an understanding and knowledge of what constitutes an unsafe, dangerous fence is absolutely necessary.

Because of the multitude of occurrences each time an entry goes on course, it is imperative the hunter judge develop and use a suitable bookkeeping system. The system must accurately place each horse relative to the others in the class, and, when done properly, should allow a judge to look back—years later, if need be—and tell exactly what each horse did over any fence in a given class. Because exhibitors can and do question a judge (whose decision is final), a good bookkeeping system that describes everything a horse did from the time he went on course until he was finished is an invaluable aid when the judge is asked to support his placings. A scorecard for working hunters, such as the sample on page 224, should include a section with a numbered box representing each obstacle on the course, and another section for a numerical grade reflecting overall performance. In addition to numbering the boxes, note the type of fence (brush, gate, oxer, etc.) as a jog to the memory when comparing close rounds, and in case you are later questioned by an exhibitor. Each box is used to describe exactly what happened on the way to and at a given fence, whether the horse took the brush box in good form, chipped in at the gate, knocked down the post-and-rail, refused the wall, and then bolted and ran right through the oxer. Keeping up with all that on each fence—before the horse reaches the next one—requires a shorthand system, an example of which is given in the appendix.

When a judge first starts scoring hunters, he probably cannot see and note everything that happens at every fence, and so should rely on relatively few symbols to record major faults. As his skill and eye improve, and he catches more mistakes and problems, he will need more symbols to note them quickly. After the horse has completed its round, and each action has been noted in the boxes, the judge goes to the second section of the scorecard and makes any additional comments, then rates the horse as to its manners and the judge's general impression of its way of going and style of jumping, and finally scores it numerically.

An excellent performer, a horse that's a good mover, cadenced, balanced, well-mannered, and jumps well, falls into the 90s, the equivalent of receiving an academic A. A good performance, from a horse that does everything reasonably well but nothing particularly outstanding or particularly poor, gets a B, or 80 to 89. The average horse, a fair mover, rates a C, 70 to 79. After that, things fall off quickly; the 60s for poor performances by horses that make minor mistakes or are bad movers, perhaps a bit cloddy or clumsy; the 50s for a major fault such as a knockdown, trot or refusal; the 40s for two or more major faults, and zero for not completing the course or for being eliminated.

In order to make these judgments—the finer points, in particular—it is best for the judge to sit outside the arena, in an elevated position from which the majority of fences are viewed from the side and the horses can be seen in profile when jumping. When marking the horses, especially in large classes, keeping a running tally of the high-scoring rounds helps facilitate matters and avoids delay when it's time to pin the ribbons.

Bear in mind that everything a given horse does is relative to everything else done by every other entry, and the class must be judged as so. Ideally, a judge should have an objective standard to go by, but each entry has to be placed against the other entries. If the judge has a round that he thinks deserves an 84, he should compare it with any others he has marked 84, and then, if possible, give it an 83 or 85. Nevertheless, some standards don't bend: Even though a horse may jump all the fences clean, one that is only a fair mover cannot get in the 90s, and bad movers, regardless of how they jump, don't make the 80s. To reach the top, to get an A, the horse must be a good mover that executes his fences properly; he must have style.

The following are examples of circumstances that may occur during working hunter classes, and how a judge should deal with them. Some of the rulings are based on written rules, and others are based on common sense, practical experience, and precedent. In all of the examples, unless otherwise specified, assume that each horse's go was good, that no errors other than those cited were made, and that all other variables are equal.

General

1. When a horse makes 2 faults at one obstacle, only the major fault is counted. However, refusals *are* cumulative; they count in addition to other refusals.

• Horse **A** had a front tick and a hind knockdown at the oxer, while **B** had a front knockdown and a hind tick at the same obstacle, and **C** had a front knockdown on the first element and a hind knockdown on the last element of the oxer.
Ruling. **A** has 4 faults, while **B** and **C** both have 8 faults.

• Horse **A** had a refusal at the gate, but circled back and jumped it cleanly. **B** had a front tick at a jump, and then knocked down the pole over it with a hind leg. **C**'s rider touched the standard with his toe, and caused the rail to fall.

Ruling. **A** and **C** both have 8 faults, while **B** has 4.

• Horse **A** had a refusal at a fence; he then circled around, came back and, upon jumping it, had a front knockdown. **B** had a refusal at another fence, but bumped the obstacle and the top rail fell down; after it was reset he jumped clean. **C** had a refusal at another obstacle, and upon jumping, a front tick.

Ruling. Horse **A** receives 8 faults for its refusal, and then another 8 for the knockdown on its second approach for a total of 16 faults. **B** receives 8 faults for the refusal. **C** receives 8 faults for the refusal.

2. When the obstacle is composed of several elements in the same vertical plane, a fault at the top element is the only one penalized.

• Horse **A** had a hard hind rub on a post-and-rail fence, which caused the second rail to fall. **B** slid into the jump and, though the top rail remained in place, the second and third rails fell; he then popped flat-footed over the obstacle and was clean.

Ruling. **A** has no faults. Because **B** neither backed up (which would have constituted a refusal) nor displaced the top rail, **B** receives no faults at the obstacle. However, **A** places over **B** at the fence, because of the awkward manner in which **B** handled the obstacle.

• Horse **A** slid into a gate with a rail over it, but managed to jump clean over the rail. **B**'s left foreleg rattled the rail, which stayed up, but the gate fell off at one end. **C** had a front knockdown.

Ruling. **A** and **B** have no jumping faults, and **C** has 8. The placing would be **B**, **A**, **C**.

• Horse **A** hit the fence with his front legs, which caused the top rail to be displaced; it did not fall, because one end landed on the rail below and the other remained in its original cup. **B** jumped from one corner over an obstacle, and its rider's toe hit the standard and caused the elements below the top rail to fall.

Ruling. **A** receives 8 faults. Even though the rail did not fall to the ground, it was not in its original position. **B** receives no faults for contact of the standard by the rider. However, this touch should be considered in close competition.

3. When an obstacle (such as an in-and-out) requires two or more fences, faults committed at each obstacle are considered separately. In case of a refusal or runout at one element, the entry may rejump the previous, and following, elements.

• At the in-and-out, Horse **A** had a front knockdown on the first obstacle and a hind knockdown on the second. Horse **B** ran out on the first, circled back and jumped clean, and was clean on the second.

Ruling. **A** receives 8 faults for the front knockdown and 4 for the hind, for 12 faults. **B** receives 8 for the runout.

• Horse **A** refused the second obstacle, and then, electing to rejump the entire combination, had a hind knockdown on the first but was clean on the second. **B** refused the first obstacle, came back over it clean and had a hind knockdown on the second. **C** refused the second obstacle, but came back and was clean when he rejumped it.

Ruling. Both **A** and **B** have 12 faults, and **C** has 8.

4. Judges shall emphasize unsafe jumping and bad form over fences, whether touched or untouched.

• Horse **A** had a clean round, but on one fence, came in too fast and had to scramble, failing to fold both forelegs. **B** had an even, consistent go, but with a light rub, pulled down a jump with a hind leg.

Ruling. An unsafe jump, whether touched or not, can end the career of both horse and rider, and it only has to happen once. Horse **B**, therefore, places above **A**.

• Horse **A** touched, or skimmed, an obstacle with its belly, and had a front and hind rub on another obstacle. Horse **B** had two front ticks.

Ruling. **A** has no jumping faults, but the skim with the belly is a major fault of form. **B** also has no faults, and places over **A**.

• Horse **A** had a clean round, but dangled its front legs on every fence, while **B** had three rubs but a very good style of jumping.

Ruling. Bad or poor form can be dangerous, and dangling is worse than rubbing. Neither **A** nor **B** receive actual faults, but Horse **B** places over **A**.

5. Incorrect leads or disuniting (cross-cantering) around the end of curves of the course are to be penalized.

6. Carrying a crop is optional. Excessive use should be penalized.

• Horse **A**'s rider had to use the stick to urge his mount over several jumps, all of which he took cleanly. **B** had a hind knockdown on one obstacle.

Ruling. Though it receives 4 faults, **B** places over **A**, unless **A** had no loss of form. If **A** maintained form, it would place over **B**.

7. In-and-outs (of one or two strides) are to be taken in the correct number of strides or be penalized.

Touches

1. Light touches are not to be considered, but when elimination is difficult, they may be scored in a comparative manner to other performances.

• Horse **A** and **B** had virtually equal rounds, even to both having a rough fence. Horse **A** had a rub, however, while **B** was clean.

Ruling. With all other things equal, and elimination difficult, **B** gets the nod.

• Horse **A** rubbed a fence, but its pace, style and manners were very good. Though it went clean, **B**'s pace was uneven, its style average and its manners only fair.

Ruling. Because of its superior way of going, Horse **A** places above **B**.

• Horse **A** cleared the eighth obstacle, and then kicked back and made contact with the rail. At the ninth, **A** had a hind rub. **B** had a light front rub on an obstacle.

Ruling. Neither horse has any faults. However, the lack of manners evidenced by **A**'s kick would place **B** higher.

• Horse **A** had two hind rubs, while **B** had no faults but twisted badly over one obstacle.

Ruling. Neither horse has any faults. However, the twist has to be penalized more than the rubs, and so should place **B** lower than **A**.

• Horse **A** had three front rubs and two hind rubs. **B** went clean, but was very strong on the bridle, and made a move and a short stride at each fence.

Ruling. Neither horse has any faults, but **A**'s manners and way of going easily place it above **B**.

Knockdowns

1. Knockdowns with any part of the horse's body behind the stifle are penalized 4 faults; with any part in front of the stifle, 8 faults; of the standard or wing by any part of the horse, rider or equipment, 8 faults; of obstacle by touching a wing or post, according to the preceding.

• Both Horses **A** and **B** had front knockdowns, **A** by making contact with a rail at its ankle, and **B** by contact above the knee.

Ruling. Though both horses receive 8 faults for front knockdowns, **B**'s knockdown was more dangerous (it's more likely to cause a horse to flip over) and thus would be placed accordingly.

• Horse **A** had a clean round, and though clean on its last fence, kicked back and knocked off the top rail. **B** had a light dragging rub with its hind legs, and pulled the top off a jump. **C** slipped on takeoff, and came down on top of a jump, catching the obstacle where the flank and stifle meet.

Ruling. **A** and **B** both receive 4 faults for hind knockdowns. **C** receives 4 or 8 faults, depending on whether the knockdown is considered in front of or behind the stifle.

• Horse **A** had two hind knockdowns, while **B** had one front knock-down and **C** had six light front ticks.

Ruling. **A** has 4 and 4 penalties, for a total of 8 faults. **B** receives 8 faults. **C** places above **A** and **B**, which are tied on faults. The cause of **A**'s and **B**'s knockdowns has to be considered when placing the two horses—manners, style, a light rub, dropped leg, bad takeoff, etc. A dangerous or chancey fence may figure in, and the horse with the knockdowns closest to dangerous would place last.

• Horse **A** knocked down the last element of an oxer with its front legs and pulled down the first element with its hind. **B** pulled down both the front and back elements with its hind legs.

Ruling. Though consisting of two elements, an oxer is one obstacle, and **A** receives 8 faults for the major error on the two committed. **B** receives 4 faults.

• Horse **A** drifted to the left over a jump, and its rider's foot touched and rocked the standard, causing the rails of an adjoining jump to fall. **B** stumbles in front of an obstacle, which caused it to twist into and over the jump; although awkward, he had only a rub. **C** had a light rub with a front foot.

Ruling. No horses receive faults. The class is placed **C**, **A**, and **B** because of style of jumping.

2. Placing any foot in a Liverpool, ditch or water obstacle is penalized 8 faults.

3. Hind knockdowns that are not the result of bad jumping shall not necessarily eliminate a horse from an award, but are scored comparatively against faults of other horses.

• Horse **A** had a rub with a hind fetlock and pulled down a rail. **B** had a rail down when he took off from too far back and caught the rail at its stifle. **C** had five light rubs.

Ruling. Horses **A** and **B** had major faults, and **B** also had an error on takeoff, while **C** had no faults. The placing should be **C**, **A**, and **B**.

1. Horse **A** had a light rub with its hind fetlocks, but pulled down a rail. **B** was clean, but on one jump its front legs were split, with a right front leg forward while the left front leg was dropped back at the knee. **C** came off the ground on one hind leg, had a light rub with that foot and pulled down a rail.

Ruling. The placing should be **A**, **C**, and **B**. Even though both horses **A** and **C** receive 4 faults for hind knockdowns, **A** had the least dangerous fence. **C**'s awkward or chancey jump, when it came off the ground on one leg, was still less dangerous than the split-legged jump of **B**.

When a horse touches an obstacle and causes the rail of an adjoining panel or wing to fall, it shall not be construed as a knockdown.

• Horse **A** slid into a gate, and caused the wing to fall on an adjoining obstacle. With its hind legs, **B** hit the top rail of a fence, which fell and bounced in such a manner that it hit the standard of a nearby jump and dislodged the top rail. **C** touched jump three with its front feet and caused a rail from an adjoining panel at jump six to fall.

Ruling. **A** receives 8 faults for the refusal. **B** receives 4 for the hind knockdown. No faults are assessed **C** for the rail falling from jump six.

Disobediences

1. Riders are allowed a circle to establish stride and pace upon entering and leaving the arena.

• Horse **A** is sent into the ring by the paddock master while the ring crew is still resetting an obstacle; the rider makes three circles before the jump is reset and the judge has given the OK to proceed on course. **B** is sent into the ring, but noting that the judge is not ready, circles until the judge nods to begin. **C** enters, makes one circle, and goes on course after a signal from the judge.

Ruling. Neither **A** nor **B** receive penalties; it is not the exhibitor's error when the paddock master is hustling in riders, or when a judge or jump crew is not ready. **C**'s procedure is standard and correct.

2. Refusals, runouts, bolting on course, showing a horse an obstacle, and extra circles on course are penalized 8 faults apiece each time they occur, with any combination of three such disobediences resulting in elimination of the entry.

• Horse **A** ran out at a fence, circled back and jumped clean. **B** was still several lengths away from a jump when it started to run out; its rider pulled it back sharply, made a quick, tiny circle and popped over the jump.

Ruling. **A** has 8 faults for the runout; the circle is not penalized, as it is merely a return to jumping position. **B** is penalized 8 faults for its circle.

• Horse **A** refused the first fence of an in-and-out, circled, and jumped it cleanly, and then ran out on the second, circled, and refused it. **B** had a refusal on the second fence, came back around to the first, refused it, and after circling again, jumped both cleanly. **C** had a refusal on the second fence, came back to jump the first and had a runout, pulled in between the two fences and then jumped the second fence cleanly.

Ruling. **A** is eliminated for three disobediences (8 faults, 8 faults, elimination). **B** has 16 faults. **C** is eliminated; the entry gets 8 faults for the refusal and another 8 for the runout, but was then eliminated for not rejumping the first fence after committing to it. Had **C** not returned to the first element, and then had been clean when it came back to the second, the entry would have received only 8 faults.

• Horse **A** refused a post-and-rail; the rider immediately pulled it away, made a trotting circle tangent to the obstacle, circled again at the center, and then the horse refused again. **B** refused the fence, the rider backed his horse ten steps and immediately jumped clean. **C** refused, and the abrupt stop caused the rider to lose his stirrups; he held the horse in place while he regained the stirrups, immediately turned, circled, and then jumped clean.

Ruling. **A** is eliminated. Though he didn't come to a halt, the tangent circle has to be considered showing the horse the obstacle. In any case, only one circle is allowed; the two refusals and the extra circle require elimination. **B** is charged 8 faults for the refusal; circling the horse is not mandatory, and backing at the option of the rider is permissible. **C** receives 8 faults for the refusal, but stopping to regain his stirrup and obviously not addressing the obstacle is acceptable.

3. Jumping an obstacle before it is reset, bolting from the ring, failing to maintain the proper course, jumping an obstacle not included on the course, and the horse and/or rider falling, result in elimination of the entry.

• Horse **A** entered the ring, in which four obstacles constitute the course. On the second fence, **A** had a hind knockdown, took fences three and four, and after changing direction, jumped fence five (which was fence two) prior to the top rail being reset.

Ruling. **A** is eliminated for jumping an obstacle before it is reset.

• Horse **A** stopped at a coop and rail, knocked down the rail with his nose, backed one step and then flat-footed the jump and continued on course.

Ruling. **A** is eliminated.

• Horse **A** had a front knockdown on the first part of an in-and-out and refused the second fence. The rider circled it, took the first element before it was reset, and then jumped out clean. **B** stopped at a vertical, demolished it, and the rider pulled up and waited for it to be reset. In the refusal, the top rail over an adjoining jump, a gate, was knocked down and fell on the landing side. The vertical was reset, **B** jumped and continued on course. The pole over the gate was not reset, but the obstacle appeared correct, and **B** jumped it clean.

Ruling. **A** is eliminated, but **B** should be whistled to a stop by the judge, the jump reset and **B** then sent on course again, starting with the gate.

• Horse **A** refused the oxer, and the rider then moved it forward, showed him the obstacle, and jumped clean, and then ran out at the sixth fence. **B** had a refusal at the third fence, circled, and jumped clean, had a runout at the fifth obstacle, circled, and jumped clean through the remainder of the course.

Ruling. **A** is eliminated after the runout. **B** has 16 faults.

HUNTER UNDER SADDLE

Remember that hunter competition in horse shows has been created to simulate the conditions found in the hunting field. When you are judging the show-ring hunter, you are judging that animal against a standard based upon ideal conditions for the field hunter. These standards are based upon athletic efficiency and getting the job done with the least amount of effort. Typical specifications for a hunter under saddle class include the statement "to be judged on performance, including way of going, manners and soundness."

The horses are to be shown at a walk, trot, and canter, both ways of the ring. Except in green classes for young horses, horses may be asked to gallop at least one way of the ring, no more than eight to gallop at one time. Light contact with the horse's mouth is required; that is, the reins are not to be loose and slack; the rider should have some tension on the reins. Contact is a way of riding which improves the performance of the horse by pulling the horse together. It is said the rider has the horse between his legs and hands, that is, he moves the horse forward with his legs (impulsion), pushing him into the bridle and the reins by having slight tension on the bit (collection), again similar to the way an accordian is pulled together. The horse should have his head and neck somewhat outward, but certainly not down on the ground by being heavy on the forehand. Rather he should have his head and neck out leaning slightly on the bit and flexed at the poll. However, his head should not be perpendicular to the ground in the manner of a dressage horse.

The walk should be spritely and ground-covering, yet not an extended walk. It should show ability to cover ground and have a little animation. It should also appear effortless.

The trot should be long strided, low, close to the ground, "mowing the grass," so to speak, and again ground-covering. It also should be effortless and flow. The trot is the gait which the horse uses to cover the most ground at a reasonable speed with the least amount of effort. It should also be reasonably comfortable to the rider. The canter should be long, low, and ground-covering, but not too fast, i.e., a mannerly horse should exhibit a canter that is calm, quiet, and relatively slow, but not so slow that it appears to be a four-beat canter—that is *very bad*. The hand gallop should show a controlled lengthening of stride. It should show the response of the horse when asked to move on; he must do it immediately, he must do it with a long, low ground-covering stride, really reaching forward, yet when asked to come back and halt he must do so immediately and with manners.

An under saddle class demonstrates a couple of very important points about the field hunter. One would oftentimes hack to the hunt meet; therefore, a horse that had a long, low ground-covering stride, guaranteeing the rider a punctual arrival at the hunt meeting while expending the least amount of effort, with enough energy to continue on a four- to five-hour fox hunt, would be most desirable. Additionally, the hunting horse needs to exhibit that same efficiency in order to have enough energy for the job to be done. The greater the height he has in his gait or the higher he lifts his legs as opposed to reaching forward in a ground-covering stride, the more energy he expends, which is not efficient. Additionally, his ability to move forward and increase speed and/or gait as well as come back mannerly is extremely important, since in the hunting field he would be moving in the company of from ten to as many as eighty horses. When hunting, if the fox is sighted or if hounds start to run, the field immediately moves on. There is no real wait, the entire field goes forward rapidly, and if the fox or hounds change track quickly, the whole field will stop and reverse equally as quickly. Manners, especially in company, are therefore highly important in the field hunter. They become even more important if the class being judged is a ladies', a children's, or an amateur class. Nevertheless, the single most important factor in under saddle classes, however, is the manner in which the horse moves, i.e., his athletic efficiency.

JUMPERS

The jumpers of today's Arabian shows have evolved from rather primitive circumstances. In the old days you didn't need a course designer. The course consisted of four fences, jumped "twice around the outside." There were no changes of direction, and no variations of course. In fact, making a change in direction was unheard of! The jumps were usually set up where they were dropped off the truck because of lack of entries or interest. The jumps themselves were not the precision-made variety we see today, but instead crude standards with poles resting on blocks or pins. Some were single-poled, topping five feet with lots of air underneath (prohibited by present rules).

But, change did come about, as happens in all progressions. The public term *grand prix* appeared because of Olympic popularity. These events combined a course of jumps much more challenging than those of the average horse show. With this surge in popularity, Arabian jumper participation has grown and jumper judges have come under closer scrutiny than in the past years.

There's a lot more to judging jumpers now than just adding up faults. Most people have the misconception that jumpers are easy to judge, when in reality many "easy" classes turn out to be complex, decision-making epics. A jumper judge must not only be knowledgeable about course designing (he or she must inspect the course prior to the class for rule violations, distances, etc.), but should be an efficient timer, know when to signal the rider to start, have a thorough understanding of the rules for each class, be mathematically correct when keeping the score-card, render a fair decision promptly whenever a judgment call has to be made, act as a schooling area supervisor when needed, and even be a psychologist when the going gets tough. The Arabian jumper riders are entitled to knowledgeable judges.

Not to oversimplify what takes place, we need to identify the situations. To clarify the start and finish of a course, a starting line at least twelve feet from the first obstacle and a finish line at least twenty-four feet beyond the last obstacle must be indicated by two markers at least twelve feet apart on each end of each line. Horses must cross the starting line (with the rider) mounted between the markers and to complete a course they must cross the finish line between the markers in the proper direction, also mounted (judges may permit or disallow mounting in the ring at their discretion). Failure to enter the ring within one minute of being called or failure to cross the starting line within one minute after an audible signal (bell, horn, whistle, gong, or buzzer) to proceed is given incurs elimination. The time limit for entering the ring is enforced by management, while the time limit for crossing the starting line is enforced by the judge. To prevent a gross unfairness to an exhibitor, the show committee may extend the time limit for entering the ring without, however, altering the jumping order.

In timed classes, time is taken from the instant the horse's chest reaches the starting line until it crosses the finish line. A whistle or horn will sound. Time is not counted while a knocked-down jump is being replaced, from the moment the rider and his mount refuse to jump and dislodge any part of the jump which needs to be replaced until after the jump is reset and the proper authority signals that the jump has been properly replaced and the rider may continue. Any elements knocked down that prevent a horse from jumping the next obstacle must be removed and time required for doing so deducted from the total. Unless automatic electrical timing equipment is used, horse show management must appoint at least two persons, other than the steward, who jointly act as timers. The show committee must furnish each of them with modern stopwatches with a time-out feature reading at least in 100ths of a second. Even when automatic electric timing equipment is used the show management must assign one person to take time manually as a backup.

It is very important that the rider does not begin his round until the judges and timekeepers are ready and the course is set. Since the announcer is often not seated with the other officials, there must be some other means of communication with the rider once he is in the ring—an audible signal (bell, horn, whistle, gong, or buzzer) that is easily heard either before or during the round as follows:

1. To give the signal to start
2. To stop a rider, in the event of an unforeseen incident (which shall also designate time out)

3. To indicate that an obstacle has to be retaken after it has been knocked down during a refusal

4. To give the signal for a rider to continue his round after an interruption (which shall also designate time in)*

5. To indicate by repeated and prolonged ringing that the competitor has been eliminated

The judge is also responsible for correct jump requirements:

1. Rails used on obstacles shall be at least four inches in diameter.

2. The only device permitted for holding all poles, rails, or like elements shall be cups, preferably metal. Devices working on a principle of tension or friction are prohibited.

3. Brush jumps shall have a clearly visible bar resting or placed above or beyond same.

4. Double-crossed poles (i.e., two pairs of crossed poles, with a spread between them) may not be used, and care should be exercised in constructing single crossed poles to prevent any abnormal difficulties.

5. Flags, when used at obstacles, must be placed at the outside extremities of the elements to be jumped.

6. All suspended components (i.e., gates, panels, etc.) must be hung not more than four inches from its top edge.

7. There must be a minimum of eight jumps except triple-bar, high-jump, six-bar, and puissance classes—twelve jumps maximum and at least three jumps in a course of eight shall be of the spread type.

The scoring in general:

1. Jumpers are scored on a mathematical basis and penalty faults, which include disobediences, falls, knockdowns, touches, and time penalties, shall be incurred between the starting line and the finishing line.

2. When a horse makes 2 or more faults at an obstacle only the major fault counts, or in the case of equal faults, only one will count, except in case of a disobedience, which counts in addition.

3. When an obstacle is composed of several elements in the same vertical plane, a fault at the top element is the only one penalized.

4. When an obstacle to be taken in one jump is composed of several elements not in the same vertical plane (oxer, triple bar, etc.) faults at several elements are penalized as one fault.

---

*Note: It is the rider's responsibility to be ready to continue on the course when the signal is given.

5. When an obstacle requires two or more jumps (in-and-out) the faults committed at each obstacle are considered separately.*
6. After the first round of the first class in any section the show or judges may excuse a horse from the ring when it becomes evident that its performance prohibits it from being in the ribbons.
7. Should a rider disregard a signal to leave the ring, the entry may be disqualified from future classes at the show.
8. In cases of broken equipment or loss of shoe, the rider may either continue without penalty or be eliminated.

Disobediences include refusals, run-outs, loss of gait, and circles.
Refusals: This constitutes stopping in front of an obstacle to be jumped, whether or not the horse knocks it down or displaces it.

1. Stopping at obstacle without knocking it down and without backing followed *immediately* by a standing jump is not penalized.
2. If halt continues, or if the horse backs even a single step voluntarily or not, or retakes course, a refusal is incurred.
3. Knocking down an obstacle in stopping or sliding constitutes a refusal, whether or not the horse goes through it. The obstacle must be retaken or the horse is eliminated.
4. The action of showing an obstacle to a horse after a refusal and before immediately retaking course is cause for elimination. The same penalty is imposed when a rider shows the horse any of the obstacles before jumping the obstacle.

Run-outs:

1. Evading or passing the obstacle to be jumped.
2. Jumping an obstacle outside its limiting markers. After a run-out or refusal horse must, before proceeding on course, rejump the obstacle at which the disobedience occurred or be *eliminated*. If the flag, standard, wing, or obstacle has not been reset when the horse is ready to jump, he must await the signal to start or be *eliminated*.

Loss of gait: Halting or stepping backward by horse after crossing starting line unless due to a refusal, run-out or on order from a judge due to unforeseen circumstances, such as a fence blowing down.
Circle: Any form of circle or circles, whereby the horse crosses its original track between two consecutive obstacles anywhere on the course, except to retake an obstacle after a refusal or run-out is a disobedience. (Note: Coming sideways, zigzagging or turning brusquely toward object

---

*Note: In case of a refusal or run-out at the second or third element of a combination, the entry must rejump the previous as well as the following elements, upon notification that obstacle has been reset, if necessary.

in jumping does not constitute a disobedience unless the horse passes the obstacle or turns back to the next obstacle or finish line.)

Some Clarifications of Confusing Situations: In fault-and-out classes, if the fall or disobedience occurs after landing, the horse will be scored as though the fault had occurred at the next approaching obstacle. When the penalty of "elimination" is incurred (as in the case of a fall) the rider will be credited with obstacles already cleared.

An obstacle is considered knocked down when a horse or rider, by contact:

1. Lowers any part thereof which establishes the height of the obstacle or the height of any element of a spread obstacle, even when the falling part is arrested in its fall by any portion of the obstacle
2. Moves any part thereof which establishes the height of the obstacle as aforesaid so that it rests on a different support from the one on which it was originally placed

Should a pole resting in a cup come to rest on the lip of the cup or on the bracket, if the bracket is an integral part of the cup, it is not considered a knockdown. Narrowing the width of a spread obstacle without altering the height of any element as defined in (1) and (2) above is not considered a knockdown. If an obstacle falls after a horse leaves the ring it shall not be considered a knockdown.

Touches shall be scored as outlined in Table I but remember that at a brush element the touch of the brush only without touching the framework or pole on top thereof is not scored as a fault.

A horse is considered off course when it deviates from the course as shown by the course diagram and then takes an obstacle prior to rectifying the deviation. To rectify the deviation, the horse must resume the course from the spot where the error was committed. Any disobedience which may be committed while rectifying the deviation must be scored.

Examples of faults and class conditions that the judge must be familiar with are shown in Table I.

Table I Touch Classes

At least two judges or one judge and a competent scorer, other than the steward, must officiate in Table I Classes.

1.	Touch of obstacle with any portion of horse's body behind stifle	½ fault
2.	Touch of obstacle with any portion of horse's body, in front of stifle, or with any part of rider or equipment	1 fault
3.	Touch of standard or wing in jumping obstacle with any part of horse, rider, or equipment	1 fault

4.	Touch of flag, automatic starter equipment, or other designated markers on starting or finishing line or flags taking the place of standards, with any part of the horse, rider, or equipment	1 fault
5.	Knockdown of obstacle, standard, or wing with any portion of horse, rider, or equipment	4 faults
6.	Knockdown of flag, automatic starter equipment, or other designated markers on starting or finishing line or flags taking the place of standards, with any part of horse, rider, or equipment during the round	4 faults
7.	One or more feet in the water or on the marking strip of the water jump	4 faults
8.	First disobedience (anywhere on course)	3 faults
9.	Second cumulative disobedience (anywhere on course)	6 faults
10.	Third cumulative disobedience (anywhere on course)	Elimination
11.	Fall of horse and/or rider (except in Fault and Out)	Elimination
12.	Jumping obstacle before it is reset or without waiting for signal to proceed	Elimination
13.	Starting before judge's audible signal to proceed; jumping obstacle before start or after crossing the finish line, whether forming part of course or not; jumping obstacle out of order; off course	Elimination
14.	Failure to enter ring within one minute of being called	Elimination
15.	Failure to cross the starting line within one minute after judge's audible signal to proceed	Elimination
16.	Jumping any obstacle before crossing starting line unless said obstacle is designated as a practice jump	Elimination
17.	Failure to jump in designated order	Elimination

Table II classes are scored the same as Table I classes with a few exceptions. Touches are not penalized, and there is a time allowed and a time limit. Penalties are assessed for going over the time allowed; exceeding the time limit results in elimination. All ties involving first place must be jumped off. The time taken to complete the course will decide between any horses tied other than for first place.

Judges should always take control of jumper classes, which are extremely easy to judge when all goes well, but chaotic when it doesn't. In Table I classes, the judge should be in the arena moving around to be able to view all the jumps. The most advantageous place to see a "touch" is from the takeoff side of the jump. If the course is long or the arena not easily set up to allow all the fences to be seen by the judge, another qualified person may assist, as well as a scribe (scorekeeper).

In Table II classes, the judge should sit preferably by the automatic timer, providing he can see all the jumps clearly. Because the riders rely on the judge via the whistle or horn to know when to start, stop, or continue on, the judge should handle his own whistle, horn, or other sounding device. It is especially important when a fence is dislodged (while the horse is refusing to jump). Time must be stopped and penalty seconds added if the fence needs to be reset. If the judge thinks the fence warrants resetting, he signals the rider to stop. If he feels the fence is jumpable, the rider is to continue on course. Therefore, it is important that the judge control the jumper ring with the whistle or else havoc can prevail.

CHAPTER
~ 7 ~

Miscellaneous Classes

NATIVE COSTUME

One of the most beautiful classes at any Arabian show is the native costume class, a very popular and exciting class. Due to color, excitement, speed, and sometimes reckless nature of the class, a large costume class can be very difficult for judges to accurately adjudicate.

When judging the performance portion the only gaits called for are the walk, canter, and hand gallop. The walk, I'm sure, takes care of itself— if the horse is truly walking and going straight. The canter is much like the canter in the English pleasure horse division, a three-beat gait, smooth, unhurried, with moderate collection and straight on both leads. The hand gallop is performed with the same long, free ground-covering strides under control as before. The hand gallop is not a faster collected canter, but a true lengthening of stride. Extreme speed will be penalized.

These criteria, as all others, leave much to the opinion of the judge: How extreme is extreme? How much do you penalize if, in the judge's opinion, it is somewhat extreme? The best way to show in this class, as in all other classes, is to your horse's best advantage or however he looks the best under control.

Because many exhibitors don't realize the costume obscures the numbers, a judge may ask show management to announce in the barn area, several times prior to the class, that numbers be worn on the back of the costume and be visible. If exhibitors desire to wear the number on the side, they should be instructed to provide a suitable second number so that there will be a visible number on each side.

Because horses are to enter the ring at a canter, I suggest that judges allow a short period of time for the horses to settle into the canter. This is possible as the class does not officially commence until the gate closes. I prefer to move from the canter directly to the hand gallop, then back to the canter prior to asking for the walk. This saves time, although I do not object to the procedure of walking after the initial canter and then asking for the canter and moving to the hand gallop. Another technique used, evidently as a check for manners, is to ask the horses to stop from the hand gallop. I have seldom noted that this proves anything but I see no objection to the procedure. In all cases, the costume class will reverse at the walk. The walk is one time when the pace is slow enough for the judge to write down a few numbers if desired. At the conclusion of the rail work, the horses are generally lined up head to tail for final inspection and backing. For safety reasons, I prefer to ask the horse to face me prior to backing rather than back in line. Backing in line may result in a problem as a horse may back too far and create a problem with the horse behind it. If the horses do back in line, it is wise to have the ringmaster nearby to ask riders to stop after backing a few strides.

The Judging Portion

The rule states that the class is to be judged 75 percent on performance and manners and 25 percent on appointments. The breed has progressed to the point that quality performance horses are being shown and judges should take the class seriously and make a real effort to closely observe the athletic ability of each horse as well as observe the manners as reflected in a steady work and lack of excessive changing of leads. It should be called to the attention of judges that, since performance is listed prior to manners, they consider allowing a very athletic and bright horse a slight error in manners in preference to a very dull performance with no infractions relative to manners. This sometimes creates problems for judges as everyone can see a change of lead, but they have trouble seeing the difference in the canter and hand gallop of a good athletic horse in contrast to a short-strided, rather rough-going horse with less physical ability. A good performance is one where the horse is collected, his rear quarter is working well under the body, and his stride is long, free, and cadenced. This would be in contrast to one that is not in the bridle, strung out, and lacking cadence and trueness of gait at all three gaits. At times an added dimension will be injected when a bright horse at the canter and hand gallop will fail to comply with the requirements at the walk. This is where weighing the facts and knowing the rules will assist a judge in rendering a judgment, which is his duty and responsibility.

Costume

The rule book calls this class the "native" costume class. Some of the outfits I've seen, however, appear to be natives of a different land where they put on everything but the kitchen sink or put on so little it must refer to the original harem costume. This particular class should be used to show good taste in both apparel and horses.

The rules allow almost any type of a headstall as long as there is no tie-down. Rider attire should consist of a native-type costume including a flowing cape (an aba) or coat, pantaloons, headdress, scarf, or sash. Seldom do we see a costume that does not contain a reasonable resemblance of the parts mentioned. Judges should also note that no objects may be carried other than a riding crop, reins, and a portion of the aba or cape. It appears impossible to literally evaluate the term "native-type costume." There are a few native types used, but the majority of attire have taken on a "show-biz" flair. This has been generally accepted, and my advice is to evaluate the costume on the basis of: Does it contain the necessary parts; is it basically in good taste, well constructed, and an appropriate color and size for the rider and horse? With these standards, the costumes in most cases leave little to choose between them, thus leaving the judge to rely on performance and manners. When a placement is justified on the basis of the costume, a judge should not hesitate to utilize the 25 percent allocated for appointments.

The rule also states that extreme and reckless speed shall be penalized. Judges should not hesitate to enforce this statement in their placing. This class is not a race; so form, cadence, and balance should be as much a part of performance in this class as in others. Excessive speed may vary according to the arena size, footing, number of horses in the class, and the control exercised by the rider. At the hand gallop the horse must be well in hand and fully under control. Depending upon whose description is used, the hand gallop is described as "slower than the gallop" and/or "definitely not a run."

The only way to judge the class is relate each entry to the others in what they do while executing the walk, canter, and hand gallop.

While this class may appear to the novice to be merely an English pleasure class with glittering frills, certain qualities make it unique unto itself. The horse should have an overall appearance of animation and alert eagerness, a well arched neck, and a lofty tail (often the only visible parts of the horse). The horse must show a combination of impulsion and collection and demonstrate good manners. Bad manners in this class, as in all the others, are still detected by sour ears, wringing tail, snapping teeth, swinging head, veering into the path of another horse (usually occurring at the hand gallop), biting, and kicking. Remember, performance and manners still count for 75 percent of the total judging.

Most mistakes in this class are made at the hand gallop, but many horses are hindered by the trappings that they are forced to carry. Tassels and beads flop around and bump the horse so that the horse is constantly changing leads. Some of the bridles (not allowed in other classes) make the horses fuss with their heads and not pay attention to what they are doing.

The other major area of difficulty is encountered when horses must stand quietly and back readily, which many do not do when standing stopped on the rail or lined up head to tail in the arena. Thus the back-up here becomes, as in other classes, a real point of judging when you have several horses doing much the same thing on the rail.

What really stands out to the judge is the horse whose rider's costume complements the theme, the horse that has a pretty way of moving, is quiet in the bridle, shows no duress when asked to do any of the gaits, and is prompt and sure in the back-up.

A native costume that complements the theme.

SIDESADDLE

Another class that is growing in popularity, both with spectators and exhibitors, is the ladies sidesaddle class. The class can be categorized as a "pleasure horse class" where manners, performance, quality, and conformation make up 85 percent of the judging, and the other 15 percent is placed on appropriate side saddle dress.

The horse's tack, however, is quite important in this class because the balance of the rider must be with the balance of the horse. Along these lines, then, the bridle should be a light show type, either single curb or single snaffle, curb, and snaffle or pelham. There should be no martingale or tie down (you will note this is the same as it is for the English pleasure horse) but you may also use any Western-type headstall without noseband in conjunction with any standard-type Western bit. You can use a curb chain but it must lie flat, the same as the Western pleasure horse. Extreme care should be taken to make sure you have good immediate response of your horse through the bridle, whichever type you choose. The saddle, while keeping you secure, should also give you maximum freedom because of the costume worn.

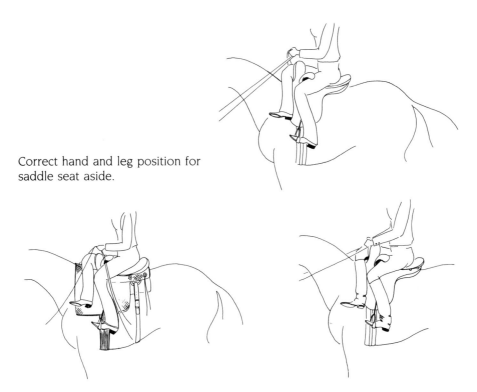

Correct hand and leg position for saddle seat aside.

Correct hand and leg position for Western stock seat aside.

Correct hand and leg position for hunter seat aside.

When judging a sidesaddle class, I pay close attention to how the horse reacts to the commands given, which is the transition period. The response must be more than just simple compliance, it should be a fluidity between horse and rider. The rider may either sit or post to the trot, however, the exhibitor should do what shows the horse to its best advantage. If your horse is rough at the trot and you try to sit to it, your smile will soon change to a grimace to keep your teeth from jarring out of your mouth. If you post, do it in rhythm, remembering that the horse must look like a pleasure to ride.

The canter is somewhat difficult because you don't have a leg on each side, so the aids are not exactly the same as the other classes. Practice giving the aids without a great deal of upper-body movement so you aren't in the habit of overreacting when trying to canter. Above all, position yourself in the ring so you stay out of trouble and can be conscious of what's going on around you.

When I judge the attire portion, I look at all the costumes and tack for period-type, "even under the skirts."

Because sidesaddle is new to many judges as well as many riders, even though it has been used for several centuries in one form or another, it is necessary to remember it is the horse that is being judged, not the rider. When judging a sidesaddle class, the first and foremost requirement for a lady's mount is manners, then performance. Soundness and general way of going need to be given particular consideration. A lady's horse should not have to be checked back all of the time.

Performance of the horse and proper tack and appointments are the two main factors that form a good team. For the rider, the principles of a good performance center on her position in the saddle. The rider's back is centered over and perpendicular to the horse's back, shoulders are level and square, hips are in a square alignment to the rider's body and the horse's back, and her head is erect with eyes looking forward. The rider's hand position in saddle seat or western is the same as if astride. Particular care should be paid to whether the rider is using romal or split reins and that they are being held properly. The hunter seat rider's hands are down on either side of the rider's right knee. The elbows in all styles should remain close to the rider's sides.

Generally, the lack of the right leg for aiding the horse on the off side at the walk, jog, or trot will present no major problems, as the leg pressure applied with the left leg will be adequate enough to move the horse on. At the canter or lope (astride) the rider normally puts the inside leg on the girth and squeezes, moves the outside leg slightly behind the girth, and drives forward with her backbone, seat bone, and weight in the outside hip pocket. However, when aside, on the left lead, the outside leg is not present. So, the rider puts the inside leg firm against the horse's side as she normally would, puts her weight in the right hip, and then drives forward off her left leg, back, and seat bones. The rider uses the same hand and bit cues that she normally uses. If your horse normally cues from turning his head to the center of the ring or to the rail, continue to do so but decrease the turn and teach the horse to work off the rider's body weight. It's important that the horse take the leads traveling straight ahead. To cue the horse for the right lead, the rider simply moves her left leg back to the normal position where she cues for head position to produce the desired canter or lope.*

For any rider to look her best, she must be mounted on a well-trained pleasure horse. The style of riding does not matter. The horse must be sound and well mannered. The transitions and gaits must be clean, even, smooth, and distinct. The horse must be reliable, one that is not going to shy or come unglued when something unusual happens. A sidesaddle horse is a lady's mount and must at all times be one that a lady feels secure on and that will if necessary "look after the rider."

---

*Be careful not to lean into the canter or lope as the horse moves along. The rider's back stays perpendicular to the horse's back with shoulders and hips square.

ATTIRE

Saddle Seat:

1. Informal: Saddleseat coat with notched lapel, of conservative colors or small pinstripes with a center vent and double inverted side pleats. The coat is fingertip length. This coat is worn for daytime and before 6 P.M.

2. Kentucky jodhpurs to match the coat and the apron.

3. The apron must match the Kentucky jodhpurs and the coat. The apron must hang level with the ground at all times. The right foot is never to show out from under the apron. The apron may come to the lower level of the left heel and be no shorter than to end at the top of the toe of the Kentucky jodhpur boots. None of the Kentucky jodhpurs should show.

4. Formal: Evening wear is worn after 6 P.M. It consists of a formal saddleseat coat with shawl collar, an apron with a matching satin strip four inches from the hemline of the apron and parallel with the ground. A matching cummerbund is always worn with modern formal saddleseat attire.

5. Kentucky jodhpur boots are black unless the rider is wearing a brown habit. Then the jodhpur boots may be brown to match the habit. For formal wear the jodhpur boots should always be black.

6. A pastel or plain white shirt is worn. Those with button down collars tend to do best. For formal wear the pleated white shirt with French cuffs is worn.

7. Vests are for informal wear only. They are matching material, though occasionally one will see a contrasting vest if quietly done.

8. The bowler derby is worn for informal classes. It must match the habit. Soft hats of any other style are not to be worn.

9. For formal wear after 6 P.M. a top hat is worn. The hat is worn level at all times. (Veil is optional and must be close fitting.)

10. The rider's hair should be tucked neatly into a bun and worn above the collar. (What if you have short hair? Get a straight hair fall to match your hair color, pin it into the hairline about two inches behind the forehead, pull it back, pin, and put the remainder into a bun. With a hat on, no one will know it's a hairpiece and not your own hair.)

11. Leather gloves of black or brown to go with the habit are required.

12. A spur is optional. (If worn it is preferred to be without a rowl.)

13. A black gaited-type whip with a white handle, thirty-three to thirty-nine inches in length. (Remember that the whip does not change hands when one changes direction in the show ring. The whip is always carried in the rider's right hand, as it is used to replace the rider's right leg.)

14. The saddle girth is to be a plain white web, either two-buckle type or Fitzwilliam. (If using a white web girth be certain that there is no stretch elastic on the girth at any point! This can cause slipping, and does not lend itself well to sidesaddle riding.)

15. The sidesaddle must be of an English type. It can be all smooth leather, or with a suede or doeskin seat, either of the modern English style or Victorian style.

16. The bridle should always be a full bridle. (Separate curb bit and snaffle bradoon.)

17. There are to be no saddlepads used, as these saddles will either have white linen or leather bottoms. (Leather bottoms should be wiped clean and conditioned after each use. The linen bottoms must also be cared for by wiping off the excess sweat and hair and arranging the saddle in such a manner as to allow the bottom to dry out. Once the bottom of the saddle is dry then go around the outer edge of the linen, that is the section of the linen that shows when on the horse, with a coat of white shoe cream. The area of the saddle that is seen should always be clean and white as should be the web saddle girth.)

18. There are to be no tiedowns, martingales, side reins, web reins, or dropped nosebands.

19. A rider may use a flower in her left lapel. It may be a feather type or a fresh flower and should always be quiet and understated.

20. As to jewelry, a tie tack, not a stock pin, is used on the four-in-hand tie. There should be no other jewelry, with the exception of finger rings which of course are covered by the rider's gloves, and therefore not seen. (No earrings of any sort.)

Western Stock Seat:

1. A western-style long-sleeve shirt, with buttons or snaps, or an equitation suit with long sleeves.

2. A western-style scarf or tie.

3. A cowboy hat. (Please keep the hatband in line with the habit. If the hatband is too loud, it is going to distract the overall appearance of the sidesaddle habit. Please refrain from multiple hat pins. One is nice if desired, but more will again take away from the overall appearance. All hats are to be worn level, not pushed back on the rider's head.)

4. Long Western-style pants to match the apron. These pants are to be worn on the outside of the rider's boot.

5. The apron must match the Western-style riding pants. It is to cover the rider's right foot, hang parallel to the ground, and may end at the rider's ankle or just come to the arch of the rider's foot. (If the apron is longer than this it can interfere with the horse and rider. It is extremely important that the apron hang level with the ground.)

6. Western-style riding boots. (Please, riding boots not disco boots.)

7. A vest is optional in accordance with the style of habit worn.

8. A jacket is optional in accordance with the style of habit worn. If worn it should just come to the seat of the saddle and no longer. It may have either a single center vent or two side vents.

9. Leather gloves are normally black or brown, but might even be gray to go with specific habit. (Please stay away from pastel habits as they will show wear very quickly.)

10. The rider's hair should be neatly tucked up on her head under her hat or up in a bun. (See instructions under saddleseat appointments.) A silver barrett may be used on the Western bun, if it is neat and small. The bun never touches the rider's collar.

11. A Western belt is optional.

12. A quirt is optional as is the spur.

13. No earrings, please. A concho pin or scarf pin is optional if worn in an understated manner.

14. The sidesaddle used for Western aside may be of the Western stock type, Victorian, early Victorian, or plantation-type sidesaddle.

15. The saddle girth must be of a string type. This is used no matter the type of sidesaddle used for Western sidesaddle riding.

16. Saddle pads of a Western style may be used under the Western-stock sidesaddle or the plantation-style sidesaddle, but are not used under the Victorian or early Victorian styles of sidesaddles. Plain white or Navaho blanket-style saddle blankets are preferred.

17. A matching Western bridle will be used. It may have either split or romal reins. If romal reins are used, the rider must carry hobbles on the front off side of the sidesaddle.

18. Mechanical hackamore, hackamore bits, running martingale, tie-downs, choke ropes, draw reins, bosal or cavasson-type noseband are prohibited.

19. Chaps are not required, as the apron replaces them to protect the rider's legs from the environment.

Hunter Seat:

1. The coat is of a dark, conservative color, having either one, two, or three buttons. The preferred colors are black or dark blue, but other dark conservative colors may be worn on informal occasions. The coat may have a single center vent or side vents. The length of the coat is just to the saddle but no longer. (The collar and lapel of the coat are to match the coat unless the lady belongs to a specific hunt and then she may wear the specific colors of that hunt. Her coat must then carry the designated buttons of the aforementioned hunt.)

2. Hunt breeches, not jodhpur, must match the apron and coat.

3. The apron must be the same color as the breeches and the coat. The hem length should be four inches above the left ankle when the rider is mounted. In no circumstances is the rider's right foot to show! The apron is to hang parallel to the ground. The apron should present a nice box appearance across the bottom of the apron. It should never tend to come to a point on the horse's shoulder. The rider's right leg belongs back according to the construction of the sidesaddle being ridden.

4. The shirt is a long-sleeved white shirt; again those shirts with button down collars.

5. Stock tie of white linen with a gold stock pin placed in a horizontal position is worn. (Ratcather or choker tie does not present the desired finesse of a lady aside.)

6. Vests are of white, buff, or canary yellow and must be worn with formal attire.

7. High black boots without tops are worn for formal occasions. Brown boots may be worn for informal riding. Garters are worn on both the left and right boot.

8. Gloves are of leather, either black or brown.

9. A spur is optional. No rowl.

10. The sidesaddle generally used is a flat English sidesaddle of smooth leather or with a doeskin seat. The Victorian sidesaddle may be used for hunting as it was so used in its own time.

11. No saddle pads are to be used.

12. The bridle can be a full double bridle, a pelham, or a snaffle. All the leather should be plain and flat.

13. No stirrup pads are ever used.

14. Girths are to be of the Fitzwilliam style either of leather or web. (Never use a girth with any stretch as it could cause slippage and be most unsafe!)

15. A leather covered "cane," similar to a modern hunt crop without the flap is carried in hack classes or hunter pleasure classes on the flat.

16. A fresh flower may be worn in the left lapel. A blue cornflower is traditional.

17. A hunting silk or black hunting bowler is worn on formal occasions.

Remember that all of the above fit together to form a complete picture that is to be both lady-like and workwoman-like in appearance.

SHOW HACK

While many refer to this class as a "dressage competition performed collectively on the rail," it is not. It is a class unto itself demonstrating the Arabian's true versatility of movement, manners, and responsiveness to the rider's aid during the many transitions required. These horses need to have a natural, free-flowing way-of-going, without a high or forced motion.

The word control appears often when describing the show hack, along with responsiveness and obedience. These horses must exhibit a high level of training, utilizing the utmost of impulsion and collection throughout each of the several gaits that are required. Many judges as well as exhibitors are not familiar with the way each gait should be performed. The judge must analyze each gait in its entirety as follows.

The walk should be a four-beat gait, straight, true, and flat footed. It is a marching pace in which the footfalls of the horse's feet follow each other. At the *collected walk*, the head approaches the vertical maintaining light contact with the horse's mouth. The hind legs are engaged with good hock action and the pace should remain marching with the feet being placed in regular sequence. Each step covers less ground and is slightly higher than the normal walk because all the joints bend more decidedly. The hind feet touch the ground behind, or at the most in the footprints of the forefeet. At the *extended walk*, the horse covers as much ground as possible without haste or losing the regularity of his steps. The hind feet touch the ground clearly in front of the footprints of the forefeet. The rider maintains a light but steady contact with the horse's mouth. The *normal walk* is a regular, unconstrained walk of moderate extension. The horse walks energetically but calmly, with even, determined steps while the rider maintains a light but steady contact with the mouth.

The trot is a two-beat gait on alternate diagonal legs separated by a moment of suspension. It is free, light, and crisp, and should be moved into without hesitation. The quality of the trot is judged by the general impression, the regularity and elasticity of the steps (supplied by a supple back and well-engaged hindquarters), and by the ability to maintain steady rhythm and natural balance; even after a transition from one trot to another. At the *collected trot*, the horse again has his head to the vertical with his neck raised and arched. The hocks should maintain an energetic impulsion, thus enabling the shoulders to move with greater ease in any direction. The horse's steps are much shorter than in the other trots, but he is lighter and more mobile. In show hack, riders always sit the collected trot. At the *extended trot*, the horse, maintaining the same rhythm, should cover as much ground as possible by lengthening his stride to the utmost as a result of great impulsion from the hindquarters. A show hack *must* exhibit a true extended trot. The forefeet should touch the ground on the spot toward which they are pointing. Riders must post at the extended trot. The *normal trot* is free moving with a moderately extended stride, but is more "round" than at the extended trot. There is an obvious impulsion from the hindquarters and the forefeet should touch the ground to which they are pointing. Rider should also be posting.

The canter is a three-beat gait, with light, cadenced, and regular strides. The quality of the canter is judged by the general impression, the regularity and crispness of the three-beat pace, and by maintaining the same rhythm and natural balance. The horse should always remain traveling straight on straight lines. At the *collected canter*, the horse moves forward with his neck raised and arched. The horse's strides are shorter than at the other canters, but he is lighter and more mobile. At the *extended canter*, the horse covers as much ground as possible without entering into a hand gallop. Maintaining the same rhythm, he lengthens his stride (without losing any of his calmness and lightness) by engaging impulsion from

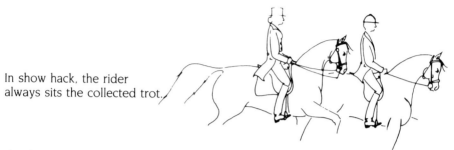

In show hack, the rider
always sits the collected trot.

the hindquarters. The *normal canter* is a pace between the collected and extended canter. The horse should be properly balanced, with even, light, and cadenced strides along with good hock action.

The *hand gallop* impels the horse forward with free, balanced, and extended strides showing an obvious impulsion from the hindquarters. He should cover as much ground as possible with a point within the horse's stride when all four feet are not in contact with the ground. This allows the horse to carry his head a little more in front of the vertical than at the other canters, and also to lower his head and neck slightly. The strides should be long and even, balanced, and unconstrained.

The *rein back* is a reversing movement in which the horse's feet are raised and set down almost simultaneously by diagonal pairs; each foot being raised and set down an instant before the diagonal foot behind, so that sometimes on hard ground four separate beats are clearly audible. The feet should be well raised and the hind feet remain well in line. At the preceding halt as well as during the rein back, the horse should remain on the bit. Anticipation, resistance to or evasion of the hand, deviation of the quarters from the straight line, spreading or inactive hind legs, and dragging forefeet are serious faults.

Transitions should be made quickly, yet must be smooth and not abrupt. Although vitality, animation, and presence are required, the horse must be under complete control and easily ridden. Obedience to the rider is of prime importance.

Judges find themselves in difficulty when they don't have a complete plan as to how they're going to handle this class. To ensure that each gait is properly called for with the extensions and collections, a method needs to be established. As this class always enters the arena at a walk, I ask for the collected, the normal (regular), the extension, and again back to the normal. I then go on to the next gait with the same routine, always returning to the normal portion of the gait before proceeding on.

Every gait called for should be distinctive, the transitions smooth, and an actual lengthening or shortening of stride, as the horse extends or collects. Many times I only see the rider working harder or easier and the horse has really never changed stride, or a noticeable change anyway. As the horse moves up with impulsion or down with collection, the rate of travel must be distinguishable, so that the show hack class is not just a catch-all class for horses that can't win in other divisions.

Appendix

TERMINOLOGY

Broodmare. Female horse kept for breeding.

Colors. Bay—reddish shades from reddish-tan to dark mahogany, with black mane and tail; Grey; Brown—various shades; Chestnut—shades from golden yellow to dark, reddish brown, with mane and tail the same color or lighter than the body. Arabians are *rarely* pure white or black.

Colt. Young male horse that is either sexually immature or has not yet reached the age of four.

Dam. Female parent of horse.

Filly. Young female horse under four years old.

Foal. Young animal that is still nursing.

Gelding. Castrated male horse.

Get. The entire progeny of a stallion.

Markings. Most common include stars, strips, or blaze faces, snip noses and a white foot or more, or white stockings.

Prepotent. The unusual ability of an individual or strain to transmit its outstanding characteristics to offspring because of genetic strength for numerous traits.

Produce. The entire progeny of a mare.

Progeny. Offspring or descendants of a horse.

Sire. Male parent of a horse.

Stallion. Mature male horse kept for breeding.

Straight. Unmixed with other bloodlines or strains.

Stud. A stallion used for breeding purposes.

Stud fees. Fees which the owner of a stallion collects when his stallion is bred with a mare.

Type. Strong and clearly marked similarity so that each is typical of the group.

219

Type characteristics in Arabians include: jaunty tail carriage, wedge-shaped head with large, wide-set eyes, relatively level croup and arched neck.

Weanling. A young horse recently taken from its mother; takes food other than by nursing.

GLOSSARY OF STANDARD TERMS DESCRIBING HUNTERS

Airy. An obstacle with large open spaces. Hunter fences should be made with plenty of material and appear so that horses and riders both may have difficulty judging airy jumps. "Airy" may also refer to the horse itself, if it overjumps and there is a lot of air and space between it and the obstacle.

Bascule. Good form; rounding the back while in arc over fence.

Chipping in. Taking off from a point too close to the fence; also called "too short."

Course pattern. A diagram that shows the arrangement of obstacles in a course, with arrows indicating direction travel and each obstacle numbered in the order in which it is to be taken. Although riders are not compelled to follow compulsory track, each obstacle must be jumped in the direction shown by arrows. The distances between fences, measured from the back of one obstacle to the front of the next, are figured on strides of approximately twelve feet. Patterns for each class must be posted at least one hour prior to the class.

Courtesy circle. A circle taken by exhibitors prior to beginning the course to establish hunting gait and pace, and again upon completion of the course, to demonstrate soundness at the trot on a loose rein. In order to save time, a judge may restrict the circle to a mandatory line, in which case a dotted line must be included in the diagram and announced one hour prior to the class, and a marker showing where the circle is to begin and end must be provided in the arena.

Cutting down. Landing closer on the far side of the fence than the takeoff point on the near side.

Dangling. Having one or more legs hanging down, rather than correctly folded, while jumping an obstacle.

Diving. Stretching the front legs far forward in an effort to clear the rails. Usually the result of taking off too far from the fence or with too much speed, diving is a severe, and potentially dangerous, form of reaching.

Drifting. Moving to either side, away from the center, of the obstacle when jumping.

Dropping a leg. Not keeping both front or both back legs up and evenly together.

Dwelling in the air. Something of an illusion; it is akin to throwing a ball in the air and watching it hang for a split second at the apex. When a horse dwells in the air, he seems to hang momentarily over the fence, the result of greenness, jumping quick but with no forward impulsion, a fear of taking off or landing, or lack of help from the rider.

Dwelling off the ground. Caused by a lack of momentum before takeoff, when the horse doesn't continue to the jump with an easy, free-flowing stride.

Element. One of the parts or components of a jump or obstacle. For instance, the top rail of an obstacle is also known as the top element.

Folds correctly. Forearms parallel, or higher, to ground, with front legs flexed at knee, front feet close to elbows and hindquarters neatly flexed and folded at hocks.

Flat back. Top line straight, rather than rounded; the horse doesn't use its back, head, neck, or shoulders.

Good arc. Takeoff and landing at points equidistant from the fence.

Ground line. A pole or rail placed on the ground approximately six inches in front of a jump. By further delineating the jump, a ground line helps the horse and rider judge the amount of effort required to clear the obstacle. Fillers such as brush boxes filled with shrubs or flowers are often used in lieu of a ground line.

Hand ridden, ridden in hand. Placed by rider's hands and legs, with stride and pace guided by subtle and sensitive aids from the rider.

Hard rub. Hitting a fence or standard with either the front- or hindquarters, and causing a loud knock or thud.

Head out. Carrying head to the outside and shoulder to the inside, instead of bending in the direction of travel.

Hunter pace. Usually twelve to fifteen miles per hour, but depends on size of course.

Impulsion. Thrust; related to collection and vertical motion, impulsion is created by the rider's legs asking the horse to go forward while his hands restrict the horse's speed.

In-and-out. A combination of two fences placed twenty-four to thirty-six feet apart, to be taken in either one or two strides. The first and second elements of an in-and-out are judged as two separate obstacles.

Inverted. A fault of jumping form, in which the back is hollowed, rather than rounded, and the head and hindquarters are higher than the back.

Iron. The term for stirrup.

Knockdown. Rail or top element of obstacle is displaced from original position, resulting in change of height or width of obstacle.

Lands in a heap. Instead of landing and going away from the fence in a smooth, flowing motion while maintaining cadence and gait, the horse stalls, literally plops down, and breaks up the rhythm upon landing.

Laying on side. Tilting of the body while in midflight over a fence, such that one side is inclined upward.

Line. Two or more fences placed in a row so as to be jumped consecutively without changing direction.

Loose form. Not folding legs tightly, but instead having more open legs while jumping, though not to the point of hanging or dangling.

Loss of forward movement. Failing to maintain a hand gallop or canter after beginning the course.

Overflexed. Breaks at withers or middle of neck, with head and neck below horizontal, and/or the face behind the vertical.

Overjumping. Jumping higher than necessary over an obstacle.

Oxer. A spread fence not exceeding three feet in width and usually consisting of rail fences placed together, one behind the other. Oxers in working hunter classes consist of two elements, and are measured from the front of the first element to the back of the second. Oxers must ascend, with the front element three to six inches lower than the back. Square oxers, those with elements of the same height, are prohibited in hunter classes, and are used only for jumpers.

Propping. An appearance by the horse of pushing back from the fence at takeoff. Though it's often a result of taking off from a point too close to the obstacle, horses may prop from any distance. A scopey horse may compensate for a takeoff point too close to the jump, but it also may become habit in horses that are allowed to slow down when approaching a fence.

Quick. Coming off the ground quickly on takeoff, or a short, rapid stride or strides immediately before takeoff.

Reaching. Front legs extended to clear the fence. Usually caused by taking off too far away from obstacle.

Refusal. Stopping in front of an obstacle, and then taking at least one step backward.

Runout. Evading or passing by an obstacle to be jumped; jumping an obstacle outside the limiting markers; horse or rider knocking down a flag, standard, wing, or other limiting marker without jumping the obstacle.

Safe jump. Horse jumps clean and in stride, with good arc and legs folded correctly.

Scope. The athletic ability required for jumping. The word is used similar to the term "cow," or cow sense, in cutting horses, though scope relates to physical ability, while cow is more a matter of mental ability.

Showing the horse an obstacle. Riding a horse up to an obstacle, without jumping it, in order to show the obstacle to the horse.

Skimming. Insufficient elevation. Also called "low belly," it is often associated with fast, flat jumps, or jumping with little effort.

Soft. The rider is able to ease off on the reins before a fence and at the finish; related to hand-ridden. Soft may also refer to an easy, or "soft," spot for takeoff.

Splitting. A horse having one leg forward and one back while jumping.

Strides. Theoretically based on twelve-foot increments. Strides are counted as the distance between jumps. (For example, sixty feet counts four strides, as in "1, 2, 3, 4, jump.")

Takeoff box. A box with small shrubs or flowers that is placed on the ground in front of a jump, and used as part of a ground line.

Twisting. Body not traveling straight while going over fence, but instead twisting to either side in order for its legs to clear the obstacle.

Unsafe jump. A style or form of jumping such that a fall could be the result.

SUGGESTED SYMBOLS FOR
DESCRIPTIVELY SCORING HUNTERS

⌒ -Good fence; leaving in stride and making proper arc

ᴎ⌒ -Propping

... -Shortened Stride on approach

> -Landing too close; cutting down

⊘ -Standing off too far and creating chancey jumps; diving

⌣ -Jumping hollow-backed; inverted

— -Jumping flat with little use of back

> -Not folding tightly enough; hanging knees, or leaving a leg

Π -Hanging legs

ʼʻ -Twisting or laying on side

ℰ -Weaving on approach or between jumps

⟨x -Cross-cantering

⌐ -Dwelling in air

ᴜᴧ -Extra stride through in-and-out

ᴘ -Hard rub

Ⓡ -Refusal or runout

Ⓧ -Knockdown

ᴌ -Rider using stick or crop on horse

hh -High head

Ⓑ -Bucks

ᴿℓ -Overflexed

ℓℓ -Plays after fence or around corner

ᴧᴧ -Sour-looking; pins ears in air

ᴧⲥ -No scope

ℛℊ -Pony-gaited or short-strided

Eℛ -Erratic pace

ᴇ -Not bending hocks and trailing hind legs out behind; storks

ᴀ -Smooth-looking, even pace; horse seemingly going on his own

ᴍᴍ -Uneven performance or pace; either jumps don't match or going fast or slow

⑨⟩ -Crash or dangerous

ℊℛ -Quick

ᴛᴧᴢ -Tense

ᴀᴛ -Strong

/// -Overchecking by rider

GM -Good mover

FM -Fair mover

BM -Bad mover

Gᴊ -Good jumper

Fᴊ -Fair jumper

Bᴊ -Bad jumper

The symbols are often used in combinations, such as:

⌒ᴼ -Good fence, but hard rub in front

ᴼ⌒ -Good fence, but hard rub behind

TWⓍ -Twisted, front knockdown

||| ⌐ -Shortened, then jumped flat

ℰMᴎ⌒ -Weaving, then extra stride and propped over fence

A TYPICAL HUNTER SCORECARD

CLASS NO. _____

CREDITS:
EVEN HUNTER PACE
FREE FLOWING STRIDE
JUMPING FENCES WITHOUT BREAKING STRIDE
JUMPING IN THE CENTER OF THE JUMP
EVEN ARC OF TRAVEL OVER THE FENCE
GOOD HUNTER CONFORMATION

FAULTS:
4 · KNOCK DOWN WITH ANY PART OF HORSES BODY BEHIND THE STIFLE
8 · KNOCK DOWN WITH ANY PART OF HORSES BODY IN FRONT OF THE STIFLE
· KNOCK DOWN OF STANDARD OR WING IN JUMPING OBSTACLE WITH ANY PART OF THE HORSE, RIDER OR EQUIPMENT
· PLACING ANY FOOT IN LIVERPOOL, DITCH OR WATER
· FIRST REFUSAL, RUNOUT, BOLTING ON COURSE. EXTRA CIRCLE, OR SHOWING AN OBSTACLE TO A HORSE
· SECOND REFUSAL, RUNOUT, BOLTING ON COURSE. EXTRA CIRCLE, OR SHOWING AN OBSTACLE TO A HORSE

AWARDS	
1	791
2	527
3	215
4	675
5	292
6	745
7	465
8	374

ELIMINATIONS:
· THIRD REFUSAL, RUNOUT, BOLTING ON COURSE, EXTRA CIRCLE OR SHOW AN OBSTACLE TO A HORSE OR ANY COMBINATION OF THESE
· JUMPING AN OBSTACLE BEFORE IT IS RESET
· BOLTING FROM RING
· FAILURE TO KEEP PROPER COURSE
· JUMPING AN OBSTACLE NOT INCLUDED IN COURSE
· HORSE AND/OR RIDER FALLING IN COMPETITION (HORSE IS CONSIDERED TO HAVE FALLEN WHEN SHOULDER AND HAUNCH ON THE SAME SIDE TOUCH THE GROUND)

JUNIOR, AMATEUR AND YOUTH: · MINIMUM HEIGHT · 3 FEET   MAXIMUM HEIGHT · 3 FEET · 3 INCHES

ALL AGE: · MINIMUM HEIGHT · 3 FEET   MAXIMUM HEIGHT · 3 FEET · 6 INCHES

SENIOR: · MINIMUM HEIGHT · 3 FEET ·3 INCHES   MAXIMUM HEIGHT · 3 FEET · 9 INCHES

A VARIATION OF 3 INCHES IN FENCE HEIGHT, DOWN FROM OFFICIAL HEIGHTS LISTED, MAY BE INSTITUTED IF SHOW MANAGEMENT AND THE OFFICIAL JUDGES FEEL CIRCUMSTANCES WARRANT, i.e., footing, weather, etc.

		Brush	Gate	~	Rail	Wall	Rail	Over	TOTAL FAULTS	WAY OF GOING	COMMENTS	SCORE
1	745									FM	uneven	70
2	893									FM	slow	65
3	791									GM		90
4	675									FM		77
5	527									GM		85
6	317		x				x			FM	drift-hang	62
7	275			R/		x		(4)		12	GM		35
8	492				(8)					8	FM		40
9	374									FM	Back off	67
10	215									GM		80
11	323			TW	R/L/					16	FM		30
12	465						x			BM	Check Back	68
13	292	TW								FM		72
14	613			TM	x		x			BM	charge	50
15	219							R	4		FM		✕

COMMON NAMES OF JUMPS

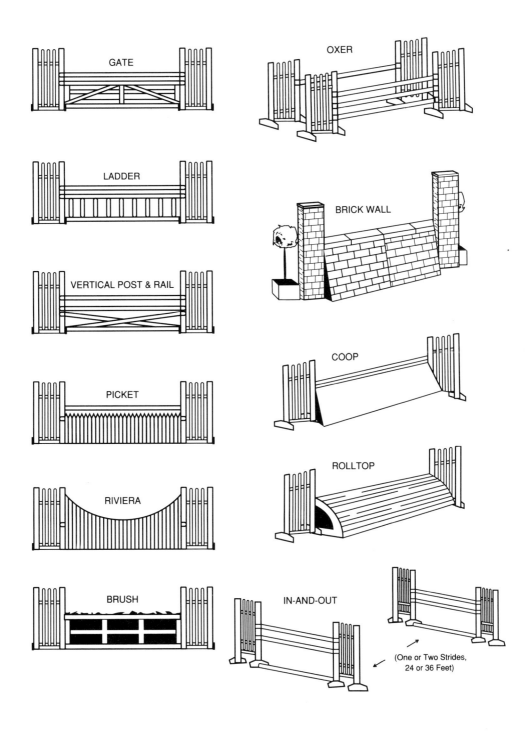

GATE

OXER

LADDER

BRICK WALL

VERTICAL POST & RAIL

PICKET

COOP

RIVIERA

ROLLTOP

BRUSH

IN-AND-OUT

(One or Two Strides, 24 or 36 Feet)

WORKING HUNTER-Basic Course

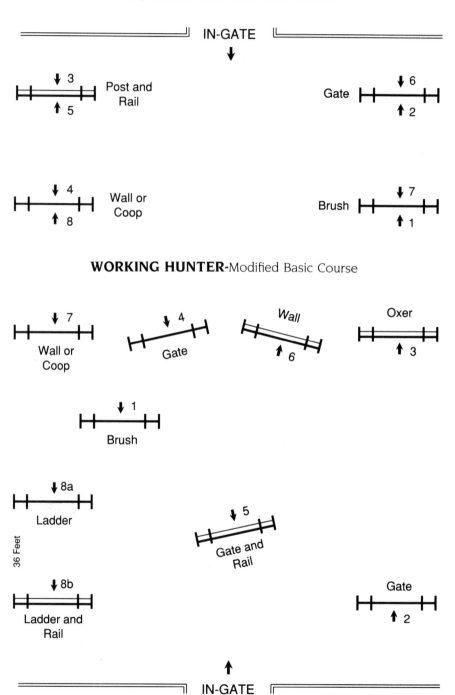

IN-GATE

↓ 3 Post and
↑ 5 Rail

Gate ↓ 6
      ↑ 2

↓ 4 Wall or
↑ 8 Coop

Brush ↓ 7
       ↑ 1

WORKING HUNTER-Modified Basic Course

↓ 7
Wall or
Coop

↓ 4
Gate

Wall
↑ 6

Oxer
↑ 3

↓ 1
Brush

↓ 8a
Ladder

36 Feet

↓ 5
Gate and
Rail

↓ 8b
Ladder and
Rail

Gate
↑ 2

↑ IN-GATE

226

Index

(**Bold** indicates illustration)